THE THEORY OF CREATION

THE THEORY OF CREATION

▼

A Scientific and Translational Analysis of the Biblical Creation Story

Jim Schicatano

Writers Club Press

San Jose New York Lincoln Shanghai

The Theory of Creation
A Scientific and Translational Analysis of the Biblical Creation Story

Writers Club Press
an imprint of iUniverse.com, Inc.

For information address:
iUniverse.com, Inc.
5220 S 16th, Ste. 200
Lincoln, NE 68512
www.iuniverse.com

ISBN: 0-595-19928-3

Printed in the United States of America

For my sister, Kathy,
who departed us too soon
but will be with us always.

Contents

▼

Introduction ix

1 The Origin of Genesis 1

2 In the Beginning, God Created 4

3 Formation of the Earth 10

4 Unformed and Void 13

5 Darkness Envelops the Earth 15

6 A Watery World 18

7 God Hovers Over the Waters 21

8 Light! 27

9 The Evening and the Morning 32

10 What is a Day? 37

11 The First Act of God 45

12 God Called the Expanse "Sky" 50

13 Land Emerges From the Sea 54

14 Vegetation—The First Life 58

15 The Lights in the Sky Above 65

16 Life Flourishes in the Sea and Air 75

17 The Convergence of Events with the Passage of Time 87

18 The Land Animals of the Sixth Day 92

19 The Creation of Man 102
20 In Our Image, In Our Likeness 119
21 Man's Dominion 129
22 The Green Plants for Food 133
23 A Day to Rest 138
24 Fulfillment of God's Commands and His Verdicts 142
25 According to Their Kinds 157
26 More Biblical Evidence for Long Creation Days 163
27 Science Supports Scripture 170
28 Natural Processes and Acts of God 177
29 Other Creationist Challenges 188
30 The Predictions of Creation 198
31 The Theory of Creation 203
32 The Meaning of Creation 233
Notes 251
Bibliography 273

INTRODUCTION

‒▼‒

It is easy to see now that the views I had once held were contradictory, and that this contradiction is pervasive in our society. There is the Bible and there is science. The former quenches our spiritual hunger, the latter satisfies our curiosity about the universe around us. Though the two may sometimes intertwine, most of us have built a mental barrier between them.

That which is recorded in the Bible cannot be questioned, for they are the very words of God. Through its books we learn the lessons of life, and of the glory and judgment of God. Its messages and promises guide us through our most joyful moments and our greatest tribulations. It gives purpose to those who would otherwise stumble through a meaningless existence. And, like the proverbial distant beacon of light on a dark and stormy night, it is a treasure chest of hope and opportunity for all that reach out to embrace its sacred words.

Then there is science—our enduring quest to explain and control our world, and our remedy for the question whose answer remains an enigma. It charts the heavens, maps the ocean floor, improves agricultural production, mines the earth for wealth, heals the sick, improves the quality of life, and postulates solutions to the enduring mysteries of the ages. Yet, science embodies so much more.

We have arrived at a period in our culture where the advancements made in science are now far removed from the comprehension of the average man. We are capable of learning to use the personal computer, but few of us could actually build one from its individual components. We do not understand how computer circuitry achieves its tasks. Yet, we are confident in the results it produces.

Whether it is the cockpit of the Stealth fighter, immunology, monetary transactions with a credit card, hi-definition television, laser technology, cloning, or quantum physics, advancements in science have been increasingly accomplished by people of scientific specialization. Most of us no longer attempt to understand how these advancements were achieved. Instead, we have grown to accept them and to expect more of them in the future.

We have grown accustomed then to science. It has produced a wealth of knowledge that quenches our curiosity and satisfies our needs. Our growing approval and confidence in science has allowed us to become comfortable seeking its solutions for answers to our problems. We ask it to solve some of our most enduring social dilemmas (birth control, addictions, unacceptable behavior), and produce solutions for a future that appears bleak (global warming, extinction of species, malnutrition, starvation, pestilence, and famine).

Since they were first written, the first eleven chapters of Genesis have stirred both the imagination and apprehension of civilizations. From the indomitable power that God manifests in the creation of the heavens and the Earth, Adam and Eve's fall from Paradise, the rebellion of man at Babel, through the iniquity of mankind that warranted the Great Flood, these chapters of the Bible are inundated with tales of morality, man's sinful nature, God's powers to create and destroy, and His patient love for all of humanity. It is in this beginning where poets, painters, writers, philosophers, Western culture, and the basis for our governments have their primary roots. But, while the stories of the first eleven chapters have had a demonstrable impact on our society, their validity has often come into question.

Science has "emancipated" mankind from such gods as the sun, the moon, the stars, and the forces of nature. It has explained away the mysteries of those false gods, whose apparent powers are now understood in natural terms rather than supernatural. With the advancement of science and technology, and man's increasing knowledge, it was inevitable that the Bible would come under closer scientific scrutiny.

Our modern, technical, science-dependent societies now turn to the Bible with skepticism. Are these truly the words of God? Or are they myths, passed down from cultures that are thousands of years old? Can the Holy Bible withstand the scrutiny of modern science? And if science finds the Bible in error, what place is left then for a collection of cherished books that scholars and readers have claimed for centuries to be the inerrant word of God?

This returns us to the contradiction that I had once held. When contemplating the Bible, I have always maintained a steadfast belief in its inerrancy. The Creation Story that is revealed to us in Genesis 1:1-2:4 tells of a creation event that occurred a meager few thousand years ago. Biblical scholars, whose opinions I have always respected, date God's creation of the heavens and the Earth from 6,000 years ago to no more than 50,000 years ago (the latter is an extreme scenario). Most are firmly committed to the younger age.

The Creation Story tells us that in six days God created the heavens and the Earth, made the Earth habitable, populated the world with countless species of animals, and finally created man. On the Seventh Day, God rested from His work. How long were the Creation Days? There is strong conviction in the Fundamentalist religious community that they were the traditional twenty-four hours.

Science has revealed to us its own creation account. From the Big Bang (ten to twenty billion years ago), through the formation of our Earth (4.5 billion years ago), through the Cambrian Explosion of life (540 million years ago), through the extinction of the dinosaurs (65 million years ago), science has uncovered a creation story that appears to contradict the Bible.

Using the scientific method, we have learned that the universe is much older than 6,000 years, and that the vast majority of plant and animal species flourished and went extinct long before 6,000 years ago. Some species survived millions of years before extinction—the dinosaurs, for example, ruled our planet for about 150 million years. By contrast, man appeared very late on the time-clock of planet Earth. Science has dated our oldest known distinctive ancestor to only four million years ago.

Man—the pinnacle of the Biblical Creation Story—has been relegated to a status only marginally above the animals. Science claims that we owe our very existence to natural processes that did not require a Creator. In contrast, the Bible claims that we hold a special place in God's plans, and that the entire Earth has been created for us.

We are thus left in a curious and contradictory position—a different type of "science-versus-religion" conflict. When many of us are discussing science, we accept the age of the Earth to be 4.5 billion years old. We acknowledge that at the end of the Mesozoic Era, some sixty-five million years ago, the dinosaurs and most species of life on Earth went extinct. When we are discussing religion, we then speak of a creation event of a few thousand years ago, and we are comfortable in our declaration that man appeared on Earth just five days after that creation event. The contradiction then is cemented in our minds and in our culture. Many people seem to accept both the scientific and the Biblical accounts of creation, despite the fact that they are hopelessly in disagreement.

Or are they?

When I first began to study the Biblical Creation Story, I searched for related materials that exhibited the following properties:

1. A sound translation of the ancient Hebrew texts.
2. Consistency in reasoning and logic, and fair and honest deductions.
3. An explanation of the creation events without bias—more specifically, a telling of the story without attempting to prove or disprove other related or unrelated theories.

Most attempts at explaining the Biblical Creation event failed to embrace all three of these basic principals. It appeared that many authors were decidedly using the story to disprove some current scientific belief. Others would "retranslate" parts of the story while ignoring the most common and obvious mistranslations—primarily, to advance some bold new theory of their own. Then there were those whose theories and explanations should best be relegated to collect dust in some forgotten section of a pubic library.

Frustrated by these misguided attempts, I decided to seek the truth of the Creation Story, using the three rules I set above as my guide. With no ax to grind and no bold new theory to offer, I began my research, uncertain whether the Bible could survive the scrutiny of science. If it could not survive such a careful analysis, then I had a moral obligation to concede defeat.

As I perused Genesis 1, I realized that what was written was a simple chronology. A point that no Biblical scholar could deny was that the events of the First Day preceded that of the Second Day, and that the events of the Second Day preceded that of the Third Day—a pattern that continued through the Seventh Day. Using this as my guide, the most important test would be to determine whether the events listed in the Bible were authenticated by science, and in the same order that is recognized by science. Only such an agreement could demonstrate the scientific validity of the Bible.

I suppose that a harmonious agreement between the Bible and science is important for the faith of many believers. In this modern, technical culture, where we often turn first to science rather than God to solve so many of our problems, such an agreement is reassuring. Others require no such evidence to sustain their unwavering faith. The Bible has, and will always be, their source of strength and their guide to salvation. Science may make its claims, but to these people, it is the Bible that possesses the ultimate truth on any given topic. Then there are those who simply desire to satisfy their curiosity. Can the Biblical account of creation be reconciled

The Theory of Creation

with current scientific beliefs? It is an interesting question that many feel needs to be answered.

Whatever guides your thoughts as you read these forthcoming chapters, always remember that divergent beliefs among God's people are to be expected. For all those whose journey leads to salvation, no two paths that guide them there are ever alike.

▼

CHAPTER ONE

THE ORIGIN OF GENESIS

THE AUTHOR OF THE CREATION STORY

It has long been accepted that Moses was the author of the first five books of the Bible, which are collectively known as the Pentateuch. More recently, Theologians have challenged that belief, and new authors of these books have been proposed. Currently, the principal writers are identified by single letters: P (Priestly), E (Elohist), and J (Yahwist), while another possible author, the Redactor, is sometimes credited with splicing these earlier authors' works together.[1]

All three (or four) authors are recognized as having contributed at least some of the text in the book of Genesis. In some cases, more than one author is believed to have produced a single story. The best example of this splicing lies in the story of Noah and the Great Flood. The text in that story often seems to be repeating facts, and it does appear that two similar stories are being told together—sometimes alternating verse by verse.

P, the "Priestly" author is credited with the Creation Story, which begins at Genesis 1:1 and ends at Genesis 2:4 (or 2:4a). This Biblical story reveals how God created the universe, and all life on the Earth in the span of six days. The proposed date of the writing of this creation account is 539 B.C.E.[2] Although P's writing contains the ancient account of creation, this date, ironically, places it after the earlier works of J (950 B.C.E.) and E (750 B.C.E.).[3] Because of this later date, P is sometimes credited as being the Redactor.[4]

While the identity of the Creation Story's author may be significant for Theologians, it does not appear to be relevant for our purposes. It is not necessarily important who wrote this account of creation, so much as the scientific validity of what was written. Rather than choose between Moses and P, I will simply refer to the principal writer of the Creation Story as "the author."

THE DATE OF THE CREATION EVENT

The first three words of the English translation of Genesis 1:1 are "*In the beginning.*" This is the only reference to the time of the creation event, and nowhere in the Bible is the date of the Biblical Creation recorded. This has not, however, prevented people from attempting to calculate it.

Perhaps the most famous attempt to determine the date of the Biblical Creation was in the 1650's when Archbishop Ussher of Canterbury calculated the date to be 4004 B.C.[5] This was accomplished by using the Biblical ages of the early humans, and the genealogy that was recorded. The theory assumes the absence of gaps in the genealogy of the Bible, something that many scholars question. Although this date is seldom accepted as being conclusive, many people today still embrace Archbishop Ussher's calculation as fact.

OUR METHODS AND ANALYSIS

There have been countless attempts through the centuries to postulate theories and propose solutions for the many mysteries of the Bible. However, it is best that we begin our endeavor with a commitment to assume nothing. We will examine the evidence for ourselves to determine the date of creation. We will thoroughly address the events of all of the Creation Days, without any inclination to accept preconceived notions. Only the facts can satisfy our probing curiosities. We will refer to the original Hebrew text when discrepancies occur, to determine the best translation. We will also reference other attempts to interpret the Creation Story, deciding which concepts we can embrace and which can be disregarded.

This attention to detail and precise translation is required for our scientific analysis. Science demands it, the people expect it, and God and the Bible deserves it.

Before we begin our analysis, we need to address our expectations. The purpose of the Creation Story was not to record every species of plant and animal life that has ever existed, nor was it meant to describe all of the physical processes that have ever influenced our world. The Creation Story is a concise, chronological listing of the highlights of the creation of the universe, the planet Earth, and the life that resides here—culminating in the creation of man, and God's instructions to him. Essentially, the Bible is a collection of religious and historical documents. Although we may gain and infer scientific knowledge from its precious words, the Bible should not be expected to read like a scientific textbook.

CHAPTER TWO

▼

IN THE BEGINNING, GOD CREATED

In the beginning God created the heavens and the earth.

Gen. 1:1 (NIV)[1]

In the beginning—a period of remote and unknown antiquity, hid in the depths of eternal ages.[2]

Jamieson, Fausset, and Brown
A Commentary Critical and
Explanatory on the Whole Bible

THE FIRST DAY

The first three words of the Holy Bible, "*In the beginning,*" reveal an origin—a beginning to our universe and to time itself. Examine the first chapter of Genesis on your own. In it, you will find no mention of the age of the universe and the Earth, nor the time and date when God created them. It tells us only that at some point there was a beginning, and at that beginning, God created the universe.

This Biblical proclamation appears to be an irrelevant claim for our modern society. Today, the scientific community widely embraces the notion that the universe had a beginning. Yet, at the time of its writing this Biblical declaration was neither known nor intuitive. Some ancient societies believed that time was eternal and that the universe had always existed (this is called the Steady State Theory). Others believed that the current universe was one of many that existed and then ended in an eternal cycle. But what the ancient people could not have known is common knowledge today.

Our universe was born between ten and twenty billion years ago in a primeval explosion called the Big Bang. At that moment, the entire universe burst into existence from a single point of origin, of infinite space-time density (such a point is known as a "singularity"). Before this momentous event there was nothing. Matter, energy, and even space and time, did not yet exist.

In 1929, Edwin Hubble (of the "Hubble Telescope" and the "Hubble Constant" fame) presented to the world the first convincing evidence that our universe had a moment of origin, when he discovered that the universe around us is expanding.[3] If we observe a universe that is expanding in every direction, we may conclude that at an earlier time the universe was much smaller. If we further pursue this line of reasoning to its logical conclusion, we then formulate the theory of the Big Bang. Mathematical equations have confirmed the possibility of the Big Bang. The physical attributes of this event are understood, and can be calculated to just a fraction of a single second upon its inception.

The first verse of the Holy Bible, of course, is not nearly as detailed as most astronomers, physicists, or philosophers would like it to be. Yet, we should not expect it to be any more revealing. The Creation Story's purpose is not to enumerate every event in the history of the universe, but rather to highlight the events that are most pertinent to man. It should also be noted that ancient man, lacking our scientific knowledge, probably was not capable of understanding more than general scientific statements.

"In the beginning, God created the Heavens and the Earth" was a fundamental statement that sufficiently recognized the Hebrew God as the sole Creator of the entire universe at the beginning of time. No more scientific knowledge needed to be imparted to mankind at the time of its writing.

We can also observe that there are no competing gods mentioned in the Creation Story—or anywhere in the Bible, either. The Hebrew God did not engage in mighty battles for supremacy with other gods. There was no god of the moon, the stars, the sun, the wind, or the seas as other cultures of that time deified—only God the Creator. The author of this story was careful not to introduce notions of false gods to the Hebrews. Instead, he chose to reveal one, omnipotent God—One that could call an entire universe into existence in the very first verse of the story.

Attempting to demonstrate the scientific significance of the first verse from a religious perspective, Scientific Creationist, Dr. Henry M. Morris, rephrased the first verse as the following:

> The transcendent, omnipotent Godhead called into existence
> the space-mass-time universe.[4]

The Creation Story, and thus the Holy Bible, begins with a declaration of enormous importance, all from the scientific accuracy of a verse that is often overlooked by the average reader.

TRANSLATING THE FIRST VERSE

To gain a better understanding of this verse, let us now closely examine the original Hebrew text for this passage. This is not something that needs to be done for every verse of the Creation Story, but I feel it is necessary to include it here to display how the original Hebrew was translated. In Hebrew, Genesis 1:1 reads:

Bereshit bara Elohim et hashamayim ve'et ha'arets[5]

Bereshit—Translated as "In the beginning."[6]

bara—Translated here as *"created."*[7] What is being conveyed here is not the customary definition of the word "create." In the true sense of the word, mankind does not actually "create"—we merely manipulate matter that already exists. Buildings, bridges, homes, automobiles, computers, and every other physical "creation" of man are all produced from preexisting materials.

Only God can create (*bara*) that from which there was nothing. No other being, including man, possesses this ability.[8] It is this particular usage that is being expressed here to the Biblical reader—that of creating something from nothing. Before the Big Bang, matter, energy, and time did not yet exist. After the Big Bang, the entire universe appeared and time began to move forward. Such a creation from nothing is referred to as *"Creation Ex Nihilo."*

This is the first of three times in Genesis 1 that the word "created" was used. The other two times include the creation of the creatures of the Fifth Day, and the creation of man on the Sixth Day.[9] Each would indicate that God produced these creations from nothing, or that which did not previously exist.

Elohim—God.[10] The word used here can also be translated in the plural and could mean "Gods."[11] Most scholars, however, accept the translation as "God" in the singular. One argument for acknowledging P, the Priestly writer, as the author of this story, is his use of the word *"Elohim"* for God throughout his credited writings in Genesis. There are other Hebrew words, which he did not use, that can also be translated as "God."

Et hashamayim ve'et ha'arets—Translated as *"the Heavens and the Earth."*[12] This expression does not refer to Heaven, where God and the angels dwell, nor does it specifically refer to our planet, the Earth. The Hebrew language did not contain a specific word that represented our concept of the universe, however, the expression, *"the Heavens and the Earth,"* is understood by scholars to encompass the entire universe.[13]

SCIENTIFIC ANALYSIS OF THE FIRST VERSE

We have now concluded that the first verse of the Holy Bible is scientifically accurate. It correctly declared a beginning to time and to the creation of the universe—something that is now the conventional belief within the scientific community.

Despite the harmony between science and the Bible, the Bible never literally described a cosmic event like the Big Bang. Biblical credibility would be enhanced if we could determine unequivocally that the first verse of the Bible is referencing the Big Bang. However, that is impossible to conclude due to the limited nature of the Hebrew text. But Biblical inerrancy will not necessarily be diminished if the Big Bang is ultimately disproved. The Bible declared only that there was a beginning to our universe and to time. That declaration is satisfactory for our endeavor.

As I noted earlier, the Bible's purpose is not to act as a scientific textbook, although it does contain some verses of a scientific nature. If our analysis of the Creation Story reveals the text to be scientifically accurate, then that should satisfy any critics. After all, what more could be asked of a religious manuscript.

THE CREATOR OF THE CREATOR

We are left with one final topic relevant to the first verse that I feel needs to be addressed. And that is an answer to the question: If God created the entire universe, who or what created God?

The common reply to such a question is that God is an eternal, omnipotent Being that needed no such creation. Yet, the answer to this question is not that simple, since the point of reference—the beginning of time—is applicable only to man and to our universe. Since we must abide by the laws governing the progression of time, we are incapable of discerning God's creation. God existed before time (as we know it) began, and will continue to exist once time ceases. He is therefore not bound by the same physical laws that govern our universe.

Who or what created God? The answer to that question can never be definitively known. However, with the knowledge that our universe was created sometime during the existence of God, and the assumption that God will survive the end of our universe, we are left with only one inescapable conclusion.

From the perspective of mankind, God is an eternal Being.

CHAPTER THREE

▼

FORMATION OF THE EARTH

The Big Bang unleashed an incomprehensible amount of energy. Initially, it was so hot that even the basic atomic particles could not form. But Einstein taught us that energy and matter are interchangeable, and what was once highly charged energy soon transformed into matter. As the energy from the explosion expanded in every direction it began to cool, and protons, neutrons, electrons, and other lesser-known particles began to form.

Hydrogen is the most basic element in the universe, possessing just one proton and one electron. It comprises nearly three-fourths of the matter in our universe. Disregarding the hydrogen isotopes, deuterium and tritium, helium is the next most basic element, and composes nearly a quarter of the remaining matter in the universe. These two basic elements, then, constitute almost the entire universe, with heavier elements existing in only trace amounts.

As the energy and matter of the Big Bang further cooled, hydrogen and helium soon began to coalesce under the pull of gravity. Hydrogen and helium are not only the most common elements in the universe but they are also the basic fuels of stars. Even as the universe continued to expand, stars and galaxies began to form from these elements. But our solar system was not among those primary creations. It would not be created for billions of years.

Stars are believed to form by "gravitational collapse." This is the process whereby a large cloud, or nebula, of hydrogen and helium (and to a lesser extent the heavier elements) in space, collapses inward due to the pull of its own gravity. As the gasses occupy less space, the density of the cloud begins to increase. Since pressure also increases, the temperature rises.

The temperature of this collapsing gas continues to increase to millions of degrees until the hydrogen atoms reach a critical point whereby they fuse together and form helium. Tremendous energy and light are emitted through this process, which is known as nuclear fusion. This is same energy that is unleashed by the hydrogen bomb. The exploding outward forces which are produced by the nuclear fusion reactions are countered by the immense gravitational pull inward, which is due to the tremendous mass of the star. These two opposing forces are in a state of general equilibrium during most of the life of the star. That is why the size of a star such as our sun remains relatively constant.

When a star converts most of its hydrogen into helium, it begins to run out of its primary fuel. It is believed that the star continues to burn hotter until the higher temperatures are reached whereby the heavier elements can be formed by the fusion process. At some point, a large star (one that is much larger than our sun) will collapse upon itself and explode—spewing its raw materials into space. Heavier elements, such as the metals, are among the debris of the explosion. This exploding star is called a "super nova."

Our solar system began to form about five billion years ago. It was created from a nebular cloud that was the remains of a super nova. Our sun is thus considered a "second generation" star because it formed from the dust and gas of an earlier star.

While our sun was formed by the same gravitational collapse described above, the planets that orbit the sun were formed much differently, by a process called "accretion."

As the nebular cloud that formed our solar system began to collapse, it also flattened into a narrow elliptical disk. Most of the matter of the disk collapsed inward and formed the sun. But some of the dust and gas remained in a flattened plane that rotated around the sun. Throughout the universe, it is common to find flattened planes of matter orbiting larger objects. Many galaxies possess this flattened property, and in our own solar system we can observe this feature in the rings of Saturn.

The plane of dust and gas soon began to coalesce into large particles, which in turn collided and formed even larger particles. It is believed that only a few million years were required before the foundations of planets, called "planetesimals," were formed. The planetesimals continued to draw in much of the remaining nebular debris that rotated around the sun.

The young Earth was bombarded in its early life by dust, meteors, comets, and even smaller planetesimals. These raw materials continuously pummeled the Earth and increased the mass of our planet. The Earth's surface was kept in a near molten state from the energy released by the continuous barrage of nebular debris, and the release of radiation from the radioactive decay of elements in the Earth's interior. But despite its hostile, violent beginnings, and its barren, inhospitable nature, a new planet had taken form.

Four and half billion years ago, the Earth was born.

CHAPTER FOUR

———————▼———————

UNFORMED AND VOID

Now the Earth was formless and empty…

Gen. 1:2 (NIV)

And the Earth was without form and void…

Gen. 1:2 (KJV)

The Earth was a strange and alien world four and a half billion years ago. Volcanoes were erupting virtually everywhere on our planet during that turbulent period. Those eruptions spewed molten lava and gasses that were trapped beneath the Earth's violent surface. Planetesimals, comets, and meteors continued to bombard our planet, depositing more gasses, water, dust, and raw materials to our world. The violent impact from those spacial rocks released vast amounts of heat and energy, further fueling our world's fiery beginning.

The Earth's early atmosphere was remarkably different from today. The outgassing of sulfur and carbon dioxide from the interior of the Earth fueled the development of a heavy, toxic atmosphere. There was no free oxygen to breathe at that time, and water molecules remained in a super-heated gaseous state.

It seems impossible that life could have ever developed on our young world. But out of the primordial chaos God brought forth order. And out of such desolation, God brought forth sustainable life. The Bible does not give us a detailed description of our young world, but it does refer to our planet as "*without form and void.*" The Hebrew words used in this verse are "*tohu*" and "*vavohu.*"[1] These Hebrew terms are meant to convey images of confusion, formlessness, and disorder.[2]

The Bible's description can be considered an accurate depiction of a young Earth. Certainly the emptiness and lifelessness of the planet are correct. And the Bible's description of a desolate, barren, chaotic world is an adroit, if not scientific, description of the violent processes that formed the Earth.

"Chaos" seems to be the integral word here. Since the very beginning of time, the Bible tells us that chaos reigned supreme throughout our universe. It is only by the will of God that order prevails.

Science has learned that four and half billion years ago the planet Earth was a turbulent, barren, desolate world. The Bible's description of our young planet has been confirmed by science.

CHAPTER FIVE

▼

DARKNESS ENVELOPS THE EARTH

darkness was over the surface of the deep...

Gen. 1:2 (NIV)

I will divide my comments on this verse into two chapters for purposes of clarity. This chapter will deal with the darkness that enveloped the Earth, while the next chapter will explore the Earth's watery surface.

Many Creationists believe that the sun's absence plunged our world into darkness. This is understandable, since the sun's creation is often incorrectly placed on the Fourth Day. The early Earth was, in fact, shrouded in darkness, just as the Bible states. The darkness, however, was not due to the absence of the sun, but rather the thickness of the impenetrable, primordial atmosphere.

Over four billion years ago, the Earth's atmosphere consisted primarily of carbon dioxide, methane, ammonia, water vapor, and hydrogen sulfide. It was a lethal mixture that could not support most life as we know it today. Several processes, including outgassing, formed the atmosphere.

Outgassing occurred when gasses trapped beneath the Earth's molten surface were released. Volcanic activity was a major source of outgassing, as was the violent impact of the nebular debris that disrupted the Earth's surface. In addition, the large rocks from space that pummeled our young world often contained gasses, which would be released upon impact.

Gravity also played an integral role in the creation of the atmosphere. In its earliest stages of formation, the Earth was a molten, thick liquid, undergoing tremendous, violent, surface upheavals. Before the rock had cooled and hardened, the heavier materials such as iron, which formed the planet's core, were drawn down to the interior of the Earth, due to the influence of gravity. Conversely, the lighter elements rose to the surface. Gasses, which were the lightest molecules, formed the atmosphere around the planet.

Some have compared the Earth's primordial atmosphere to the dense atmosphere of Venus today. This is a fair comparison because our young planet's atmosphere was also comprised of gasses like carbon dioxide. It is believed that the level of carbon dioxide in the Earth's primordial atmosphere was hundreds or perhaps thousands of times greater than today.[1] Carbon dioxide is a greenhouse gas, and as it blanketed the Earth it trapped both the heat emitted from our world, and the warmth the Earth received from a young, weak sun.[2] Greenhouse gasses on Venus have impeded heat there from dissipating into space, thereby raising the surface temperature to a sweltering 900 degrees.[3]

The impenetrable, thick atmosphere shrouded the surface of our planet from the light of the sun. For tens of millions of years, the Earth was cloaked in darkness, while being relentlessly bombarded by spacial debris. Its surface was a hot, molten liquid and its atmosphere was lethal.

Over time, however, the atmosphere began to dissipate and the sun's warm rays finally extended to the surface of our world. Millions of years would pass before the atmosphere became transparent as it is today.

There are other theories that have been proposed to explain the darkness that is mentioned in this Biblical verse. The primary theory, as I have mentioned, is that the sun had not yet been created (this erroneous belief will be discussed in a later chapter). Another popular interpretation defines the darkness as being "evil." This particular translation supports other theories that perceive the entire Creation Story as being allegorical as opposed to the more common literal interpretation. While such a metaphorical translation might be permissible, Bible scholars do not generally accept it. Darkness may be a reference to evil, however, the darkness stated in Genesis 1:2 is best understood as an absence of light.

The Bible does not specifically state what produced the darkness that blanketed the young Earth. We have turned to science to reveal one possible answer—that being the impenetrable, primordial atmosphere. Some may be troubled that it was science, and not the Bible, that solved this age-old enigma. But using the tools of science to explain Biblical mysteries does not remove God from the process. Darkness was the original state of the young Earth. Without the creation of light (or light-giving bodies) by God, it would have remained in eternal darkness. The very fact that the Bible records the darkness that initially enveloped the Earth—regardless of the processes involved—only strengthens the Creation Story's validity.

CHAPTER SIX

▼

A WATERY WORLD

As we observe our world today, it is difficult to believe that the Earth's surface was ever completely submerged under water. Vast regions of deserts, rain forests, savannahs, mountains, and plateaus occupy millions of square acres of land, while supporting billions of humans, and millions of plant and animal species. The great mountain ranges of our world that tower thousands of feet above sea level only strengthen our certainty that land must have always existed. But the Bible reveals that this was not always true. Most Biblical scholars agree that the Creation Story describes an Earth that was completely inundated by water. Two passages in particular indicate a watery world.

> *darkness was over the surface of the deep...*
>
> Gen. 1:2 (NIV)

> *"...Let dry ground appear."*
>
> Gen. 1:9 (NIV)

The first passage tells us that during the early development of the Earth, the water was shrouded in darkness. How prevalent was the water? Did it cover the entire Earth? This Biblical passage answers neither question. It tells us only that water *did* exist on our world at that time.

The second passage reveals that God called forth the dry ground to appear. Since this passage makes little or no sense if land had previously existed, we are left to conclude that the world was completely or nearly completely covered by water. Where did all of the water come from? The Creation Story never addresses God's creation of water.

From a scientific perspective we immediately must ask: Was there ever a time when the entire Earth was enveloped by water?[1]

The water that exists on our world today came from the formation of our solar system and our planet. The great nebular cloud of dust and gas that formed our solar system also contained chunks of ice. Liquid water may have existed throughout the solar system as early as 4.5 billion years ago—or shortly after the formation of the Earth.[2] The water on our planet, like the metals and the gasses, owes its existence to the very formation of the Earth. When the Bible states that God created the Earth, this probably included the creation of water.

Before four billion years ago, the Earth's atmosphere maintained a temperature well above the boiling point of water. Consequently, the water on our world was trapped as super-heated steam. As the Earth cooled, water vapor began to condense into rain.[3] Soon the rain turned into a torrential downpour. For millions of years, the primordial atmosphere relentlessly yielded water to the surface of the Earth.

Tectonic plate movement, which is the process that formed the great mountain ranges of the world, had not yet begun, and the Earth's surface was relatively smooth. Water steadily poured from the sky, filling the shallow valleys, and eroding areas of higher elevation. Volcanoes continued to release more gasses and steam into the atmosphere. Comets, which are primarily composed of ice, added even more water upon impact with our planet.[4]

Soon, the Earth was virtually covered by one large body of water.[5] The continents that we take for granted today did not exist four billion years ago. Volcanoes would occasionally rise above the ocean surface to spew forth their molten materials. But the Earth was essentially in the very condition that the Bible declares—the land was submerged under a global ocean.

▼

CHAPTER SEVEN

GOD HOVERS OVER THE WATERS

*Now the earth was formless and empty, darkness was over the surface
of the deep, and the Spirit of God was hovering over the waters.*
                                                    Gen. 1:2 (NIV)

*Over the waters was only darkness, and the Spirit of God brooded over
them preparing the earth and the waters for the production of life.*[1]
                                    A Catholic Commentary on Holy Scripture

The prevalence of life on planet Earth is a wondrous mystery that no
scientist working in a research laboratory has ever been able to duplicate
or explain. Life seemingly exists everywhere on our planet. It has been
found in the thin air atop the peaks of the highest mountains, in deep
oceanic trenches where the sun's rays cannot penetrate, in the boiling
water of hot springs, and even in the most barren, desolate deserts of the
world. Virtually everywhere that we search we find life teeming on our
wonderful planet.

How has such a diversity of life maintained itself through the billions of years of Earth's history? Why hasn't it been extinguished in all of this time?

Cataclysmic events have nearly decimated our world throughout the eons. The most widely known global catastrophe—the extinction of the dinosaurs at the end of the Mesozoic Era—was probably caused by the impact of a large meteor. But there is evidence of other meteors from different eras that have bombarded our planet—and just as life continued to thrive after the demise of the dinosaurs, some form of life always found a way to survive each disaster. Violent volcanic eruptions have wiped out life in whole regions, only to have the area miraculously rejuvenate with life a few years later. Frigid Ice Ages have come and gone. Earthquakes, floods, hurricanes, and other violent acts of nature have all attributed to the extinction of countless species of life that have inhabited our planet. But life always persevered.

Even such natural factors that we perceive as being permanent have changed through the ages. The 23 ½ degree tilt of the Earth on its axis has not been permanent, nor has its elliptical orbit around the sun always been precisely the same. The amount of energy that the Earth receives from the sun has varied throughout the billions of years of its existence. Even the speed of the Earth's rotation has not been consistent. These factors change as time passes, effecting the temperature, atmosphere, and sea levels of our planet. Billions of years ago our atmosphere was void of oxygen. Yet today much of the life on the Earth requires oxygen to exist. In all that time, through all of the countless species of life that have inhabited the Earth through the ages, life of some variety has always found a way to endure and flourish.

Some believe that the Earth itself is, in a sense, alive, and that the complex web of life here is maintained through a "life force" that emanates from our mother planet. The existence of a divine Being is not necessarily required in such a concept. In this theory, the life force may have originated by a series of natural accidents or by pure chance.

Science, too, has sought to understand how life began on our planet. Scientists have attempted to duplicate the conditions that existed on the Earth billions of years ago, and the mechanisms involved that created the building blocks of life. Some type of natural process is largely recognized as initiating a sustaining life cycle that has successfully perpetuated for billions of years.[2] The exact details of that process has so far eluded science.

After all of the incredible advancements and discoveries made by science through the centuries, today we are still puzzled by the origin of life on planet Earth. And we still cannot explain how life has endured through the billions of years of Earth's history.

In previous chapters, we have turned to science for answers to questions that the Bible has not fully explained. Now it is time to turn to the Bible for possible answers to these enigmas that have puzzled science.

When I first read the passage "*and the Spirit of God was hovering over the waters*" in verse two above, I paused in deliberation. I then continued to read the remainder of the Creation Story, yet this one phrase still puzzled me. It simply did not seem to conform to the spirit and purpose of the story. What was God's Spirit doing, hovering over the waters of the Earth? And why would such a phrase be included in the story? I examined other Bibles for variations in translations. Some Bibles replaced "*the Spirit of God*" with "*the Wind of God.*" The word "*hovering,*" which is in the NIV, is sometimes interpreted as "*moved*" or "*moving.*" The King James Version translates this phrase as: "*And the Spirit of God moved upon the face of the waters.*"

Most Theologians would agree that if a phrase is included in the Holy Bible it must possess a purpose. Despite its imposing size, the Bible is actually a compact collection of manuscripts with little room for superfluous phrases. Thus, the author of the Creation Story must have intentionally chosen to include this mysterious phrase. Buy why?

One of the pertinent words in question here is the Hebrew word "*ruah.*"[3] This is what is being translated as "*wind*" or "*spirit.*"[4] With this in mind, here are some possible explanations for the intended meaning of this passage.

1. THE WIND[5]

Is this phrase merely reporting God's creation of the wind and possibly the seas? Light and darkness were also introduced on the First Day, so the purpose of the text may be to demonstrate that God created the natural elements, like the wind and the sea. However, there is little evidence that this was the objective of the author. If the purpose of this phrase was to announce the creation of such elements, the author probably would have phrased the words differently. When you read the verse, it is not at all apparent that God is creating the wind or the sea.

2. GOD'S SPIRIT

Many scholars believe that this word is better translated as *"spirit"* than *"wind."*[6] This passage may be describing an action that has less to do with chaos (or a natural element such as a powerful wind) and more to do with God's creative ability.[7] However, we are then left with the image of the Spirit of God mysteriously hovering or moving over the waters.

3. THE HOLY SPIRIT[8]

Some Christian sources maintain that the Spirit of God in this phrase is a reference to the Holy Spirit, the third Godhead of the Trinity. While it may be possible to interpret this from the text, such a translation is indirect and not necessarily warranted. Still, such an interpretation is plausible and should not be dismissed just because the word is located in the Old Testament.

"HOVERED" OR "MOVED"

As we continue to gain a deeper insight into this passage, let us examine God's activity—that of *"hovering"* or *"moving"* over the waters. *"Hovered"* or *"moved"* is the translation of the Hebrew word, *"merachefet."*[9] This word occurs only one other time in the Bible, in Deuteronomy 32:11 (as *"hovers"*).[10]

like an eagle that stirs up its nest and hovers over its young, that spreads its wings to catch them and carries them on its pinions.

Deuteronomy 32:11 (NIV)

The action being described in Deuteronomy is that of an eagle protecting or caring for her young as she hovers over them.[11] In the same way, God is described in Genesis 1:2 as hovering over the waters of the Earth. This could be a metaphorical phrase, indicating God's care for His creation of our planet. It also could be describing God's actual interaction with the water. Although the text is not more specific, God may be creating or fostering life in the Earth's global ocean.

THE ELUSIVE MEANING

It is not clear what is happening in this phrase or why it was included in this story. One common theory is that this phrase may be leftover from an earlier draft of the Creation Story, where the God of the Bible conquers a god of the sea. Most of the ancient civilizations associated specific gods with the various natural elements, such as the wind, water, fire, the sun, the moon, and even the stars. In the mythologies, the gods often battled among themselves for supremacy. If this phrase was leftover from an earlier text, it may have been included to display God's supremacy, by hovering over a defeated god of the sea.

This argument is unlikely, however, since throughout the Creation Story the author appears to be very careful to acknowledge the existence of one and only one God. It would have been uncharacteristic of the author to introduce another, lesser god.

Another theory is that God is described here preparing the Earth for the life that He would soon create.[12] It is not known specifically what it is that God is doing, but the fact that His Spirit moved over the Earth's surface must indicate some action of great significance and concern. God's creation of life would be a significant event.

During the Earth's early history—over 3.8 billion years ago—simple, single-celled forms of life appeared in the seas. Before that time, science believes that some natural process was slowly creating the building blocks of life.

There are many theories that attempt to explain how life first originated on our planet. But what I find interesting is that this mysterious phrase in the Bible is describing an act of God that takes place very early in the history of the Earth—around the time that life first appeared.

God may be hovering above the water in order to seed the world with the first forms of life. I acknowledge that this theory is not clearly explained in the text, nor is it a commonly held view. Of all the beliefs that I embrace in this endeavor, this one is probably based on the least amount of tangible Biblical evidence. Nevertheless, it is certainly within the realm of possibility, from both a theological and scientific perspective.

Was God creating the mere building blocks of life, such as amino acids? Or did God begin with single-celled organisms? We may never know the answer to either question. The process that God used to create life from lifelessness may never be found. Most Biblical scholars would disagree with the scenario that I am suggesting, and many scientists would prefer a natural mechanism for life's origin. However, God certainly did *something* with the water at about the time that life first appeared there. This is either an interesting coincidence or an intriguing answer to the origin of life on planet Earth.

▼

CHAPTER EIGHT

LIGHT!

And God said, "Let there be light," and there was light. God saw that the light was good, and he separated the light from the darkness. God called the light "day," and the darkness he called "night." And there was evening, and there was morning—the first day.

Gen. 1:4-5 (NIV)

But by the command of God, light was rendered visible; the thick murky clouds were dispersed, broken, or rarefied, and light diffused over the expanse of waters.[1]

Jamieson, Fausset, and Brown
A Commentary Critical and
Explanatory on the Whole Bible

When the primordial atmosphere first formed, the entire world was cloaked in total darkness. As the Earth began to cool, the steam in the atmosphere condensed into water. Eventually, a massive deluge commenced, which created the global ocean. The very process of precipitation, which formed the ocean, helped to dissipate the impenetrable cloud cover, and sunlight penetrated the murky atmosphere. Light had finally reached the surface of planet Earth.

We are left to conclude that the First Day, as described in the Bible, is scientifically accurate. While the Bible may not fully explain every stage of these "natural" processes, nothing that the Bible claims is in error.

Before we continue with our examination of the next Biblical verse, there are still some remaining issues of the First Day that need to be addressed.

THE BIG BANG

Some Creationists believe that the light described on the First Day did not emanate from the sun. Instead, they believe that it originated from the creation of the universe, or the Big Bang. Their reasoning seems sensible at first. Before the Big Bang there was nothing, which they interpret to be a state of darkness. After the Big Bang, energy and light suddenly existed in the universe.

Even if we choose to ignore some of the logical, scientific, and meta-physical problems with this argument (For example, can darkness exist without a universe or in a state of nothingness? Or is darkness merely the absence of light?), the theory does not withstand careful scrutiny and logic. The Bible declares that the universe was created *"In the beginning."* It then moves forward in time and describes the conditions of the Earth, revealing that it was in a state of darkness and covered with water. The Earth is first described in verse 2, while light is first mentioned in verse 4. Since the Earth clearly existed before light is first referenced, then the light cannot be attributed to the Big Bang. The Big Bang and the birth of our universe certainly preceded the formation of the Earth.

SYMBOLIC LIGHT

Some scholars believe that God's creation of light on the First Day was symbolic, and not a physical event. They believe that chaos, or darkness, originally reigned throughout the universe. It was only after God created order, or light, that the universe began to develop organization.

In a sense, the introduction of light to our planet does bring order. It gives us day and night, warmth, and allows plants to grow from the ground.

There is no real reason, however, to assume that any event of the First Day was symbolic. As I have already demonstrated, the Bible can be taken literally here, as it accurately describes the formation of our world. The Bible should not be taken symbolically unless the passage in question clearly requires it.

HIDDEN LIGHT

Another interesting but symbolic interpretation of this passage is one that interprets the light to be a "Hidden Light," rather than a light that generated luminosity. This "Hidden Light" is a light of truth or justice that cannot be seen by human beings. It was created at the beginning of time, and perhaps will some day be seen by God's faithful believers. This "light" will reveal the purpose or meaning of our existence, and bestow a higher understanding of God to all who witness it.

There are many variations on this theory, yet none of them should be accepted as valid interpretations. Once again, this is because the Biblical text is not symbolic in nature and should be taken literally.

THE LORD SPEAKS AND THE GIFT OF LIGHT

It is interesting to note that this was God's first recorded command of the Bible. In an earlier period (billions of years earlier, in fact), He had created the entire universe, including the Earth. But it was with the creation of light that He was first quoted. This magnifies the significance of God's action, and with good reason. Natural processes and life itself cannot be maintained on Earth without the light from our nearest star.

The stars that occupy our night skies are sometimes breathtaking in their beauty. Travelers traversing the land, and seamen sailing the seas, have long used the stars to help navigate them to their destinations. Even today, a simple glance up at the North Star points us in a definitive direction. The stars have been helpful to mankind over the centuries, and perhaps someday we will journey out to them and discover yet more of God's wondrous creations.

There are over 100 billion stars in our galaxy, but despite the prodigious number, one star in particular is preeminent in importance. It is evident that the greatest gift that God gave us on the First Day was not the magnificence and vastness of the universe, but the light from our sun. Without light there could be no life on planet Earth. Without the engine of that light, the sun, there could be no solar system.

The Bible was written for the benefit of mankind. It would only be logical for the Bible to highlight that which is most pertinent to man. Thus, God's first command is one of special importance to us. The prior creations of the First Day are certainly important, but you cannot help but read the first five verses and gain some sense of buildup to the creation of light. Nothing that occurred prior to that moment can match its significance.

THE EVENTS OF THE FIRST CREATION DAY

The stages in the formation of our planet are now considered "natural processes." We are told in our science textbooks that this is the natural way that solar systems and planets are formed in our universe. This is probably true. The formation of the sun and the planets as I have described them may be a common model found throughout the universe. But it is also likely that God formulated the grand design.

Consider the odds involved, that the author of the Creation Story could describe in general terms, the nature of the events in the creation of the universe and our world. The author lived thousands of years ago when scientific knowledge was minuscule and in its infancy. Yet, consider what he declared:

1. The universe had a beginning.
2. Time had a beginning.
3. The young Earth was desolate and void of life.
4. The surface of the Earth was blanketed in darkness.
5. The Earth was covered by water.
6. Light finally illuminated the Earth, but only after all of the above had occurred.

All of these statements are known to be scientifically accurate. Yet the author should not have known any of these scientific facts. If we were to disregard divine inspiration, we could not begin to explain how an author that lived so long ago could have acquired such knowledge. However such accuracy was achieved, the First Day of Creation has survived the scrutiny of science.

CHAPTER NINE

▼

THE EVENING AND THE MORNING

And there was evening, and there was morning—the first day.
Gen. 1:5 (NIV)

The Hebrew word *'ereb*, translated *evening* also means "sunset,"
"night," or "ending of the day." And the word *boqer*, translated
morning, also means "sunrise," "coming of light," "beginning of
the day," or "dawning," with possible metaphoric usage.[1]
Dr. Hugh Ross
Genesis One: A Scientific Perspective

Each of the first six days of Creation end with the Biblical phrase above—
except, of course, the number changes with each advancing day (the Seventh
Day has no such closure, and is a topic that will be discussed later).

The evening-followed-by-the-morning sequence at the end of each
Creation Day may not seem natural today. In our culture, the morning
hours begin at midnight. In contrast, each Creation Day continued

through the evening hours, and did not end until dawn, when the next day began. Since the phrase announced the beginning of the evening, we can infer that God only created during the daylight hours. Although it is not explicitly stated here, this may be a case where God set an example for us to follow. We are expected to work during the day and cease from work at dusk. Since societies at that time were largely agrarian, working the land and tending the herds, this was a wise pattern to follow.

There are some logistical problems with the standard interpretation of this phrase that may indicate something unconventional is taking place here. When and where does dawn arrive on a planet that is in constant rotation? Where is the reference point on the Earth that experiences the rising sun? At any time during a 24-hour day, the sun is both rising and setting somewhere on our planet. As experienced from the barren world of the First Day, without any reference point, it is impossible to differentiate between evening and morning. Both events are occurring simultaneously somewhere on our world. The problem is that these terms can only possess their traditional meanings from a particular location on the Earth. Since no such place is mentioned anywhere in the Creation Story, and the only stated reference point is the entire planet, these terms—as understood by the general reader—are illogical. The entire Earth cannot experience a morning or an evening.

This is the most compelling reason that I believe we should abandon the most common and popular definitions of "*evening*" and "*morning*" in this story. The word "*evening*" is not describing the setting of the sun, which is followed by twilight and then darkness. "*Morning*" is not the introduction of dawn, followed by a rising sun. Neither would make sense in this passage since the world experiences both events simultaneously, all of the time. Since the primary definitions produced illogical results, it is necessary to turn to secondary definitions. "*Evening*" can be thought of as an "end" or an "ending" to a period of creativity, while "*morning*" can be perceived as the "beginning" of another period of creativity.[2]

The terms "*evening*," "*morning*," and "*day*" in the Creation account are considered by many to be conclusive evidence that the days of Creation were 24-hours long. But even in our English language, the words "evening" and "morning" (and possible metaphors) are not limited to specific times in a 24-hour day. Consider such terms as "The dawn of the Roman Empire," "Morning in America," "Our twilight years," and "The dawn of man." There are many phrases in the English language that contain the words "morning," "dawn," "twilight," and "evening." Many of them, like the examples above, denote the beginning or ending of an unspecified period of time. Their usage is not restricted to a standard 24-hour day.

Remember, the goal of any Biblical translation should be to properly interpret the message of the author. Since the primary or popular definitions failed to produce any coherent message, it is reasonable to search for alternative meanings for the Hebrew words.

The author wrote the Creation Story in a manner that allows the reader to understand God's actions. We learn that God worked—or created—during the day, and ceased to work at night. This is essentially God's "workday" and is something that mankind has experienced since the dawn of time—work all day, relax, and sleep at night. It is certainly not meant to convey the notion that God works as humans do. He is not bound by such restrictions as a 24-hour clock, or the rising and setting of the sun. The entire purpose of introducing concepts such as "*day*," "*evening*," and "*morning*" was to allow us to relate to God's activities. Without this humanization of the account, there is probably no way that we could ever understand the workings of a Creator Whose time is boundless and Whose capacity is limitless.

If the Creation Days did not span twenty-four hours, then must we still believe that they occurred in consecutive, or continuous, units of time? Hebrew scholar Dr. Gleason L. Archer observes:

> There were six major stages in this work of formation, and these stages are represented by successive days of a week. In this connection it is important to observe that none of the six creative days bears a definite article in the Hebrew text; the

translations "*the* first day," "*the* second day," etc., are in error. The Hebrew says, "And the evening took place, and the morning took place, day one" (1:5). Hebrew expresses "the first day" by *hayyom hari'son*, but this text says simply *yom 'ehad* ("day one"). Again, in v.8 we read not *hayyom hasseni* ("the second day") but *yom seni* ("a second day").[3]

The original Hebrew text reveals that the days of Creation were certainly sequential in nature—each event followed the preceding event—however, they were not necessarily continuous. There may have been long periods of time between the Creation Days, and possibly between the events occurring within each day. The distinction here is that "*evening*" and "*morning*" are not necessarily definitive chronological boundaries. They were included in the text to distinguish between creation events that were sequential. It makes little sense to bind them to an arbitrary period, such as the twenty-four hours it takes for our planet to complete one rotation.[4]

As for the rest of the passage, I have already explained that "*morning*" and "*evening*" may encompass long periods of time. The Hebrew syntax of the passage, as noted by Dr. Archer, suggests that the Creation Days were indeed sequential but were not necessarily continuous. The days are better translated as "a second day" or "a third day" rather than using the definite article, "the," before the day number.[5] Unfortunately, the most egregious error in the translation of this passage occurs in the popular King James Version. For example, it translates the closing passages of the first two days as:

And the evening and the morning were the first day.
And the evening and the morning were the second day.

The translation is admirable for its brevity, and is adequate for the average Bible reader. For our endeavor, however, the error in the translation cannot be disregarded. What is missing is the second "to be" verb (The Hebrew word is *vayehi*).[6] A preferable translation of the original Hebrew text would acknowledge the verb following "*the evening.*" Here is an alternative translation of these phrases, patterned after Dr. Archer's observations:

*And the evening took place, and the morning took place, day one.
And the evening took place, and the morning took place, a
second day.*[7]

The proper interpretation of the passages may not seem significant—it
only alters a few words. But the message conveyed is dramatically different
from the King James Version. The *"evening"* and the *"morning"* in the
King James Version seem to be contained within one unit of action, since
they share the same verb (*"the evening and the morning* were *the first day"*).
The proper interpretation, however, reveals these events to be distinct, and
occurring separately, albeit consecutively (it could also be written as
"evening was, morning was...") The phrases, "A second day...A third
day..." display possible non-continuous events with lapses of time in
between. The traditional translations, *"The second day...The third day..."*
gives the reader the false impression that Creation events were continuous
with no passage of time between them.

It is hard not to notice the unusual syntax used by the author in these
passages. This may be additional evidence that we are not dealing with
days of creation that were twenty-four hours in length.

The initial evidence involves common sense and the point that I raised
earlier. At this stage of the Creation Story no cities had been built and no
countries had been established on our barren planet. The only reference
point mentioned on the First Day is the planet Earth. We are thus left to
conclude that it is the *entire* Earth that experienced *"the evening"* and *"the
morning."* But how is that possible? When is the beginning and the end of
a day on a planet that is rotating, and is simultaneously experiencing a rising sun on one side of the world and a setting sun on the opposite side?

Since there is no reasonable answer to such a question, we are compelled
to seek alternative interpretations for the terms. It is much more sensible to
view *"the evening"* as the end of God's creative work for the Day, while
understanding the term *"the morning"* to indicate the beginning of a new
Creation Day. The strict 24-hour perspective makes little sense.

▼

CHAPTER TEN

WHAT IS A DAY?

When I first read the Creation Story, I embraced the view that most readers hold today—that the days of Creation were six, consecutive, 24-hour days. This seemed to be a reasonable interpretation, and I held that view for much of my life—until this endeavor.

Since that time, my views have been altered by the facts, and I now support the beliefs of a Day-Age Creationist. As a Day-Age Creationist, I still believe in a special creation by God, however, I do not believe that the days of Creation were confined to twenty-four hours, but periods of time that range from thousands to hundreds of millions of years. From my perspective, the Creation Day is not the 24-hour day that we have all been taught to accept, but a "Day of God" or a period of God's activity.[1]

Even now that I have altered my understanding of Creation, I still cannot comprehend the significance that some attach to the rigid interpretation of the 24-hour day. Why is it so important that each Creation Day equals the time it takes the planet Earth to complete one rotation?

Certainly this cannot be a fundamental of our faith—not when there is so much more to be gained from the hallowed passages of the Scriptures.

The Holy Bible instills in each of us a sense of understanding of God and His expectations. Faith in His divinity appears to be paramount, for it is the belief in His unerring guidance that comforts us along our journey through a difficult and challenging life. The Ten Commandments are always a good place to begin, when seeking the path to righteousness. The Commandments are the moral foundation of most Western cultures. They instruct us how to interact with others, and how to properly honor the Lord our God. Learning from your mistakes, hard-work, humbleness before God, and treating others as you wish to be treated are more lessons that we are taught from the Scriptures. And yet the Bible reveals so much more—a virtually endless list of philosophical, theological, and moral arguments, messages, and examples that can be gained from anyone who chooses to embrace its wisdom.

I find it difficult to accept that a strict interpretation of 24-hour Creation Days must be embraced to attain salvation. It does not seem reasonable to require strict adherence to this time-frame—especially when we compare it to other moral commands that God has directed to each of us in the Bible. In my opinion, it is simply not important whether we believe that the Earth is 4.5 billion years old, or the 6,000 to 12,000 years of age that many Creationists claim. Either belief probably holds no bearing on our salvation. Of course, only God truly knows what is required of each of us, and I decline to challenge the rationale behind any of His judgments—as we all must.

Although the age of the Earth and the length of Creation Days may be irrelevant for salvation, this does not render either argument to be inconsequential. The infallibility of the Bible is very important—and is the primary focus of this endeavor. If the Bible contains even one ascertainable error, then the validity of the Scriptures may be called into question. But a proper understanding of its contents is the first obstacle that we must hurdle, if we are to properly assess its message.

The problem with this first obstacle is that the Old Testament was not written in modern English or any other modern language that could be easily translated. It was written in ancient Hebrew, a language that is thousands of years old. The antiquity of the language complicates our ability to translate the Bible. Even when a precise translation is achieved, it is often difficult to understand the message that the author intended to convey.

Recall the first time that you read something written by William Shakespeare. Shakespeare wrote his works in the English language. Yet, a casual, initial reading of his text is very confusing—it actually appears to be written in a foreign language. Not only has the English language significantly evolved in several hundred years but the colloquialisms, the culture, and the knowledge of mankind has changed dramatically through the centuries.

The Hebrew language that was used in the Old Testament is much older than Shakespeare's English, and it *is* a foreign language. As such, its translation into any language may slightly differ depending on the translator. There are many versions of the Holy Bible, and the proponents of each of them maintain a loyalty to their Bible's specific translations.

We have already discussed the translations and interpretations of the words "evening" and "morning," and have concluded that their meanings are not necessarily confined to the "ending" and "beginning" of a 24-hour day. This has already altered our understanding of the Biblical passages. The word "*day*" in the Creation Story is a similarly misunderstood term. Like "evening" and "morning," and like virtually every word in the English language, it possesses more than one definition. The Hebrew word that is translated into "day" is *yom*.[2] *Yom* is actually similar to the English word "day" in the ways it may be used. So let us examine some of the meanings of the word "day."

1. TWENTY-FOUR CONSECUTIVE HOURS

Twenty-four consecutive hours is probably the first definition of "day" that comes to mind, because it is the most common definition, and it is the subject that we are discussing. As I have noted before, there is nothing particularly special about a 24-hour Earth day that would compel God to limit His creative activity to accommodate that time-frame. One complete rotation of the Earth may be important to human beings and even the animals. But no animals appeared until the Fifth Day, while human beings were created on the Sixth Day. Why would God be constrained by the rotation of a planet that remained lifeless until the Fifth Day? On such a world, it would be pointless for God to complete His work within twenty-four hours—or one complete planetary rotation.

2. DAYTIME

The first time that the word *yom* is used in the Bible is when God named the light "*day*" in Genesis 1:5.[3] In this instance, "day" is referring to the daylight portion of the day. This varies in length but may average ten to fourteen hours. An interesting point can be made about this definition. Above the Arctic Circle or below the Antarctic Circle, "daylight" and "night" extend for several consecutive months of the year. Twilight also lasts longer in the polar regions. The length of "day" in this example is relative to the position on planet Earth where the measurement is made.

Creationists have often used this particular passage in the Bible, where God names the light "*day*," as evidence for 24-hour Creation Days. They are correct in their observation that *yom* is first defined here. They are also correct in their argument that this particular usage does not reflect the millions or billions of years that a Day-Age Creationist embraces. They are clearly wrong in their assessment, however, that this proves that Creation Days spanned twenty-four hours.

The first appearance of the word *yom* represents only the daylight hours, not the entire day. If this is used as evidence to determine the length of Creation Days, then those days would only average twelve hours—depending on the location on the Earth and the time of the year. It is true that God named the daylight "*day*," but that reveals nothing about the actual length of a Creation Day.

3. AN ERA

A "day" may also refer to an era. Some examples of this are found in the expressions: "The day of the automobile" or "The day of the Lord." We often hear older people say, "Back in my day..." In these examples, the period of time that is encompassed in a "day" may be years or even decades.

The use of the word "day" in this circumstance almost never represents twenty-four hours. It can designate a period of time that may span weeks, months, or even years. In these examples, a "day" represents a period of time (an "era") that is generally not recognized by specific chronological boundaries, but by the activity that it contains.[4]

4. A UNIT OF WORK

Before this era of rapid transportation, people would often think of distance in terms of "days" of travel: "Three days distance by horse" or "Two days march to the enemy fort."[5] In these examples, "day" does not actually represent twenty-four hours of continuous activity. Instead, it represents the time to complete a designated task—traveling a particular distance. While the distance remains constant, the time to traverse the distance depends on the form of travel.[6]

In today's modern office, it is not uncommon for employees to refer to the completion time for projects as "a few days of work" or "a whole day of work." People of all employment today often put in a "full day of work" at their jobs. In these modern examples, a "day" is actually referring to an eight-hour workday and not the entire day. In addition, it is assumed that for those employed from Monday through Friday, weekends and Holidays are not factored into any assessment of project completion. Consequently, entire "days" are excluded.

In all of these examples, a "day" is a measurement of the time involved to complete a task, and not the passage of twenty-four consecutive hours. Just as we discuss "a day's work" (which is seldom twenty-four hours but more likely an eight-hour workday), God has revealed His "day of work" in each of the days of Creation.

ORGANIZING A TASK

How could man understand all that God had accomplished over a period of billions of years? One way would be for God to divide His creative process into recognizable units, each one containing highlights of that time period. Each of those units would then be called a "day."

Suppose that you have a major project to complete over a period of time. A common organizational method used to complete the project is to divide it into a series of steps or tasks. Each step comprises all of the work that needs to be completed before moving onto the next step. The work involved within each step is generally related or similar in some manner, which is the reason that they would be grouped together. You would then label each step to identify them. When "Step 1" is completed you move on to "Step 2." When "Step 2" is completed you move on to "Step 3," and so on, until the final step is completed and the project is finished.

The steps involved may take varying lengths of time to be completed. If you have a proficient understanding of what you are doing, you may even begin the next step before the current step is finished. In this manner, each step is a unit of related work completed over a period of time.

I believe that this analogy is similar to what God did in describing Creation. Each step of Creation was comprised of many tasks, but only one or two major achievements were recorded in the Bible. The major tasks of each day were grouped into a step, or a unit of work. Since there was a beginning and an end to that step, the Hebrew words *voker* (meaning "dawn" or possibly "beginning") and *erev* (meaning "twilight" or "ending") were used.[7] The Hebrew word *yom* represented the time to complete each task. What other method could God use to relate these events to the ancient Hebrews? The people of that time were certainly unaware that the universe was billions of years old. Such an enormous amount of time would have seemed like eternity to them.

CONCLUSION

The purpose of this chapter is to demonstrate that the Hebrew word *yom*, in general, represents a period of time—the length of which is determined by its use in the sentence. As illustrated above, the word *yom* comprises several definitions in the Hebrew language—very similar, in fact, to the English word "day." This is important to know, because so many people assume that the very use of this word is definitive confirmation that a Creation Day *must* be twenty-four hours in length. That belief is clearly not true. Even the conservative reference, *Nelson's Illustrated Bible Dictionary*, acknowledges:

> Skeptics have ridiculed the creation story in Genesis because it reports that the creation occurred in six days. But the indefinite meaning of day takes care of this objection.[8]

My analysis of each Creation Day in the following chapters will be from the perspective of a Day-Age Creationist. We will determine if the initial story of the Bible can withstand the scientific scrutiny from this acceptable interpretation. Later, I will give Biblical evidence that demonstrates that a long Creation Day is not only an acceptable interpretation but a preferable interpretation.

ALTERNATIVE INTERPRETATIONS

There are two other interpretations of the Creation Story that should be addressed here. Both acknowledge a universe and a Creation that span billions of years.

One belief is that the days of Creation in the Bible are not describing the actual history of creation, but instead were the seven consecutive days that God revealed the Creation Story to the author—generally acknowledged to be Moses. In this scenario, one day God revealed to Moses the initial creation events that occurred in the distant past. Moses categorized those events as belonging to the "First Day" of Creation. The very next day God revealed more of the Creation Story to Moses. Moses in turn classified those events as occurring on the "Second Day" of Creation. The revelations would continue for five more days, and each day Moses merely categorized the events as belonging to a corresponding Creation Day. Consequently, the duration of God's Creation was never actually being recorded, but rather the day of the revelation.

Another theory is that all of the events in each day of Creation did, in fact, span 24-hours in length. However, long gaps of indeterminable time bridged the recorded days. This belief appears to be an intriguing attempt to harmonize science with the Bible. It concedes to science a universe that is billions of years old while satisfying the Fundamentalist's belief in 24-hour Creation Days.

While both theories might be plausible, most Biblical scholars do not support either belief. Such imaginative attempts at Bible-science reconciliation are not necessary. The Theory of Creation that I am proposing needs only to accept that the Biblical Creation Day is not the 24-hour day that we have come to embrace, but rather a period of time that the Lord recognizes as one of His days.

CHAPTER ELEVEN

▼

THE FIRST ACT OF GOD

Most Bible readers are familiar with the opening phrase of the Book of Genesis. As previously noted, "*In the beginning*" is the translation of the Hebrew word, *Bereshith*.[1] By analyzing the first several Hebrew words and noting the context in which *Bereshith* is used, the translation, "*In the beginning, God created,*" is considered to be acceptable by most scholars.

It is not, however, the only translation possible. Some Bibles translate the initial verse as "*When God began to create*" or "*In the beginning of God's creating.*" Most Biblical scholars also consider these translations to be acceptable. For the average reader, such translations are not significant and do not alter the overall theme of the first chapter. However, for our purposes these differences produce unexpected consequences on our scientific analysis of the first three verses of Genesis.

Here is *The Jewish Publication Society of America's* translation of the first three verses of the Bible:

When God began to create the heaven and the earth—the earth being unformed and void, with darkness over the surface of the deep and a wind from God sweeping over the water—God said, "Let there be light"; and there was light.[2]

A careful analysis of this translation reveals that God's first act was the creation of light, and not the creation of the heavens and the Earth. It further reveals that the Earth already existed when God created light, and that the Earth was unformed, void, shrouded in darkness, and covered by water at the time light was created.

This interpretation is very different from the one that we have examined in this endeavor. When the first phrase is translated as "*In the beginning,*" what follows is a very short chronology. It is revealed that God first created the heavens and the Earth (the entire universe). The Earth was initially unformed and void, shrouded in darkness, and engulfed in water. Then the Spirit of God moved (or hovered) over the water. It was only *after* all of those events had transpired that God created light.

What is the reader left to believe? Was God's first act the creation of the universe? Or did God begin by creating light? Was there preexisting material before the creation event? Or did God create the entire universe from nothing (*creation ex nihilo*)?

It is interesting that both translations are considered to be acceptable by scholars, especially since their differences render the order of events on the First Day to be virtually in reverse of each other. But there is always some latitude allowed when translating an ancient foreign language. Even *The Jewish Publication Society of America* includes a footnote with this first phrase, noting that "*In the Beginning*" can also be used.[3] If we are to base our understanding of these events entirely on linguistic interpretation, then the discrepancies cannot be resolved. That is why we must turn to logic and science for the answer.

First we must understand what is meant by light. The only source of appreciable light that our planet receives comes from the sun. The sun is a yellow dwarf star through which all life on the Earth depends; it is the engine that fuels our solar system. The light that we receive from the moon is reflected light from the sun. Starlight, though inspiring in its beauty, is negligible as a source of light.

Some Creationists believe that the light created on the First Day was not sunlight. Instead, they attribute the ancient light to an unknown source of illumination that God has long since removed. This argument may have been developed to support the misguided belief that the sun, the moon, and the stars were created on the Fourth Day (I will discuss the Fourth Day in a later chapter). However, anyone who attempts to associate the light of the First Day with a source other than our sun must surely be expected to provide some evidence to support their conviction.

There is no doubt that a God Who created an entire universe would certainly be capable of producing a source of light that illuminated the Earth until the sun was created three days later. No one is questioning God's creative ability. However, there is no evidence that such a source ever existed, nor is there any reason that it would be needed—not when the most obvious source of light, the sun, still exists today, located some ninety-three million miles from our planet.

Without any tangible evidence, we are left to conclude that the light the Bible describes is the light from the sun. This is the most elementary solution to the problem posed, yet it is one that too many Bible scholars either disregard or refute. No other miracle is needed for this source of light. No other theories or unscientific proposals need to be postulated.

Now that we are certain that the light of the First Day emanated from our sun, we are able to draw another reasonable conclusion. The initial phrase of the Bible should be translated as *"In the Beginning"* rather than the linguistically acceptable, but logically faulty phrase, *"When God began to create."*

The reasoning behind this is indisputable. Since God created the *"heavens and the Earth"* (the universe includes all of the galaxies, stars, and our sun and Earth) the creation of light (from our sun) could not be His first act of creation. If we rephrase the words of the "*When God began to create*" argument, to better convey the meaning of the passage, we have:

> When God began to create the universe—which includes our solar system and our Earth—and the Earth was in the condition described in verse 2, then God created light.

If we were to accept this translation, we would be faced with a peculiar dilemma. These verses describe an Earth that already existed before God created the universe. But how is that possible? How could the Earth exist without a universe? If we say that the universe already existed with the Earth, and it was only light that God created, then what kind of universe was it? The universe consists of billions of galaxies, which in turn consist of billions of stars. Consequently, if the universe already existed, then stars also existed—and the light that they radiated. It is impossible for the universe to exist without light. Since the light described emanated from our sun, and our sun is a star, then it too must have existed. The Earth could not possibly exist without the sun. Certainly there could be no liquid water (*the deep*) without the sun.

The translation, "*When God began to create*" also introduces another problem. Such a translation diminishes the power of the God of the Bible, and He is rendered inferior to the preeminent status that we have come to embrace. If the universe and the Earth were already in existence before God's initial act—the creation of light—then to whom do we attribute the creation of the universe and the Earth? How did they originate? If God created the universe, then the Bible would not disregard such a magnificent miracle and begin with the creation of light. The very chapter that explains the Creation event should include God's creation of the universe.

I believe that the Holy Bible did not exclude God's initial act. It was recorded, and it included the birth of our universe out of nothing (the Big Bang), the formation of the galaxies, and the development of our solar system. All of these events are recorded for posterity, and are included with the simple and succinct phrase: *In the beginning God created the heavens and the earth.*

This seemingly modest phrase possesses extraordinary meaning. It encompassed a time-span of billions of years, from that first moment of the Big Bang some ten to twenty billion years ago, to the time of the Earth's formation—some 4.5 billion years ago.

When God said, "*Let there be light,*" light from our sun finally penetrated the dissipating cloud cover that had previously shrouded the young Earth in darkness. The Holy Bible has recorded this event and science has confirmed it.

"*In the beginning God created the heavens and the earth,*" is the correct translation of the first verse of the Bible.

▼

CHAPTER TWELVE

GOD CALLED THE EXPANSE "SKY"

And God said, "Let there be an expanse between the waters to separate water from water." So God made the expanse and separated the water under the expanse from the water above it. And it was so. God called the expanse "sky." And there was evening, and there was morning—the second day.

Gen. 1:6-8 (NIV)

And God said, Let there be a firmament in the midst of the waters, and let it divide the waters from the waters. And God made the firmament, and divided the waters which were under the firmament from the waters which were above the firmament: and it was so. And God called the firmament Heaven. And the evening and the morning were the second day.

Gen. 1:6-8 (KJV)

THE SECOND DAY

I have included both the New International Version (NIV) and the King James Version (KJV) of the Second Day for us to make comparisons, and to enhance our understanding of the Biblical text. The dissimilar translations of two words comprise most of the real differences in the verses. It is essential that we gain a better understanding of these terms before we can determine the correct meaning of the passage.

"HEAVEN" OR "SKY"

In the KJV, the word *"Heaven"* is used where the NIV uses the word *"sky."* Theologians have no problem understanding the King James Version of this text. However, many readers of the King James Version may form the wrong impression from this passage. Heaven—the home of God and His angels—was not being created here. Such a translation would make little sense, since the passage that we are discussing is clearly a continuation from the First Day, and the further formation of our planet. The New International Version translation is preferable here. God created the atmosphere, or what could be called the *"sky."*

"FIRMAMENT" OR "EXPANSE"

The second difference is the King James translation of the Hebrew word, *"rakia,"* into *"firmament."*[1] The NIV translates *rakia* as an *"expanse,"* which God named the *"sky."*

There has been much debate about the term *"firmament"* and its exact meaning in this verse. Many believe that what is being described here is consistent with an erroneous concept of the people of that time—that there existed a metallic dome ceiling above the world, which supported a repository of rainwater. In this case, the "firmament" would be a hammered-out, metal sheet that stretched across the sky. It separated the waters on the surface of the Earth from the repository of water that existed above it.

If this were the only definition of *rakia* then the passage would clearly contradict established science. No such dome exists, of course, and it is our atmosphere that separates us from space. However, *rakia* also possesses other meanings that do not necessarily imply a stretched-out, metallic substance; they are "an expanse" and "thinned out."[2,3]

The "*expanse*" or "*firmament*" in question is the area between the surface of the Earth (water under the expanse) and the clouds (the water above it). This is a layer of the atmosphere that we call the troposphere. It supplies the air that we breathe, and the clouds that yield the rain.

THE HYDROLOGIC CYCLE

The formation of the hydrologic cycle, which is also known as the water cycle, is also being described on the Second Day. The basic flow of the water cycle works like this: surface water is taken up into the air by the process of evaporation; the moist air then condenses to form rain, a process called condensation; rain water returns to the surface via precipitation. The Creation Story does not elaborate on the hydrologic cycle, and the text is essentially an allusion to the process. Other Bible verses, which I will list later, do describe the cycle in greater detail. However, the Biblical text does reveal that at that time in the Earth's history, the hydrologic cycle began.

The events of the Second Day are scientifically accurate. As I have previously explained, the atmosphere of our young planet was like a thick blanket suspended over the Earth's dark surface. It obstructed all light from the sun. The super-heated steam in the air was too hot to condense, and remained as a gas in the heavy atmosphere. As the Earth cooled, water vapor condensed into rain, thereby precipitating and creating the global ocean. The dissipation of the dense atmosphere allowed some sunlight to finally reach the Earth's watery surface. Sunlight is the catalyst of the hydrologic cycle—warming the surface waters to the point where evaporation can occur. Although the early Earth was warm enough to induce immediate evaporation (volcanoes were probably ubiquitous on our planet), the sun's rays were essential for the process to continue. Once the thick atmosphere dispersed, water existed on the surface of the Earth as the sea, and in the atmosphere as clouds. The atmosphere, or "*sky*," of the young Earth, separated the waters.

The Bible only tells us that the "*sky*" (a very generic term) was created on the Second Day. But it is interesting that at that time in the Earth's history, the young atmosphere of the Earth was already beginning to form into a more stable layer of gasses. The atmosphere was in fact being created, confirming the Bible's claims.

THE ATMOSPHERE

It should also be noted that at that time in the Earth's history the early atmosphere still contained no oxygen, and could not support human life.

Around 3.5 billion years ago, single-celled organisms called "Cyanobacteria" appeared. They were one of the earliest forms of life on the Earth. Cyanobacteria (commonly called "blue-green algae") are photosynthetic organisms. This means that they are similar to plants, and convert sunlight into energy. These organisms may not have been the very first form of life on our planet, but their existence played a significant role in the development of our atmosphere. While the Earth's early atmosphere did not contain any free-oxygen, Cyanobacteria release oxygen as a byproduct of their metabolism. The existence and success of Cyanobacteria generated an increasing amount of oxygen into our early atmosphere. Eventually, Cyanobacteria greatly altered the atmosphere of the Earth, providing us with the very oxygen that we require to breathe today.

▼

CHAPTER THIRTEEN

LAND EMERGES FROM THE SEA

And God said, "Let the water under the sky be gathered to one place, and let dry ground appear." And it was so. God called the dry ground "land," and the gathered waters he called "seas." And God saw that it was good.

Gen. 1:9-10 (NIV)

THE THIRD DAY

Around the same time that light first reached the Earth's watery surface, and the hydrologic cycle was just beginning, the reign of bombardment from small planetesimals, meteors, and comets was coming to an end.[1] In addition, the interior of our world—which had consisted of thick, swirling, molten metals—was slowly cooling. It was also around this time (between 4 billion and 3.8 billion years ago) that tectonic plates began to form and the process of continent-building began.

Our planet was probably never completely covered by water, although for the sake of argument, it was, essentially, a watery world. Volcanic eruptions undoubtedly formed islands that would rise above the water's surface from time to time, but they were not permanent and erosion would soon submerge their remains.

Around four billion years ago the continents were only about one-tenth of their size today.[2] The cornerstones of the continents—granitic rock called "cratons"—began to buoy out of the water at that time.[3] Cratons are the oldest remaining rocks on our planet.[4] While the sea-floor mostly consists of dark, heavy, basaltic rock, the land is composed of lighter, granitic rock, which tends to rise above sea-level like an object floating on water.[5]

Initially, the young Earth was too turbulent to support the horizontal process that we recognize as plate tectonics. The interior of the Earth was still very hot and the process was more vertical and more violent. As more cratons formed, they were thrust violently upward and moved quickly and freely above the Earth's watery surface. The moving cratons often collided, merged, and formed large landmasses. Eventually, the Earth's interior cooled and the craton's vertical movement subsided. It was then, some 2.5 billion years ago, that the horizontal, or sliding, process we understand as plate tectonics truly began, and the continents began to form.[6]

The continents are formed on large plates of rock, which move very slowly around the Earth's surface. Areas where the plates collide are generally regions of volatility. The western coasts of North America and South America are located at the edges of such plates, and are often areas of violent earthquakes. The subcontinent of India rests on its own tectonic plate. It was once part of the African continent but moved independently across the Indian Ocean and collided with Asia. It struck Asia with such tremendous force that the land there was thrust upward, and produced the world's highest mountains, the Himalayas.

Tectonic plate movement is a relatively recent addition to the annals of science. Alfred Wegener, a German meteorologist, was the first to propose the theory in 1915.[7] The process of plate tectonics (and continental drift) was not understood until the middle of the twentieth century. Even today, there are still many questions about the process that remain unanswered.

However, there is now enough evidence to support the theory that science has accepted it as fact.

Of all the theories and established facts of science that I am presenting to support the Biblical Creation, this one is the most impressive, and comes closest to comparing with the Biblical text. The Bible clearly states that the continents emerged from the sea. This revelation is neither anticipated nor intuitive—certainly the author would not be expected to know this. And yet, this Biblical assertion correlates closely with the scientific facts.

Today, we possess a more comprehensive understanding of how the continents formed and how the tectonic plates move. This has led us to a greater understanding of the Biblical text. It also allows us to conclude that the Creation Story has once again been verified by the expanding knowledge of science.

PANGAEA

There has been at least one major misinterpretation of the Biblical text of the Third Day. It involves the phrase: *"Let the water under the sky be gathered to one place."* This is an unusual phrase, and I can see where it may cause some confusion. Where was this water that gathered in one place? Does this represent all of the water in the world?

It is very clear to us today that the water on our world is not truly gathered in one particular area. We are not referring to a lake, or an inland sea, where the water is distinctly separate from the land in one particular location. Water on the Earth both surrounds the continents and lies within the continents. This must have been clearly evident to the author of the Creation Story. If the author viewed the water in the Mediterranean Sea as water that gathered in one place, how would he perceive all of the water that makes up the streams, rivers, lakes, and ponds? Certainly these bodies of water were created by God, too, and would not be disregarded by the author.

One of the common interpretations of this phrase is to view the water and the land as being distinct. This would essentially require that all of the land on the Earth would have to be gathered into one location with water surrounding it. Such a scenario may have occurred several times in the history of the Earth, however, the further back in time we travel the less certain we are of the exact positions of the tectonic plates.

We are certain that this scenario did occur at least once in the Earth's history. Around the end of the Paleozoic Era, some 250 million years ago, all of the continents came together and formed one large supercontinent called Pangaea. Pangaea was one huge landmass, encircled by the ocean like an island. At that time, it could literally be said that the water had gathered into one place (disregarding inland bodies of water), while the land had also gathered into one place. This scenario seems to conform to the Biblical phrase, and many recognize Pangaea's existence as confirmation of the Biblical text.

From a chronological perspective, however, Pangaea's existence is incompatible with the Third Day. Pangaea formed long after tectonic plate movement began, and the existence of the supercontinent does little to enhance the authenticity of the Bible. In addition, there is evidence that other supercontinents existed before Pangaea.[8] The entire supercontinent scenario is simply a case where people are reading too much into the text. While it is true that the existence of Pangaea does compare favorably to the Biblical description provided, there is no need to search history for such an unexpected scientific event.

The author of the Creation Story was certainly aware that water, other than the oceans, was found throughout the land. The unusual phrase is probably being over-interpreted by most people today. If we think about it, water does tend to amass as it moves. Streams lead into rivers, and rivers generally lead into the oceans, as water always seeks its level. The general purpose of these Biblical verses is to announce the emergence of the land from beneath the surface of the sea. That is all that is really necessary for us to understand the first major event of the Third Day.

▼

CHAPTER FOURTEEN

VEGETATION—THE FIRST LIFE

*Then God said, "Let the land produce vegetation: seed-bearing plants
and trees on the land that bear fruit with seed in it, according to their
various kinds." And it was so. The land produced vegetation: plants
bearing seed according to their kinds and trees bearing fruit with seed
in it according to their kinds. And God saw that it was good. And
there was evening, and there was morning—the third day.*

Gen. 1:11-13 (NIV)

According to the Creation Story, the Third Day consisted of two major
events: the emergence of land from beneath the sea, and the creation of
plants on the land. Two types of plants in particular were introduced on
this day: seed-bearing plants and fruit-bearing trees. It is also on this day
that the term *"according to their kinds"* is mentioned for the first time.

It could almost be anticipated that plants would be introduced at this
time in the Creation Story. Land had just appeared, so plants—the lowest
rung of the food chain in the eyes of ancient man—could not have been

introduced before this time. Plants could not have been created any time after the Fourth Day either, for on the Fifth Day, animals were introduced. Since many animals consume plants for food, plants would have to be introduced prior to their creation.

There are some differences among Bibles in the translation, and thus, interpretation of these verses. There are also some additional points that I feel should be addressed here.

THE "LAND" VERSUS THE "EARTH"

While the NIV Bible translates the text as "*Let the land produce vegetation…*" many other Bibles do not use the word "*land.*" Instead, the word "*Earth*" is used. Here is one example:

> And God said, Let the earth bring forth grass, the herb yielding seed, and the fruit tree yielding fruit after his kind, whose seed is in itself, upon the earth: and it was so.
>
> Gen. 1:11 (KJV)

The word "*Earth*" (the Hebrew word is "*ha'arets*"[1]) in the Bible does not necessarily refer to the entire planet. It may be a reference to dry land, which may encompass a region, kingdom, something equivalent to a country, or simply the dry surface where man resides.[2] Similarly, the word "earth" in English could also mean the soil or dirt—and not the entire planet.

It is generally believed that the Bible is referencing just the dry land in these verses. The primary reason for this is the context in which the word "*land*" or "*Earth*" is used. Earlier on the Third Day the land emerged from the sea upon God's command. Continuing with that theme, God then commanded the land to produce vegetation. This interpretation implies that God restricted the creation of plants to the land, and excluded vegetation in the sea. This may not be significant to the average reader, but if the Bible is saying that land plants were the first forms of life, and preceded marine vegetation and sea animals, then the scientific validity of the

Creation Story must be brought into question. This creation order does not concur with the scientific record.

If we were to understand these verses to reveal that God commanded the "planet Earth" to produce vegetation, then it would be acceptable for us to declare that marine vegetation, such as seaweed and algae, could be included. The consensus translation of the text, however, is that of dry land only—indicating that only vegetation on the land was produced.

This consensus, however, does not necessarily preclude us from expanding the realm of God's creations. Most commentaries and analyses of the Bible are primarily focused on the theological implications of the text, and not its scientific consequences. Such methodology makes sense, since the overwhelming majority of those that turn to the Bible are seeking God's message, and not answers to the mysteries of science. I suspect that when pressed for a definitive interpretation, most Theologians would include the creation of sea plants on the Third Day.

The Bible excludes many types of plants and animals in the Creation Story. That does not necessarily imply that God deems them unimportant or does not recognize their existence. But in the eyes of ancient man, for whom this story was first revealed, it was inconsequential that something like algae or seaweed may have been excluded from the Creation Story.

"VEGETATION" OR "GRASS"

The King James Version's translation of this text differs from most Biblical translations. It declares that three types of vegetation were produced: grass, seed-yielding herbs, and fruit trees. Other versions of this text (like the NIV at the beginning of this chapter) substitute the word *"vegetation"* for the word *"grass,"* and reduces the seed-bearing plants and the fruit trees to subsets of the "vegetation" that was produced.

Critics of the Bible believe they have gained valuable ammunition with the King James Version's translation of this passage. From a scientific perspective the Bible is in error. Grasses appeared on the Earth after the creation of sea creatures and birds (which were created on the Fifth Day). The King James Version is probably the most popular version of the Holy Bible, and it is the primary version that most skeptics read and quote when analyzing the Creation Story. From a critical perspective, this passage proves that the Creation Story does not agree with science, since the order of creation is clearly inaccurate.

There is nothing necessarily wrong with the King James Version's translation of this phrase. It is a reasonable translation and might, in fact, be correctly stating the author's true intentions. The Hebrew word being used here, "*deshe*," is translated as "*grass*."[3] However, most Bibles interpret "*deshe*" to represent all types of vegetation, or plants in general.

It is pointless to debate the date that grasses appeared on the Earth, since that translation does not appear in most Bibles. Most translations concur with the New International Version's interpretation: God called forth the land to produce vegetation, and the two types of vegetation that were produced were seed-bearing plants and fruit-producing trees.

PLANTS ARE NOT LIFE

You may notice that the text does not say that God "created" the plants, only that He commanded the land to produce them. Apparently, God had placed within the fertile soil all the properties necessary for the production of plants. All that was required was His command to initiate the process. It should also be noted that the Hebrews did not consider plants to be alive like the animals.[4]

ACCORDING TO THEIR KINDS

This is the first time the phrase "*according to their kinds*" is used. It suggests that there is a limiting property in the types of offspring that these plants can produce. Fruit trees have always been and will always be fruit trees, possessing the same properties of their progenitors. The same is true of seed-bearing plants. I will discuss the phrase "*according to their kinds*" in more detail in a later chapter.

THE SCIENTIFIC RECORD

Even if we were to disregard the King James Version's translation of *"grass,"* the introduction of plants on land at this stage in the Creation Story is still problematic. Angiosperms, or flowering plants, are among the most popular and prevalent plants in the world. Most plants that human beings cultivate for food and medicinal purposes are actually flowering plants—including those that we would consider to be "grasses." Yet, Angiosperms did not appear until approximately 120 million years ago, which is somewhat late on our planetary clock.[5]

Plants in general may have first appeared on land during the upper Silurian Period.[6] That is a geological period of time that spanned from 438 to 412 million years ago.[7] But plants probably did not achieve prodigious success until the Devonian Period, which extended from 412 to 354 million years ago.[8,9] Even if we were to extend this date to its extreme limit, the earliest that we are able to date any rudimentary plant life on land may only be 476 million years ago.[10]

Here we appear to stumble upon a major scientific discrepancy in the Bible, regardless of the version that we are reading. The sea creatures initially created two days later, on the Fifth Day, probably represent the tremendous explosion of diverse marine life that is called the "Cambrian Explosion" (a point that I will argue later). But that profusion of new life occurred some 540 million years ago—tens of millions of years *before* any life had appeared on land.

Plants actually preceded animals in the seas. However, the fruit trees and the seed-bearing plants that we naturally classify as land plants appeared long after animal life thrived in the seas on the Fifth Day. Consequently, the Bible appears to be hopelessly inaccurate. From a scientific perspective, what the Bible declares to be created on the Fifth Day actually occurred before the creation of plants on the Third Day.

When we envision a fruit tree, there are several types that come to mind. Apple trees, cherry trees, and pear trees are just a few examples. These are all *"trees on the land that bear fruit with seeds in it"* as God commanded (remember, the Hebrew word that is being translated as "*land*" could also be referring to the entire Earth). Seed-bearing plants may include many of the vegetables grown in the garden, or some of the various grains—since to man, many of these appear to be seed-like vegetation.

As we read the Bible today, we are inclined to place our modern concepts of words and phrases upon the words we read. This is completely reasonable and generally harmless, since the Bible and its messages tend to transcend the science, the cultures, and the knowledge possessed through the ages. In our endeavor, however, this natural inclination may lead us astray as we carefully and thoroughly examine the scientific validity of the Creation Story, and the correct translation and interpretation of its passages.

Our modern perception of fruit trees and seed-bearing plants may simply not apply to the Biblical text stated here. We may, in fact, be too rigid in our understanding of these plants. This is attributable to the passage of over two thousand years since the writing of this story. But what then does the Bible mean when it refers to fruit trees and seed-bearing plants? Dr. Hugh Ross explains:

> Clearly, most of these life-forms were relatively primitive; the words *seed*, *trees*, and *fruit* need not be interpreted as narrowly as they are defined today. Centuries ago *seed* denoted any kind of embryo from which a new plant would grow. Similarly, all plants produce something that would be termed *fruit*. *Trees* would include shrubs, bushes, and plants with wooden stalks.[11]

It is probably acceptable to interpret these Biblical verses in a more general sense, rather than limiting them or restricting them to any plants in particular. Essentially, what is being revealed here is the creation of plants on our world.[12] So while it is true that animal life in the seas had already appeared before the fruit trees and the seed-bearing plants on land, it is also true that plants always preceded animals, in the seas and on the land. Evidence of seaweed and planktonic algae in the oceans date back tens of millions of years before sea-dwelling animals appeared there.[13] Plants on land also predated animals by millions of years. If we can accept that what was created on the Third Day simply represents all plant-life, then the Bible corroborates with the scientific facts.

I have stated that my purpose in this endeavor is to give an objective and honest scientific evaluation of the Creation Story. My analysis of the Third Day may appear disingenuous—reinterpreting the text to harmonize the Bible with current scientific knowledge. However, it is difficult to determine if the Bible has excluded sea plants from the Creation Story.

Scientists may debate the taxonomy of marine vegetation, but the Bible does not categorize its creations in the same manner as modern man. Ancient man would have been unconcerned if plants in the seas were officially members of the "Plant Kingdom." If it was green and appeared plant-like, whether it was washed ashore or was caught in the fisherman's net, it would have been considered a plant.

We must also recognize another possibility here, and that would be the author's aspiration of brevity in the text. It is true that a more precise chronology of the creation of living things would have plants created in the sea first, followed by animals in the sea, followed by plants on the land, and completed by animals on the land. However, a more precise recording of events adds little to the general theme of the Creation Story, while appending needless lines of text. The significance of the second major event of the Third Day is to declare that God had introduced plants or vegetation onto our world. It would serve little purpose to expand upon the exact order and details of every creation of God. How many readers would be willing to scrutinize the thousands of pages of text that such an inclusive listing would entail?

Other forms of plants would appear on our world much later than the time-frame allowed for the Third Creation Day—flowering plants are an example of this. However, if it is acceptable to understand the Third Day as the day that plants in general first appeared on our world, then this day, too, has withstood the scrutiny of science. I believe that the majority of Biblical scholars would accept such an interpretation.

▼

CHAPTER FIFTEEN

THE LIGHTS IN THE SKY ABOVE

And God said, "Let there be lights in the expanse of the sky to separate the day from the night, and let them serve as signs to mark seasons and days and years, and let them be lights in the expanse of the sky to give light on the earth." And it was so. God made two great lights—the greater light to govern the day and the lesser light to govern the night. He also made the stars. God set them in the expanse of the sky to give light on the earth, to govern the day and the night, and to separate light from darkness. And God saw that it was good. And there was evening, and there was morning—the fourth day.

Gen. 1:14-19 (NIV)

We are so far removed from the world of Genesis that we can scarcely comprehend how revolutionary was such a statement uttered to those who were habituated to a universe whose heavens were peopled with gods and demons, benign and malign tutelary spirits. [1]

Bruce Vawter
On Genesis: A New Reading

THE FOURTH DAY

The events of the Fourth Day pose another problem for the Biblical reader. Many Creationists believe that the sun, the moon, and the stars were created on this day. But if the sun was created on the Fourth Day, what was the source of the light that God created on the First Day? Here are some common answers to this intriguing question.

1. ORDER FROM DISORDER

What was created on the First Day was not "light" that we perceive as illumination. It was "order," created by God to conquer the "disorder" or "chaos" of the young universe.

I have already discussed this theory. Most Biblical translators do not accept this interpretation, since it is reasonably clear that "luminosity" is being described here, and not something symbolic.

2. A TEMPORARY "LIGHT"

There are some that believe the light of the First Day emanated from a luminous source other than the sun. For some inexplicable reason, God created a temporary source of light that illuminated the Earth for the first three Creation Days. When He finally created the sun on the Fourth Day, there was no longer any need for the mysterious, temporary light. God has since removed it from our solar system (or universe) without leaving behind any evidence of its existence.

This belief is arguably the most common interpretation among young-Earth Creationists. Regardless of the rationale they use to explain or justify such a questionable interpretation, this theory simply cannot be given any credence. From a physical perspective, such an imaginative interpretation requires some evidence that the alternative light source ever existed. However, no such evidence exists. From a logical perspective, we must question why God would create a temporary source of light and then wait for three days until He created the sun. The sun is a star, and—like other stars throughout the universe—it produces the light that illuminates the planets that revolve around it. What purpose is served by delaying the creation of the sun and creating a temporary light source? Why wouldn't God merely create the sun on the First Creation Day and make *it* the source of light?

I will acknowledge that God often works in mysterious ways, and His divine purpose cannot always be ascertained or understood by human beings. However, the "temporary light" theory of the First Day certainly challenges the credibility of the Scriptures. This theory requires us to accept the existence of something that no longer exists and left behind no evidence of its existence. It is never directly addressed nor explained in the Bible, and it performed the function of something that was created just three days later. When Creationists embrace this theory, it is little wonder that skeptics insist that the Scriptures can be interpreted in any manner the reader chooses.

I also find it intriguing that many of the same people that believe in strict 24-hour Creation days could place the creation of the sun and the stars on the Fourth Day. How could a day be determined on our planet without reference points? It is the sun and the stars that provide us with those very points of reference. If they had not been created until the Fourth Day, it would be impossible to distinguish between the prior three days.

3. A YOUNG SUN

Some people make a distinction between a star that was in the process of forming on the First Day (a proto-star), and a fully formed sun of the Fourth Day.

As the sun was forming from the gravitational collapse of gasses from the nebular cloud, the temperature of those gasses began to rise. In the "proto-star" scenario, the light that was created on the First Day was the light that emanated from the hot, nebulous gasses before nuclear fusion commenced, and the sun was fully formed. By definition, you could not call such a nebulous entity a "star" or a "sun." This explains why God did not reveal the sun's creation on the First Day—referring to it only as "light." By the Fourth Day, after hundreds of millions of years, the sun had completely formed and could properly be called "*the greater light.*"

I suppose that such a theory is scientifically plausible, especially since I am proposing Creation Days that span millions or billions of years. The maturing stages in the sun's formation would certainly be discernible given such long passages of time. Yet, it is difficult to believe that such an irrelevant distinction would be made to mankind thousands of years ago. Since human beings were not created until the Sixth Day, what purpose would be served for the author to distinguish between the stages in the development of a star? Light is light, whether its origin is a nebulous proto-sun or a fully-formed, mature star. It does not seem likely that God would make such a scientific distinction.

CREATION OR FORMAL INTRODUCTION

It is interesting to note that the Hebrew verb "*bara*" that was used in the very first verse of the Bible is not present in the original Hebrew text of verses 14 through 19.[2] The word "*bara*" is translated as "*created*" in Genesis 1:1, and represents a special creation that can only be achieved by God. But in Genesis 1:16, the text does not state that God "created" the sun and the moon; instead, it reveals that He "*made*" them.

> God made two great lights—the greater light to govern the day and the lesser light to govern the night.

The Hebrew word for "*made*" is "*vaya'as.*"[3] Some Biblical translators note the distinction being made on the Fourth Day by using "*vaya'as*" (or *wayya'as*[4]) instead of "*bara.*" Dr.Gleason Archer observes:

> The Hebrew verb *wayya'as* in v.16 should better be rendered "Now [God] *had made* the two great luminaries, etc.," rather than as simple past tense, "[God] *made.*"[5]

And Nathaniel Kravitz notes:

> The phrase "Let there be" in this verse was not intended to
> be construed as describing a creationary act. Those
> "lights"—sun, moon, and stars—were not created on the
> fourth day—the verb "create" was not even employed in
> this verse. Here only "be," "made," "put" (or "placed")
> were used.[6]

The light that was created on the First Day emanated from the sun,
which is the most obvious source of luminosity. It is the same sun that has
illuminated the Earth since the beginning of our planet's history. This is
the most logical and easily defensible conclusion that we can develop and
embrace from the Biblical and scientific evidence that we possess. It makes
little sense to conjure up alternative explanations.

It is commonly believed that the stars were also created on the Fourth
Day. This is curious, since star-creation should have been included in the
first verse of the Bible. When the Bible reveals that God created "*the Heavens
and the Earth*" in Genesis 1:1, there is a broad consensus among Biblical
scholars that the phrase refers to the creation of the universe, and the galaxies and the stars that reside within it. Since the creation of the stars was
recorded at the very beginning of the Bible, their mention on the Fourth
Day only adds to the growing enigma concerning the events of this day.

In addition, the moon is introduced on this day. It is not clear, from a
Biblical perspective, whether the moon's creation would be included in the
opening verse of Genesis. It is certainly part of the cosmos (the "*Heavens
and the Earth*"), yet it might be more closely associated with the formation
of the Earth. We simply cannot determine its day of origin by reading or
analyzing the Biblical text.

When were these celestial bodies created? In the case of the sun and the
stars, the Bible has already told us of their creation in the distant past, during the First Day. The creation of the moon may or may not have also
occurred on the First Day.

But if the creation of the sun and the stars was chronicled on the First Day, why are they being mentioned here on the Fourth Day? What is the purpose of the Fourth Creation Day?

There are many possible answers to these questions. One is derived from a scientific analysis, while others are attained from a theological perspective.

THE SCIENTIFIC SOLUTION

It is intriguing that only celestial bodies are referenced on this day—that is, they are all visible in the sky above. Because the author addresses them together, this might be evidence that he is not describing the "creation" of these celestial bodies. God could have created the moon, the stars, and the sun on any day He chose. It is somewhat less likely that He would create them all on the same day (it is certainly not impossible, just less likely). Perhaps the moon could have been created on the Second Day, and the stars on the Third Day, just after the introduction of plants on our world. Any combination could have been used, but instead it was decided that their introduction should be together. Such a combined presentation, however, may assist us in resolving this riddle.

The first three days of Creation dealt primarily with the planet Earth. The focus of the Fourth Day, however, has suddenly shifted upward—to the celestial bodies in the sky. All three bodies (the sun, the moon, and the stars) make their formal introduction at this time. Is this their moment of creation? Or is it the first time they are all visible? Since the focus of the Creation Story so far has been almost exclusively confined to events on planet Earth, consistency compels us to maintain an Earth-based perspective. From this position, we may conclude that these celestial bodies have suddenly appeared to the surface of the Earth for the first time—thus requiring a formal introduction.

As I have previously explained, it is believed that the thick atmosphere that had formed around our young planet, some four billion years ago, impeded the sun's rays, and submersed the Earth in darkness. Over the course of hundreds of millions of years the opaque atmosphere slowly dissipated, until light finally reached the Earth's surface. At that time, the atmosphere had still not completely cleared, and was translucent. Eventually, the atmosphere became transparent like it is today. At that moment the sun, the moon, and the stars all became completely visible for the first time.[7]

This scientific solution to the enigma of the Fourth Day tells us that the Earth's slowly dissipating atmosphere finally became transparent, rendering space visible to the surface of our planet. The sun, the moon, and the stars were completely visible once the sky had finally cleared, and the Bible formally introduced these celestial bodies.

THE THEOLOGICAL SOLUTION

While the scientific solution for the Fourth Day is certainly plausible, it does not seem complete. The Biblical text does not just announce the appearance of the sun, the moon, and the stars. It also denotes their purpose, both explicitly and implicitly.

One of the expressed purposes of the sun, the moon, and the stars is to cast light onto our planet, and to separate the day from the night. The sun is the primary source of light on planet Earth. Without it, life could not be sustained. The moon emits no light of its own but reflects the light from the sun. The moon is not always visible in the night sky. As it revolves around the Earth it is just as often visible during the daytime as the night. However, when the moon appears during the night, it does govern the night sky and is a considerable source of reflected light. The light we receive from the stars is negligible.

Another declared purpose of the sun, the moon, and the stars is to *"serve as signs to mark seasons and days and years."* This is essentially declaring that these luminaries can be used as markers on a calendar. This natural calendar—given to us by God—consists of signs that mankind has depended on for thousands of years. The four seasons, planting time, and harvest time can all be determined by the positions of the sun and the stars.[8] Religious festivals were also determined by the positions of these celestial bodies.[9] The festivals were important to the people for mandating regular worship of God.

These celestial bodies have also aided sailors and travelers for centuries.[10] Because of the Earth's rotation, the sun, the moon, and the stars appear to rise from the east and set in the west. Familiar stars and groups of stars have aided travelers at night since the beginning of recorded human history.

There is another, more powerful purpose of the Fourth Day that is not directly addressed but merely implied. A careful review of the passage reveals that the sun and the moon were not mentioned by name. Instead, the sun was designated "*the greater light*" and the moon was referenced as "*the lesser light*." By deliberately avoiding their names, the author was ignoring the divine and astrological significance often attached to the sun and the moon.[11]

Ancient man ignorantly believed that the sun, the moon, and the stars were of a divine nature or governed by individual gods. The ancient Egyptians worshipped the sun god, Re (or Ra).[12] In Greece, the sun god was called Helios.[13] The Romans referred to their sun god as Sol.[14] The Romans often borrowed their divinities from the older, ancient Greek culture. Generally they renamed them and attributed to them slightly different divine powers. Selene was the ancient Greek goddess of the moon, while in Rome, she was called Luna.[15,16]

The primary concept that the author was attempting to convey on the Fourth Day is that the God of the ancient Hebrews—the One and only true God—was the Creator of the sun, the moon, and the stars. He created these heavenly bodies to benefit mankind, not to govern over us or falsely influence our decisions. The sun gives us light for life and warmth, and enables us to witness the wondrous creations of God around us. The lights in the sky above have guided travelers for thousands of years, and still serve as religious markers for Holy Days today.

These celestial bodies possess no divine powers of their own. They hold no ability to portend any future event—nor are they capable of controlling man's destiny. There were no great ancient battles between the various gods for supremacy. There was no division of power among any group of competing divine beings, as the ancient peoples of the world believed. The sun, the moon, and the stars are creations of God, and are sacred only in the sense that they were created by God to benefit mankind.

THE FOURTH DAY RESOLUTION

Both the scientific explanation and the theological solutions provide us with many answers and implications concerning the Fourth Day. Perhaps in their multiple solutions, we have been provided answers to a day that possesses several meanings and messages.

The Earth's ancient atmosphere may have finally cleared and allowed the surface of the planet an unobstructed view of these celestial bodies that dominate the sky. This would explain their sudden appearance in the Creation Story (as opposed to their alleged creation). Since we know that the sun and the stars existed long before that stage in the Earth's history, it is scientifically impossible for them to have been created on the Fourth Day. In addition, the Bible has already told us that light was created on the First Day. From a scientific perspective, it makes little sense to conjure up a mysterious, temporary source of light when the sun is located just ninety-three million miles away, and has been casting light onto our world for billions of years.

The scientific explanation for the Fourth Day is plausible, yet, it is not nearly inclusive enough for all that is directly stated or implied in the Biblical text. For this endeavor, I believe it is acceptable to disregard the scientific solution for this Creation Day. While there is nothing wrong—scientifically or theoretically—with the scientific solution, I do not believe that the messages being conveyed in these verses are related to any natural or physical process in the Earth's history. The real power of this passage does not reside in anything that is science-related.

The purpose of the Fourth Day is best understood from the theological perspective. Ancient man had long worshipped the sun, the moon, and the stars as if they were gods, or were controlled by deities. Here, the power of those imaginary gods was exposed as nonexistent, as the Hebrew God declared that the celestial bodies were His creations. They were not even addressed by their formal names, but were merely designated as the "*greater light*" and the "*lesser light*." They were commanded by God to cast their light onto the Earth during the day and the night, and they further benefited man by serving as signs and markers for our calendar.

These ancient "gods," having been reduced to one of the many creations of the Hebrew God, were, in fact, given a divine purpose on the Fourth Day. They were appointed by God to serve man in all the ways that I have mentioned—not to rule over man as ancient people believed. This then, is the primary objective of God's work on the Fourth Day.

▼

CHAPTER SIXTEEN

LIFE FLOURISHES IN THE SEA AND AIR

And God said, "Let the water teem with living creatures, and let birds fly above the earth across the expanse of the sky." So God created the great creatures of the sea and every living and moving thing with which the water teems, according to their kinds, and every winged bird according to its kind. And God saw that it was good. God blessed them and said, "Be fruitful and increase in number and fill the water in the seas, and let the birds increase on the earth." And there was evening, and there was morning—the fifth day.

Gen. 1:20-23 (NIV)

And God said, Let the waters bring forth abundantly the moving creature that hath life, and fowl that may fly above the earth in the open firmament of heaven.
And God created great whales, and every living creature that moveth, which the waters brought forth abundantly, after their kind, and every winged fowl after his kind: and God saw that it was good.
And God blessed them, saying, Be fruitful, and multiply, and fill the waters in the seas, and let fowl multiply in the earth. And the evening and the morning were the fifth day.

Gen. 1:20-23 (KJV)

THE FIFTH DAY

On the Fifth Day, God turned His attention to the sea and the air. At His command, all manner of sea life and flying creatures were created (the Hebrew word "*bara*" is used[1]), filling the seas and the air with their tremendous multitudes. God blessed these creatures and instructed them to reproduce.

To gain a greater insight into what was accomplished on the Fifth Day, we must once again examine the original text of the document. I have included both the New International Version and the King James Version for comparison. These are the key terms, in order of appearance.

1. THE LIVING CREATURES

According to the Bible, the first animals were created in the waters—a fact that has since been confirmed by science. Whether this life was confined to the oceans or included fresh water sources is not revealed. However, most Bible commentaries generally restrict the initial creation of animals to the oceans. There are two key words in this passage that require a closer examination. They are the Hebrew words "*sherets*" and "*nephesh*."[2]

Sherets—Refers to the word "*teem*" in verse twenty, and suggests that these creatures existed in "swarms" and reproduced in prodigious numbers.[3] The word also implies movement, and is associated with sea creatures, insects, and even rodents.[4]

Nephesh—Translated as "*living creatures*," and represents creatures that possess some type of soul.[5] This is the first time that life of any kind is mentioned in the Creation Story, since plants were not recognized as living creatures like animals and human beings.[6]

The Biblical text does not chronicle the specific types of species that were created, however, the phrases that were used suggest that they were probably relatively small sea creatures that appeared in prodigious numbers. This would include ancient forms of fish, and possibly animals like the extinct trilobites, which once existed in large numbers.

The Bible declares that plants were created on the Third Day and sea creatures were created on the Fifth Day. However, scientific research has revealed that the seas were swarming with animal life tens of millions of years before any plants appeared on dry land. Consequently, the Bible appears to be inaccurate.

Some Biblical supporters argue that the first "true" fish (or modern fish) appeared in the seas *after* many fruit-bearing trees and seed-bearing plants had invaded the land. There might be some scientific validity to this claim, depending on which species of life are included or excluded. But to argue from such a perspective certainly gives the appearance of a disingenuous interpretation. Fish are not the sole form of sea life. The Biblical text would certainly include fish, but we should not disregard all other marine life just to harmonize the Bible with the scientific facts.

2. THE FLYING CREATURES

On the Fifth Day, God also created winged creatures—or creatures that were capable of flight. Many critics will see the word "*bird*" written in the

Bible and instantly declare the Biblical order of creation to be inaccurate. The Bible is correct in placing the initial appearance of birds after plants and trees had taken root on the dry land (if we accept the land plants argument of the Third Day). However, birds did not appear at the same time the oceans first teemed with animal life. Fish, sharks, trilobites, and a multitude of ancient marine life thrived for hundreds of millions of years before the first bird soared through the air.

Birds were not the only flying creatures that were created on the Fifth Day. The New International Version uses the word "*birds,*" while the King James Version uses the term "*fowl*" to describe God's creations. These translations are acceptable when discussing the Bible in a general sense, but for our purposes they are much too restrictive. Any creature that is capable of flight, or possibly any winged creature, could be included among the creations of the Fifth Day.[7] Birds, flying insects, Pterosaurs, and bats are all possible candidates. Pterosaurs are the extinct flying reptiles that lived during the era of the dinosaurs.

As we expand the list of flying creatures, we observe yet another problem. The four types of flying creatures listed above all initially appeared at different times in the Earth's history. In fact, bats did not appear until about fifty million years ago.[8] This seemingly further contradicts the scientific facts, until we remember that this Creation Day could have extended for hundreds of millions of years.

3. THE GREAT CREATURES OF THE SEA

The King James Version translates the Hebrew word "tannin," in verse twenty-one, as "whales."[9] This is yet another translation that critics use as evidence of Biblical inaccuracy, since whales were not among the first creatures to reside in the oceans. In fact, primitive whales did not appear in the oceans until fifty-three to fifty million years ago.[10] However, most Bibles translate "*tannin*" in a broader, more general sense, as "*great creatures of the sea*" or "*great sea creatures*." This word represents all the large creatures of the sea. This may include whales, sharks, large fish, giant squids, or any of the great extinct creatures of the past that dwelled in the oceans, such as the Plesiosaurs (the Loch Ness Monster is allegedly said to resemble a Plesiosaur) and the Ichthyosaurs (the "fish-lizard").

It is also interesting that the word "*tannin*" is often translated as "dragons."[11] We have all heard the legends of the mighty dragons that lived in the past, and we rightfully dismiss these stories as being fabrications of imaginative writers. But many scholars find it peculiar that the Hebrew word for dragons is included here. Could this word be describing the great dinosaurs of the past? The physical descriptions of dragons in ancient writings are very similar to the scientific reconstructions of some dinosaurs (based on their skeletal remains). Although no one has ever seen a fire-breathing dragon, perhaps the Creation Story author included this term as evidence for the existence of dragon-like creatures that lived in the distant past. Some scholars believe this is exactly the author's intent, and include the creation of dinosaurs on the Fifth Day.

We can never be certain whether the great reptilian dinosaurs were meant to be included among the creations of the Fifth Day—or even the Sixth Day as some would argue. The Sixth Day argument is primarily based on the erroneous belief that land animals were only created on the Sixth Day. While a Sixth Day creation can actually be dismissed (which I will explain in a later chapter), it is not clear whether dinosaurs would be included among "*the great creatures of the sea.*"

In addition to grouping animals for a brief zoological listing, there may be another significant, theological purpose that the "*great creatures of the sea*" were included. Once again, the author reveals a God Whose power cannot be challenged, even by the most ferocious and feared of mythical creatures.[12] The terrifying, mighty sea monster is but another of God's many creations, manifesting no threat to the One, true God.

OTHER FIFTH DAY CREATIONS

The "*living creatures*," "*flying creatures*," and "*the great creatures of the sea*" were the three types of animals that God created on the Fifth Day. The general terms used to describe these creations allowed us to expand our list to include other related animals. But even that list may not be all-inclusive. Are there other creatures that might be considered a part of the Fifth Day's creations?

1. SINGLE-CELLED ORGANISMS

Prokaryotic life (simple, single-celled organisms that do not possess a cell nucleus) actually thrived alone for nearly half of the Earth's history. It was not until one and a half billion years ago that more complex, single-celled organisms, called "eukaryotes," appeared. Nearly another billion years would elapse until larger organisms, such as trilobites, would debut on planet Earth.

Since microscopic, single-celled organisms dominate much of the Earth's history, their absence in the Creation Story is sometimes cited as evidence of Biblical inaccuracy. Their creation should have been included no later than the Third Day, before the introduction of plants, or possibly earlier. Instead, the first recorded animal life were the swarming, living creatures and the great sea creatures that God created on the Fifth Day. Why then does the Bible exclude single-celled organisms? Is this legitimate evidence of Biblical fallacy?

The fact that any creature was excluded from the Creation Story is actually a blessing. Try to imagine the size of the Bible if God had included every species that had ever existed on our planet. Many scholars believe that dinosaurs and insects were omitted from the Creation Story. Most scholars would also argue that bacteria and viruses were definitely excluded. The only possible place where bacteria and viruses might be included is in the phrase "*and the Spirit of God was hovering over the waters,*" which I have previously explained.

In addition, there is the argument of common sense. What would be the point of recording the creation of microscopic organisms? At the time the Bible was written, humanity was not aware of bacteria or viruses. Much like the dinosaurs, a convincing argument could be made that the Bible needed to include only creatures that its readers would recognize. Dinosaurs, bacteria, viruses, and other microscopic or extinct creatures would remain undiscovered for thousands of years after the writing of the Creation Story.

2. INSECTS

The question of including insects in the Creation Story has also been highly debated. Many scholars believe that insects were part of the Fifth Day creations—some grouped with flying creatures and others associated with swarming creatures.[13] Other scholars include them with the land animals of the Sixth Day—as *"creatures that move along the ground."* Still, others maintain that insects were completely excluded from the Biblical story.

Scholars have debated all three viewpoints, and each point does possess credible arguments. But despite the merit that each argument exhibits, there does not appear to be a convincing resolution to the classification of the insects.

In my opinion, the least acceptable of these beliefs is to include the insects with the creation of the land animals and man on the Sixth Day. This is because the Creation Story reveals each of God's creations in an increasing order of importance (relative to both God and man) with each passing day. God's final creation was man, demonstrating that human beings are the most significant of God's creations. The land animals, which I will argue are mammals (such as horses, cattle, bears, lions, and rodents), were created just before man on the Sixth Day. This is logical, since man has developed a relationship with many of these animals. In addition, these animals possess some degree of measurable intelligence. For these reasons, it is problematic to group insects with the Sixth Day land animals.

If we were required to designate a Creation Day for insects, it would have to be the Fifth Day. Flying insects could be included among the flying creatures. Bees, flies, gnats, locusts, mosquitoes, and moths are some of the common winged insects. Most scholars would probably accept their creation on the Fifth Day since they are capable of flight. But how do we classify insects that are incapable of flight? Should we include them with the swarming creatures? Many non-flying insects such as roaches, termites, and ants do appear to exist in extraordinary numbers. But is it reasonable to place their creation with the sea creatures and flying creatures, which were the primary creations of the Fifth Day? Perhaps. The word "*sherets*" in this passage is often translated as "creeping things" in the Bible.[14] Consequently, it is probably acceptable to classify crawling insects under the category "creeping things," or in this Biblical passage, as a member of the "swarming" creatures.[15] In addition, it would make little sense to designate one day for the creation of flying insects and another day for the creation of non-flying insects. So the Fifth Day would be the best candidate for the creation of insects.

Yet, it is probably just as reasonable to acknowledge that the Creation Day for insects cannot be determined by the Biblical text. This may be an unsatisfactory conclusion for some readers, however, there is little consensus among scholars on this subject. Remember, we are attempting to produce an objective and honest interpretation of the Creation Story. Theories can be argued, but it is not our goal to classify every species of animal that has ever roamed planet Earth.

3. AMPHIBIANS

Amphibians should probably be included among the creations of the Fifth Day. These are creatures that begin their life in the water, but may spend their adult life on the land.

Frogs are arguably the most popular amphibians. Typical of amphibian creatures, the female frog lays her soft eggs in the water. A male frog then releases sperm over the eggs, which fertilizes them. The result is the baby frog or tadpole, which is strictly an aquatic creature. Once the tadpole matures into an adult frog it is capable of dwelling on the land. Such a close relationship with the water would justify placing the creation of amphibians on this day.

4. REPTILES

Reptiles are cold-blooded vertebrates that generally produce offspring by laying eggs. The most well-known reptiles are snakes, crocodiles, lizards, turtles, and probably the dinosaurs. Unlike amphibians, reptiles are generally able to spend their entire lives on land.

The problem with the Biblical classification of reptiles becomes evident when we consider the abundant and distinct types of reptilian creatures. Crocodiles, for example, would probably be categorized as water dwelling creatures by ancient man. Many turtles and snakes also spend most of their lives living in or near bodies of water. Yet, it would be inaccurate to classify turtles and snakes as strictly aquatic creatures since they are generally terrestrial animals. The extinct Pterosaurs only serve to further complicate reptilian classification, since they were flying reptiles.

Reptiles are considered a distinct scientific class of animals today (Reptilia), but thousands of years ago ancient man would not have grouped these creatures together. The Creation Story does not classify animals by their reproductive similarities, their respiratory systems, or the existence of vertebrae. Instead, it divides the animals into water dwelling creatures, creatures capable of flight, and land dwelling creatures. The animal's overall relationship with man is also a factor.

Since many reptiles are associated with water (like the crocodiles), and the Pterosaurs were capable of flight, it could be argued that some reptiles were created on the Fifth Day. But like the insects, it is very difficult to designate all reptiles to any particular Creation Day.

THE SCIENTIFIC RECORD

Now that we have defined the terminology, and the scientific and Biblical characteristics of the creatures that were created on the Fifth Day, we can compare this day with the scientific record. Until this day, no other animals were mentioned in the Bible. Yet, the Fifth Day began with the seas suddenly swarming with life, and the creatures of flight filling the sky. Is this Biblical description comparable to any historical event known to science? With regards to life in the sea, there may be such an event.

I believe that the phrase, *"Let the water teem with living creatures,"* is a description of a period in the Earth's history known as the "Cambrian Explosion." This sudden and virtually miraculous explosion of diverse life in the seas occurred during the Cambrian Period of the Paleozoic Era, around 540 million years ago. In a period of just ten million years (which is the passing of but a few minutes on the time-clock of planet Earth), virtually every animal phyla that exists today abruptly appeared in the Earth's oceans.[16] *The McGraw-Hill Encyclopedia of Science & Technology* explains:

> Following some still unexplained event, the seas were suddenly populated by a rich fauna of shell-bearing invertebrates after 3 billion years of supporting only simple plants and perhaps 100 million years with shell-less invertebrates.[17]

Discover magazine also describes this event:

> Then, within just 10 million years, almost every major group, or phylum, of animals appeared. Almost all the major body plans seems to have sprung into existence—including phyla such as arthropods (which came to include insects and crustaceans), annelids (leeches and worms), mollusks (squid and clams), echinoderms (starfish and sea urchins), and chordates (fish and humans).[18]

While life had yet to appear on the land, the seas literally teemed with all manner of life by 530 million years ago. The extinct trilobites were the most prevalent species of sea life that existed at that time. Primitive clams and snails had also appeared.[19] By 520 million years ago, vertebrates made their appearance.[20] Jawless fish soon followed by the Ordovician Period— about 500 million years ago.[21] Jawed fish would appear by 460 million years ago.[22] Around 400 million years ago, larger marine creatures such as sharks followed them.[23] Amphibians would venture onto the dry land during the Devonian Period (between 412 and 354 million years ago[24]).[25] The Mesozoic Era—or the "Age of Dinosaurs" (250 million to 65 million years ago)—saw the rise of giant marine creatures such as the Ichthyosaurs, Plesiosaurs, Mosasaurs, and crocodiles.[26]

In the air, flying insects were the first to appear, about 300 million years ago.[27] The reptilian Pterosaurs traversed the skies during the "Age of Dinosaurs," while birds finally appeared some 150 million years ago. By the time the first bird took to the air, the creatures of the seas had increased in number—under God's blessing—and filled the waters. Soon, the birds flourished and filled the air.

When the dinosaurs went extinct, some sixty-five million years ago, all of God's commands for the Fifth Day had been fulfilled. The seas were literally teeming with life and the birds were the kings of the air.

While the Biblical text focuses on marine animals and flying creatures, it should not be assumed that no animal life appeared on the land during that time. Birds, in fact, are generally terrestrial creatures, and many do not spend a great deal of time near bodies of water. This is also true of the flying insects. The author was certainly aware that not all of God's creations of the Fifth Day spent their time in the water or in the air. Consequently, by naming flying creatures, the author was acknowledging that some land animals were created on this day. There are many Biblical scholars that believe life did not appear on the land until the Sixth Day. The creation of flying creatures certainly refutes that conviction.

The Fifth Day spanned at least 400 million years, and was a time of tremendous change in the life that inhabited our planet. Single-celled and simple organisms had dominated life on the Earth for nearly three billion years. But on the Fifth Day, the seas were filled with an abundance of large, multicellular creatures. The barren land gave rise to great forests, amphibians, insects, dinosaurs, and reptiles. The skies were filled as flying insects, Pterosaurs, and birds soared above the land and sea below, traversing great distances.

The Biblical record of the Fifth Day may or may not include the creation of the dinosaurs, insects, or certain types of reptiles. Amphibians, animals capable of flight, and the ancestors of much of the sea life that still exists today, were created during this day, as the Bible records. Late-arriving animals such as the bats and the Cetaceans (which includes whales and porpoises) do present some problems for the Biblical record. These mammals appeared after the demise of the dinosaurs, and it is debatable whether to include their creation with other flying creatures and marine animals.

Most scholars will acknowledge that the Biblical record for this day is certainly incomplete from a scientific perspective. Yet, what the Bible does reveal in no way contradicts the scientific evidence. The Biblical recording of a pivotal scientific event like the Cambrian Explosion only enhances its credibility.

From the perspective of what the Bible has recorded on the Fifth Creation Day—and not what it has excluded—the events of this day are in complete agreement with the scientific record.

▼

CHAPTER SEVENTEEN

THE CONVERGENCE OF EVENTS WITH THE PASSAGE OF TIME

One common argument against a Biblical Creation and the Day-Age Theory is the simultaneous creation of the animals described on the Fifth Day. If Genesis 1:20 is meant to convey concurrent creations of God, then the passage is scientifically inaccurate. The major groups of creatures that comprise the Fifth Day all made their initial appearances on our planet at different times. The Fifth Day is unique in this respect, since the events of the other days are more time-discernible.

The events of the First Day, for example, can be clearly distinguished from each other. God first created all space, time, matter, and energy, which we recognize as the known universe. He then turned His attention to a young Earth that was in a state of turbulence and disorder, and void of life. Out of the chaos, He brought forth order and the light of the sun. Each of the events are recognized by Biblical scholars as being distinct and distinguishable from each other. They are also recognized as occurring sequentially over the course of time.

The Second Day witnessed the formation of the water cycle and the creation of the sky. God initiated these two "natural" processes in a time-frame that is generally accepted as overlapping. The creation of the water cycle was indirectly involved in the creation of the sky. Although these two events may be considered simultaneous, there are no scientific facts or theories that invalidate the scientific legitimacy of the Second Day—at least not in the context of the alleged inaccuracies of the Fifth Day.

The events of the Third Day are also clearly distinguishable from each other. God's first command was for the land to emerge from the sea. Once this process was initiated, God then issued His second command, which produced vegetation on the Earth. These events are definitely separate actions performed by God on the same day. A careful reading of the text confirms that these acts were not simultaneous.

The Fourth Day includes the introduction of the sun, the moon, and the stars, and the many purposes defined for them. These celestial bodies are all mentioned together for several reasons that I have already addressed.

The Sixth Day, which we have yet to examine, will include the creation of land animals and man. Virtually all Biblical scholars recognize these events as also occurring separately. The land animals were created first, followed by the creation of man.

The Fifth Day stands alone then in the apparent simultaneous creation of creatures that we know appeared at different times in the Earth's history. But does this draw into question the legitimacy of the Bible? Or, is there another way of understanding the events of this day that transpired so long ago?

Let us consider God as playing the role of an artist in the Creation Story. The universe, the Earth, and all of the creatures that dwell here are merely His artistic creations. In a sense, this perspective can be considered legitimate. There is both great beauty and grand design in the world around us, and I find it difficult *not* to acknowledge God as being the ultimate artist.

One morning, on a special Fifth Day of His workweek, God, the Artist, decided to create sea creatures. With a mere command, all manner of wondrous sea creatures were created, and His artist's den (the Earth) literally teemed with an abundance of diverse creatures. God's work was so awe-inspiring that even He would later acknowledge the goodness of His own work. The afternoon came and God then decided to create birds and other flying creatures. For good measure, He also decided to create even more sea creatures. Again, with just a simple command, a tremendous variety of flying creatures and sea creatures were created. He paused to admire their beauty, and declared His creations to be good—going so far as to bestow His blessing upon them. Having completed all that He had desired to accomplish, God the Artist, concluded His work for the day.

Now let us imagine that some time later someone asked God, the Artist, what He had created during that Fifth Day. God revealed to the questioner that in the morning He had created a tremendous diversity of wondrous sea creatures. He created small sea creatures, which existed in vast swarms, and the great creatures of the sea, so that the oceans teemed with a multitude of incredible life. In the afternoon, He continued to explain, He had decided to create remarkable flying creatures. In addition, He created even more wonderful sea creatures. God even disclosed to the questioner that the life that He had created was so prodigious and so diverse that He marveled at His achievements, and at the end of the day He blessed His creations.

Let us suppose that even more time had passed and the same question was again asked of God, the Artist. But the events of that Fifth Day had transpired in the distant past, and God had created many other wonderful creatures since then. In the morning, He revealed to the second questioner, He had created many types of sea creatures. God further explained that in the afternoon, He had created flying creatures and even more sea creatures. He noted that He was quite pleased with His work of that day.

Naturally, the questioners never actually existed. I have only included them in this endeavor to assist us in understanding the Biblical account of the Fifth Day. Their imaginary purpose was to act as intermediaries as to what would finally happen. Notice that the first time God revealed His work, He described His actions in great detail. But as time passed and other events had transpired, God's description to the second questioner was abbreviated. Of course, God is not accountable to anyone and was never required to explain what He had accomplished during that memorable Fifth Day. Yet, what follows did, in fact, transpire when God decided to reveal His word to His final creation.

Millions of years had passed since that Fifth Day ended, and God decided to record the history of His workweek and the events of Creation. He even decided to include advice, warnings, and His expectations to His final creation—a creature that God regarded so highly that He fashioned him in His own image. As God recorded this information—called the Scriptures—He arrived at the time of the Fifth Day. God realized that the historical record that He was endeavoring to complete must be succinct, despite the grandeur of His work, and the many important historical events that had occurred. Like any author of a book, God chose to emphasize only certain events.

As He wrote down the happenings of that day, the words He chose were very brief but effective in capturing His main points. Essentially, they said:

On the Fifth Day, God created sea creatures and flying creatures.

With the passage of time, events that have transpired in the past seem to converge together. This does not mean that they occurred simultaneously—only that they can be grouped together for purposes of clarity or that the distinction between them is not necessarily significant.

We can all recall specific events of our childhood. Often we perceive of those isolated events as a type of summation of those years. They comprise a specific period of time in our lives—our childhood. Similar summations often reflect various periods of our lives: our "teenage years," our "high school years," "that memorable summer," and our "first job." The individual memories that we have of those periods in our life were probably separated by months or possibly years of forgotten or relatively unimportant events. Yet we still categorize them together because they happened during a specific period of time.

I summarized the actual text of the Fifth Day above to demonstrate the brevity of the Bible. Essentially, the Bible is revealing to us that the Fifth Day was a period of time—or day—when God created the sea dwelling (or sea-related) creatures and flying creatures. The fact that they are joined in a sentence does not necessarily mean that they occurred simultaneously. Remember, the Fifth Day spanned hundreds of millions of years. The seas literally teemed with all sorts of life over that time. Sharks, birds, trilobites, fish, amphibians, and a multitude of other creatures were created at various times during that period. It would only make sense that God, Who is ultimately the author of the Creation Story, would consolidate them together in one all-inclusive statement.

Scientific facts then, pose no threat to the events of the Fifth Day—once we recognize that the creations of that day are being summarized for purposes of clarity for the reader. As I have demonstrated, historical events appear to converge over the passage of time.

▼

CHAPTER EIGHTEEN

THE LAND ANIMALS OF THE SIXTH DAY

And God said, "Let the land produce living creatures according to their kinds: livestock, creatures that move along the ground, and wild animals, each according to its kind." And it was so. God made the wild animals according to their kinds, the livestock according to their kinds, and all the creatures that move along the ground according to their kinds. And God saw that it was good.

Gen. 1:24-25 (NIV)

And God said, Let the earth bring forth the living creature after his kind, cattle, and creeping thing, and beast of the earth after his kind: and it was so.
And God made the beast of the earth after his kind, and cattle after their kind, and every thing that creepeth upon the earth after his kind: and God saw that it was good.

Gen. 1:24-25 (KJV)

THE SIXTH DAY

The Sixth Day is highlighted by two major creation events: the creation of the land animals, and the subsequent creation of man (which will be discussed in the next chapter). Adhering to the hierarchy of the Creation Story, the land animals created on the Sixth Day would generally be of higher intelligence than the flying creatures and the sea creatures of the Fifth Day. The fact that they were created on the same day as man, albeit before him, would also suggest that these creatures have the ability to form a relatively close relationship with man.

Most Biblical translators agree that the primary creation here is the "*living creatures,*" (the Hebrew word is "*Nephesh*"[1]) and what follows in the text are three types of "*living creatures.*" Verse 25 strengthens this argument by including only those three subsets—the "*livestock,*" "*creatures that move along the ground,*" and the "*wild animals.*"

It is interesting to note that the order of animals listed in verse 24 differs from verse 25. It is not clear why the list is dissimilar, however, even if they were identical it would probably not indicate any appreciable difference in their order of creation. All three are still grouped as subsets of the "*living creatures.*"

Let us examine the three types of "*living creatures*" that were created on this day.

1. "LIVESTOCK" OR "CATTLE"

Of the three categories of animals that were created on the Sixth Day, the interpretation of this one has attained the greatest consensus among Biblical translators. The phrase "*livestock*" or "*cattle*" (the Hebrew word is "*behemah*"[2]) clearly refers to all domesticated animals.[3] Upon reading this passage, the reader undoubtedly conjures up images of cows feeding in the pasture. Although it would be correct to include cows, such a narrow interpretation is too restrictive. The animals that were created probably included goats, sheep, oxen, pigs, horses, donkeys, mules, camels, and possibly dogs. Any large animal that is capable of being domesticated by man could be considered a part of this group.

As we review the types of animals in this category, it is apparent that this group consists exclusively of mammals. Mammals are animals that are grouped under the scientific class, *Mammalia*. Human beings are mammals, as are most of the animals that we associate with on a daily basis, such as cats and dogs. Mammals are warm-blooded vertebrates that possess some body hair or fur. Female mammals are able to produce milk in their mammary glands, which allows them to directly feed their young. Animals under the classification *Mammalia* are arguably the most intelligent creatures in the world, possessing relatively large and somewhat complex brains. Gorillas, chimpanzees, orangutans, horses, pigs, and dogs are all very intelligent animals—and all are mammals. Even where we find mammals in the sea—creatures such as porpoises and whales—we discover a high degree of intelligence.

While I still maintain that we should not attempt to categorize Biblical groups of animals into modern scientific classes, this particular category does seem to consist exclusively of mammals. This is because mammals are generally the only animals that can be domesticated.

2. "WILD ANIMALS" OR "BEASTS OF THE EARTH"

The animals that are being described here are the large animals that man is not capable of domesticating (the Hebrew word is *chaitho*[4]). These may include dangerous carnivores such as lions and tigers, and other animals such as bears, elephants, and possibly even the hippopotamus. While it is true that professionals or specialists can tame some of these wild animals, their general nature is one of freedom and wildness.

There is some consensus on the animals that constitute the "*wild animals*" or "*beasts of the Earth*" described here. However, I have seen the dinosaurs listed in this group. To include dinosaurs here is probably inaccurate, and many Biblical translators and scholars reject this belief. As I have previously stated, the dinosaurs are probably not a part of the Creation Story.

The "*wild animals*" should also be recognized as predominantly mammalian. Since the preceding category, "*livestock*," is exclusively mammalian, it is reasonable to assume the Bible would remain consistent here.

3. "CREATURES THAT MOVE ALONG THE GROUND" OR "CREEPING THING"

Quite often, scholars and translators strongly disagree over the translation of a particular Biblical passage. While many hold great conviction in their own personal interpretation, it sometimes remains unclear which is the most credible interpretation. It is this type of dilemma that impedes our literal understanding of the animals that comprise the final group of land animals.

The Hebrew word used here is "*remes*," which suggests creatures whose movement consists of a crawling or creeping motion.[5] Here are some of the possibilities for these creeping creatures:

> ...various forms of creeping things–from the huge reptiles to the insignificant caterpillars.[6]
>> Jamieson, Fausset, and Brown
>> A Commentary Critical and
>> Explanatory on the Whole Bible

> ...creeping thing, including all kinds of insects.[7]
>> Liberty Bible Commentary

> *creeping thing.* Reptiles.[8]
>> The Pentateuch and Haftorahs

> ...the short-legged mammals, such as the rodents.[9]
>> Hugh Ross
>> Genesis One: A Scientific Perspective

> *Creeping thing, remes,* all the different genera of serpents, worms, and such animals as have no feet.[10]
>> Adam Clarke
>> Commentary on the Holy Bible

I believe that some of these interpretations are implausible. It is probably inaccurate to classify all of the animals in this category as reptiles. There are some reptiles, however, which could be included in this group. Snakes are the first creatures that come to mind, since they slither along the ground. Lizards are creatures whose movements could be considered creeping, and turtles are crawling animals. When we consider the means by which these aforementioned reptiles move, they might be considered for inclusion.

To suggest that these creatures are insects is problematic. If insects are to be included at all in the Creation Story, then flying insects probably should have been a Fifth Day creation, along with other flying creatures. Non-flying insects might be included here on the Sixth Day, since they are creatures that creep or crawl along the ground. However, it is also possible (and some might argue, preferable) to place them among the swarming creatures of the Fifth Day.

In both cases, there is no compelling evidence that either insects or reptiles, as a group, belong with the creations of this day. Furthermore, if we claim that insects and reptiles were created with the other land animals of the Sixth Day, we immediately pose several dilemmas—thematically and theologically.

We have already established that "*livestock*" are animals capable of domestication—such as cows, oxen, and horses. The "*wild animals*" are most likely the large undomesticated animals. This would include lions, bears, and elephants. Can we legitimately place insects and reptiles among the creation of these mammals that possess such a higher level of intelligence? Which insect is comparable to a horse? Which reptile is comparable to a lion or an elephant? These large mammals may be inferior to human beings, but they certainly possess far greater intellectual ability than any insect or reptile.

The hierarchical theme of the Creation Story reveals the creation of creatures with progressively higher intelligence. The insects (ants, termites, and flies) and the reptiles (turtles, snakes, and lizards) just do not possess the intellectual capacity of mammals. Based on this thematic principal, the Creation Story would not include the creation of such lesser creatures with mammals.

There is also the personal-theological argument. Dogs, horses, cats, and even cows possess the ability to interact with human beings. It is possible to form relationships with these animals, and some might argue that these animals are capable of possessing a personality. Theologians believe that these types of animals possess a "soul," or are "soulish creatures." This is not to be confused with the soul that God has endowed in men and women. The soul, or spirit, that human beings possess is made in the very image of God. But there is clearly a difference between a horse or a cow and any insect or reptile. Insects and reptiles appear capable of only action and reaction. Gaze into the eyes of a turtle or a snake, and there does not appear to be anything "there" looking back. It is possible that these differences between mammals and the insects and reptiles might be the result of contrasting intellectual capacity. However, it is just as likely, from a theological perspective, that God has endowed these higher creatures with souls that do not merely give the animal life but allow it to possess some level of consciousness, and the capacity to form a relationship with man.

It is important to remember that all three groups of animals created on this day are a subset of the "*living creatures.*" That means they fall under the category of the *nephesh*. In the Bible, the Hebrew word "*nephesh*" refers to animals that possess some type of soul, and is generally reserved only for mammals and birds.[11]

Even if we were to expand the definition of *nephesh* to include animals other than mammals, it is still improbable that insects and reptiles would be created on the same day as the more intelligent mammals—which includes human beings. Given the evidence, it is best to exclude insects and reptiles from the creations of the Sixth Day.

What animals should be included then among the "*creatures that move along the ground*"? If we must choose, then we would have to select the smaller mammals, such as mice, rats, shrews, moles, and other rodents.[12] These animals appear to best fit the criteria, thematically and theologically.

There is really no consensus as to which animals comprise the "*creatures that move along the ground.*" This last category remains elusive, and is not as clearly defined as the prior types of creatures created on this day. This elusiveness has allowed some latitude for spirited debate. Given the broad disparity of translations among scholars, it is tempting to label this category as "inconclusive" and move on to analyze subsequent Biblical text. I will instead maintain that the smaller mammals listed above are probably the animals that best fit the Biblical concept of "*creatures that move along the ground*" or "*creeping things.*"

THE FIRST LAND ANIMALS

As I have noted previously, many scholars argue that all of the land animals were created on the Sixth Day. This argument is so popular, and embraced with such conviction that, at first, I found it difficult to refute this nearly universal belief. Yet, it is quite clear that life on land was created on the Fifth Day with the birds (and possibly insects, amphibians, and some reptiles), since birds are generally terrestrial creatures. Ancient man, and thus the author, was certainly aware of this fact.

THE TRANSLATION OF BIBLICAL ANIMALS

It is often difficult to develop a precise translation of the ancient Biblical text. We are not only dealing with an ancient foreign language but also ancient people whose cultures bear little resemblance to the industrialized societies that have since developed. In addition to these difficulties, the translation of animals mentioned in the Bible has proven particularly challenging. Some of the animals that I have mentioned no longer inhabit the areas in which they were once found (lions in the Holy Land, for example[13]). Another problem is that some of the words and phrases used to describe animals can possess multiple meanings (as many as ten in some cases[14]). When we view the Bible from this perspective, the challenge of deciphering the precise animal or animals described in the text is magnified. *The Nelson's Illustrated Bible Dictionary* observes:

> Scores of specific animals are named in the Bible. But many of these names are simply the educated guesses of translators. In some cases, the meaning is obvious to translators, and in others the passage gives helpful clues. But other passages offer no clue at all to which specific animals are intended. In those cases, the meaning of the animal names has been lost.[15]

This problem is exemplified by the confusion that we encountered when interpreting the phrase *"creatures that move along the ground."* Although the conclusion that we reached is based on sound reasoning, many scholars could pose equally impressive arguments supporting their particular interpretation of this phrase. Their interpretation may greatly contrast ours and still be an acceptable translation.

THE SCIENTIFIC RECORD FOR THIS DAY

The most famous (but not the largest[16]) mass-extinction of life on planet Earth occurred some sixty-five million years ago. Nearly three-fourths of all animal species, including the dinosaurs, went extinct. Scientists attribute that prominent natural disaster to a meteor, an asteroid, or a comet striking the Earth.[17]

But life on planet Earth did not end with that catastrophe. New life-forms appeared, and some life-forms that survived the cataclysm continued to thrive. The period of time from that mass-extinction, sixty-five million years ago, through today is known as the Cenozoic Era (Cenozoic means "recent life"). This era has been nicknamed "The Age of Mammals," since mammals became more prominent and more dominant on our world during this time.[18] Mammals are among the last animals that appeared on our planet.

Although many mammals lived during the age of the dinosaurs, they did not grow in prominence and size until the famous mass-extinction.

The Paleocene Epoch, which is the first epoch of the Tertiary Period (in the Cenozoic Era), is a time in the Earth's history that spanned from sixty-five million years ago to fifty-five million years ago.[19] This was the first epoch that followed the extinction of the dinosaurs. During those ten million years many new mammals made their first appearance on planet Earth.

The Biblical "*livestock*" may be represented in part by an order of mammals known as Artiodactyla (which includes pigs, camels, bison, cattle, goats, and sheep), whose origin dates to the late Paleocene Epoch.[20] Other members of "*livestock*" might include horses and asses, which date back some fifty-seven million years ago.[21]

Some of the "*wild animals*" might include the order of mammals called the Carnivora—the dogs, the cat family, bears, and other carnivores—which first appeared in the early Paleocene.[22] The origin of two other "*wild animals*"—the elephants and the rhinoceroses—are also dated to that epoch.[23,24]

The rodents (an order of mammals called "Rodentia", which also appeared in the late Paleocene[25]) comprise many of the "*creatures that move along the ground.*"

It may appear that I am being excessively specific in placing these Biblical animals into their modern scientific classification. The relevant point, however, is that all of these animals originated in a 10-million year span (the Paleocene Epoch), which began after the demise of the dinosaurs. While the exact scientific classification might not be comprehensive for each Biblical category of animal, the dates that all of these animals first appeared are strikingly similar—validating the Biblical grouping of these animals on the same Creation Day.

It is true that many new animals filled the seas, and new types of birds soared through the air during the so-called "Age of Mammals." Although plants were introduced on the Third Day, some plants, such as flowers, grew in prominence during the Cenozoic Era. But arguing from an acceptable

Biblical perspective, and using the most reasonable interpretations of these animal groups, it is difficult to find any fault with the Biblical grouping of "*livestock,*" "*creatures that move along the ground,*" and "*wild animals*" on this final day of creating. The rise of these great mammals did in fact occur more recently than God's previous creations. The plants of the Third Day, and the diverse sea creatures of the Fifth Day, both preceded the appearance of mammals. There is some debate over the origin of birds on our world, but again, all scientific scholars agree that the appearance of birds predates the great mammals.

Consequently, the Biblical record of the creation of the land animals on the Sixth Day has been scientifically verified. The first portion of the Sixth Creation Day—the rise of the mammals—is consistent with the scientific facts.

CHAPTER NINETEEN

▼

THE CREATION OF MAN

*Then God said, "Let us make man in our image, in our likeness,
and let them rule over the fish of the sea and the birds of the air,
over the livestock, over all the earth, and over all the creatures that
move along the ground."
So God created man in his own image, in the image of God he
created him; male and female he created them.*

Gen. 1:26-27 (NIV)

THE SIXTH DAY CONTINUES

After God created the land animals of the Sixth Day, He turned His
attention to what most Theologians believe is the primary objective of the
Biblical Creation—the creation of mankind (the Hebrew word for man is
"*adam*"[1])

The notion of man's preeminence above all of creation was not a prevalent concept in ancient cultures. At that time, most cultures assumed that

humans were made to serve the gods, and to toil endlessly in an attempt to honor and please them. It was believed that human beings were subjected to the whims of the gods, falling into disfavor for sometimes no apparent reason. The gods were even said to use human beings for sexual relations. Drought, disease, death, infertility, earthquakes, floods, and other natural disasters were all attributed to the anger of the gods. In the ancient world, man was deemed little higher than a beast of burden—a mere toy to be enjoyed and abused by the numerous gods.

The Hebrew Bible embraces none of those beliefs. Although man was created on the same day as many land animals, he was set above all of God's creations, and was given dominion over all of God's creatures. Man's position on the hierarchy of creation is so high, that the Bible states we were made in the "image" and "likeness" of God. Psalm 8 reveals our "spiritual rank" to be just below that of the angels.

Man is God's final creation in this historical account. While some may view the lateness of our creation to be demeaning, it really is a matter of perspective. It might just as well be considered an honor that all of creation was completed and ready for us when we were created.[2]

THE ORIGIN OF MAN

Science and the Bible are in agreement on one aspect of man's creation— human beings made a very late appearance on planet Earth. Hundreds of millions of years, and a countless number of animals would appear, flourish, and disappear, before man—*Homo Sapiens*—finally arrived.

But while science and the Bible agree on man's place in the chronology of creation, there is a great division in explaining how mankind came into existence. The Bible declares that human beings are a special creation, created in the very image of God. Science theorizes that modern man is a descendant of primitive Hominids that date back millions of years. From the scientific perspective, man is just another animal that has descended from the same common ancestor as all other life on planet Earth.

AUSTRALOPITHECUS AND HOMO HABILIS

If we were to travel back in time, some four million years ago, and visit the continent of Africa, we might encounter what most scientists recognize as our oldest known ancestor. At that time, our ancestors were believed to be small, hairy, ape-like creatures that possessed some human physical traits. They were capable of walking upright—a physical achievement that only human beings are believed to have accomplished—and possessed brains no larger than a modern chimpanzee. Science has placed man's oldest recognized forerunners in the genus *Australopithecus* (as opposed to *Homo*, which is man's genus).

That the *Australopithecines* existed is not in question. These creatures certainly lived on the Earth from two to four million years ago.[3] It is not known how populous they became, however, every discovery of their fossilized remains has been confined to the continent of Africa.

I find it difficult to accept that these primates were ancestors of man. They had very small brains, were incapable of speech, and possessed many ape-like qualities. In fact, it is generally accepted that some of these creatures were probably not our ancestors. But those that are classified by science as forefathers to the human race pose an interesting dilemma for creationists. Can this scientific theory be reconciled with the Bible? Most Theologians agree that it can not. Biblical scholars are in near universal agreement that man's first appearance must have been in the form of a modern human being. The story of Adam and Eve, beginning in Genesis 2, is an account of the first man and woman. Although I will not examine the details of that story, it is impossible to interpret any of the first couple's actions as being "primitive" in nature. They possessed the ability to speak to God, to name the animals, and to understand the difference between right and wrong. Adam and Eve were certainly far more intelligent than any animal that has ever dwelled on planet Earth.

Before we determine the accuracy of the Bible, based on this scientific evidence, let us first better understand the type of creature that we are discussing. It is true that the *Australopithecines* possessed some human-like qualities. Their bone structure suggests bipedal movement (upright walking). Their arms and legs may have resembled modern humans more than modern apes, and even their jawbone possessed a human-like quality. Regardless of the physical similarities between the *Australopithecines* and modern man, I contend that unless their DNA is analyzed and compared to human DNA, it is impossible to conclude that they were truly man's ancient ancestors.[4] Their brain-size is unconvincingly small, and their bodies possess too many ape-like qualities to be of any threat to the Bible. Chimpanzees, gorillas, and orangutans also possess many human-like physical qualities; that does not make them direct ancestors of modern man. This uncertainty is also supported by the passage of millions of years and the paucity of transitional fossils.

The existence of these ape-like creatures, and their possible descendants, *Homo Habilis* (which existed sometime between one and three million years ago), has never impressed me. *Homo Habilis* possessed a larger brain than *Australopithecus* and may have been the first Hominid to use tools. However, its brain-size is within the acceptable range of the largest modern apes—or at least, it is reasonably close.

Many creatures traverse the landscape of planet earth. Some are capable of using tools, and many possess large .brains that are capable of some organization of thought. Neither of those traits are exclusively human, and most Creationists would agree that these distant "relatives" of man were nothing more than extinct species of apes.

Even from a scientific perspective, such a belief would not be dismissed. There is a paucity of fossilized bones of these ancient creatures, making it difficult to determine their lines of descent. It has not been proven that *Homo Habilis* really descended from *Australopithecus*. Excavations continue to be undertaken in Africa. Because so few fossils exist of these creatures, nearly every discovery unearths some new information.

Perhaps the very next fossil will dramatically alter our perception of *Australopithecus* or *Homo Habilis*. Perhaps we will learn that neither of these creatures were man's ancestors, and that some other "ape-man" was the true progenitor of today's modern humans. If such an event transpires, it would still prove that the Biblical account of man's origin is in error. However, it would also prove that the accepted scientific theories of today are also inaccurate—and that is the point of this argument. Until more fossils are uncovered and some scientific test can prove conclusively that any of these ancient creatures were the direct ancestors of man, the Biblical Creation's record remains unblemished.

However, more interesting questions and more intriguing creatures remain to challenge the Biblical claim of man's special creation.

THE LESS MODERN MAN

We may be able to dismiss the more ancient species of apes that science recognizes as early ancestors of man, but as we move forward in time the fossil-record becomes more problematic.

It is difficult to dismiss *Homo Erectus* (the famous "Peking Man" and "Java Man" are part of this species), since they possessed many human-like qualities. They first appeared about two million years ago and dwelled in various regions throughout the world, before disappearing some 300,000 years ago. The fossil records for these creatures are much more numerous and more revealing than either *Australopithecus* or *Homo Habilis*. The average brain-size of *Homo Erectus* was much larger than any modern ape—although it was still smaller than the average modern human brain. They may have been capable of some rudimentary speech, used stone tools, were most certainly bipedal, and were nearly as tall as modern man. They are also believed to be the first Hominids to venture beyond the continent of Africa. Far from being ape-like, some of these creatures could be better described as "primitive man." Their existence in the fossil record poses a dilemma for Creationists.

Perhaps even more problematic (and more puzzling) are the *Neandertals*, which appeared around 200,000 years ago. Again, the lineage is unclear, and it is not known if the *Neandertals* were direct descendants of *Homo Erectus*. The *Neandertals* were brawny beings, with thick, heavy bones and stocky, muscular bodies. They crafted fine stone tools that were more advanced than anything produced by *Homo Erectus*. They were also bipedal. Of all the Hominids, they were probably the most similar to modern humans, even in terms of facial appearance. Surprisingly, the brain-size of the *Neandertals* often equaled, and sometimes surpassed, modern man. Greater brain-size does not necessarily indicate greater intelligence, however, it is agreed that there is some correlation. At the very least, we can be certain that they were highly intelligent beings—certainly more intelligent than any ape that has ever lived.

The *Neandertals* were probably the first Hominids that buried their dead, and cared for their sick and elderly. This may or may not indicate a belief in some deity, however, some would argue that it strongly suggests it. But if the *Neandertals* did believe in God, they left behind no legacy that exhibited such a belief. No cave paintings, no artwork, and no evidence of decorative ornaments have ever been attributed to these beings. The *Neandertals* may have possessed significant intelligence and displayed compassion toward each other, yet, the absence of any artistic expression is somewhat disappointing. This may be evidence that the spirit that God has endowed in modern man was absent from these prehistoric beings.

About 30,000 years ago, the *Neandertals* went extinct. The exact cause of their demise remains a mystery today. Their place in the genealogy of human beings has always been debated, and many experts categorize them under the same genus and species as modern man—that being *Homo sapiens*. The *Neandertals*, however, would be placed in a separate Variety, and would be classified as *Homo sapiens neanderthalensis*. Accordingly, modern man would be reclassified as *Homo sapiens sapiens*. This separate classification represents a scientific distinction between the two.[5]

Apart from the *Neandertals*, fossil remains that are classified as "primitive" human beings date back about 100,000 years. This indicates that human beings and the Neandertals existed together for some time, and some scientists believe that humans may have been responsible for the *Neandertals*' extinction. The disappearance of the *Neandertals* does coincide with the appearance of a people that most experts agree denotes the beginning of modern human culture (at least in Europe)—that being *Cro Magnon*.

The *Cro Magnon* appeared in Europe some 30,000 years ago. There is speculation that they may have migrated to Europe from either the Mid-East or Africa, pushing back the date of their true origin. Their skeletal structures are almost identical to modern humans, which indicates that they were intelligent and capable of speech. *Cro Magnon* buried their dead like the *Neandertals*, but, they appeared to have been superior hunters and produced more sophisticated stone tools. *Cro Magnon* also created personal adornments such as jewelry, and their fine artistic skills are visible in cave paintings that still exist today.

No one knows if the *Cro Magnon* were the descendants of Adam and Eve. The date of their appearance, however, is not necessarily inconsistent with the Biblical record. Many fundamentalists place the creation of Adam and Eve at about 6,000 years ago (Archbishop Ussher's chronology is the most popular example). As I noted earlier, however, other scholars believe that gaps may exist in the Biblical genealogy. The existence of such gaps would place the first couple's creation further back in time.

How far back can we place modern man's origin without compromising the Biblical text? The fundamentalist *Liberty Bible Commentary* believes that it is acceptable to place our creation as long ago as 10,000 B.C. (or 12,000 years ago).[6] But can we accept an origin of 30,000 years ago, which would be required for *Cro Magnon*? It is difficult, but not inconceivable, to accept a Biblical creation of man occurring 30,000, or even 40,000, years ago. While the date of 30,000 years ago is widely accepted for *Cro Magnon's* appearance, a range of error of 5,000 years or more may exist.

An extreme limit of between 6,000 and 50,000 years would be acceptable to many Biblical scholars.[7] If the scientific dates for the appearance of human beings can be accepted, then the Biblical creation of man and the scientific origin of modern man may overlap in time—theoretically supporting the Bible.

This scenario, however, leaves me ambivalent. The Bible clearly places man's origin in Mesopotamia. If we are to take into account *Cro Magnon's* migration from the Middle East (assuming the Bible to be accurate) to Europe, that would push man's origin even further back in time. All of this might be acceptable under the Biblical timetable, however, the further back in time we place modern man's origin, the greater strain we place on the Bible's credibility.

Of course, none of this has answered the greatest question of all. Even if we are to accept *Cro Magnon* as the earliest culture of modern humans, what are we to make of the Hominids? Assuming that the Bible is correct, and that man has been the beneficiary of a divine, special origin, what are primitive "ape-men" doing on a world where the Bible has clearly separated man from the animals? Does the Bible provide us with any clues to solve the origin and purpose of the Hominids? Here are some of the common speculations to this question.

1. ADAM'S FIRST WIFE

Some scholars believe that Eve may not have been the first woman created. On the Sixth Day of the Creation Story, it is revealed that a man and a woman were created together. In the next Biblical story (Adam and Eve) we learn that Adam was created first, and Eve was subsequently created from a body-part of Adam. Consequently, the two stories appear to contradict each other in their account of the first man and woman. Some believe that the woman of the Sixth Day and Eve are two different people (an erroneous conclusion that I will explain later). Eve is credited as being the mother of all humanity, but the woman of the Sixth Day is never mentioned again. There has been some speculation about the fate of this mysterious woman. Could she and Adam have produced offspring? Did that offspring include some of the Hominids—possibly the *Neandertals*?

2. LUCIFER'S FALLEN ANGELS

In Ezekiel 28:11-19 is an intriguing story about a mysterious King of Tyre who had dwelled in Eden, the garden of God. The King is said to have possessed tremendous wisdom and was perfect in beauty. He is also said to have been the model of perfection, blameless since the day he was created by God, and was an anointed cherub (or guardian), selected to guard the Throne of God.[8] Eden is described as a magnificent garden of enormous wealth, possessing precious stones, jewels, and gold.

The King of Tyre had grown vain, corrupted, and evil because of his great beauty and elevated position. God then drove him out of the Throne of God and cast him to Earth where he was made a spectacle before kings. The King of Tyre was then consumed by fire and reduced to ashes. All who had known him witnessed these events and were appalled by him.

Many scholars believe that these passages are a direct reference to Lucifer, or Satan, and not some evil, Earthly king that lived during the time of Ezekiel. No true human being could ever be described in such a manner (perfect and blameless).

The Bible does not reveal the time of Lucifer's rise and fall. But it is interesting that he is said to have walked in a garden called Eden—the very name given to the land where Adam and Eve first dwelled. The garden described in Ezekiel, however, does not seem to resemble the garden described in Genesis.

There is a theory that Lucifer once dwelled on our world, long before man's creation. He was the ruler of the Earth, with dominion over all of his followers. This was before his fall from grace and his rebellion against God. This story is never fully explained in the Bible, except for the allusions in Ezekiel and similar passages in Isaiah 14:12-15. If this theory is correct, and Lucifer once dwelled on planet Earth, what did he look like?

Scientists believe that they are unearthing the fossilized remains of man's ancestors in Africa. These fossils are millions of years old, and suggest that primitive man once possessed many ape-like characteristics. But is science misinterpreting their finds? Is there an alternative explanation for the existence of these fossils? Based on the verses in Ezekiel and Isaiah, some scholars believe that the fossilized bones of the Hominids are actually the remains of Lucifer's fallen angels.

There is really a paucity of physical and written evidence to support this belief. The Bible gives no time-frame of this account, nor the location of the ancient garden of Eden. It is entirely possible that this story contains symbols, such as precious jewels and stones, only to convey to man what richness and wealth Eden possessed. That wealth may not have consisted of actual metals and minerals, but may have been some heavenly opulence that we would be unable to comprehend.

I do not know if any of the fossils found in Africa are actually the remains of Lucifer's race of fallen angels—although it is hypothetically (and quite remotely) possible. But it is one theory that I have heard used to explain the Hominid fossils. In any event, Ezekiel 28:11-19 is certainly an interesting and enigmatic passage. Perhaps we will not learn its true meaning until the end of time.

3. THE DESCENDANTS OF CAIN

After Cain killed his brother, Abel, the Bible states that God "marked" Cain in some way, to protect him from others who might seek retribution. It is not clear what the mark was, however, it does appear that it was physical, so that Cain, and his descendants, could be easily recognized. In this theory, the cursed descendants of Cain were the Hominids, which would easily be distinguished from human beings.

4. A SATANIC DECEPTION

Some scholars claim that the Hominid fossils are a satanic deception. It has long been acknowledged that God has granted some power to Satan here on Earth. For reasons that will not be discussed in this endeavor, God has allowed Satan to deceive human beings, and to entice us into sinful acts. There are limits to Satan's abilities and actions—but confusing us with physical evidence that appears inexplicable may not be one of them. Illusions are Satan's most effective temptations against mankind.

Has Satan misled mankind again? The discovery of fossils that exhibit physical properties of both man and ape has led science to conclude that we have descended naturally from ape-like ancestors. This scientific revelation has produced demonstrable consequences on our modern society—a society that has developed ever-increasing confidence and reliance in the benefits that science has yielded. If man descended naturally from ape-like creatures, then what significance does God hold in our creation? Because the Bible claims that we are the primary purpose of God's creation, its credibility is seriously strained if man descended naturally on the Earth.

Perhaps no discovery has had a more profound effect on the way we view ourselves than the unearthing of the Hominid fossils, and the theories that they have inspired. Many scholars attribute the rise of sadistic Nazism and militant Communism to this belief. Others argue that man's inhumanity toward man has always existed. God and religion have been on the defense against the growing forces of science, materialists, and naturalists for over a century. The Bible has come under considerable scrutiny, and God's very existence has been challenged.

Satan could create few illusions of greater effectiveness than the Hominid fossils. Their existence has persuaded us to question our very purpose and creation, and our understanding of the universe around us. If these fossils are the products of a satanic deception, then the cleverness and tenacity of Satan must never be underestimated—for they have been manifestly effective.

5. THE GIANTS OF THE BIBLE

The Old Testament reveals that mysterious giant beings once roamed the Earth. The exact origin of the giants remains unknown, however, it is known that they posed a continuing threat to ancient man, and the two cultures often clashed in battle. Despite the endless archaeological excavations that have uncovered countless ancient relics in the Holy Land, no colossal, skeletal remain has ever been discovered to support the existence of these enigmatic giants. Science and the Bible appear to be irreconcilable on this point, since there is no evidence to support the Biblical claim.

There is one theory, however, that might solve this riddle and reconcile the Bible with science. Perhaps the remains of the mysterious giants have been found, but they have been misinterpreted by modern man.

The Biblical references to giants may actually be describing the extinct *Neandertals*. The *Neandertals* may not have been as vertically imposing as the physical descriptions of giants in the Bible, however, they were believed to be extremely muscular, very strong, and much larger than ancient man. The *Neandertals* may have possessed as much as thirty percent more body-mass than human beings.[9]

Scientists are convinced that both the *Neandertals* and early human beings resided in the Middle East at about the same time. It is not known how or if they interacted, but since competition for resources has always been central to man's existence, some interaction was highly probable. How would human beings view the *Neandertals*? When we take into account the *Neandertals'* greater body mass and tremendous strength, it seems plausible that ancient man would consider these large, muscular beings to be giants.

6. OTHER MEN

There are some mysteries in the Bible that have always puzzled scholars. Why did Cain need a "mark"? From whom was he being protected? At the time of the first murder, the Bible recorded the existence of only four people in the entire world. It has long been accepted that Adam and Eve had many children after Cain and Abel (Seth is named for certain). But how large could the human population have grown so early in our history? Had the known world become so populated that Cain needed a mark to be identified?

What of the city that Cain supposedly built (or at least began to build)? No scholar would suggest that the city consisted of millions of people like the overpopulated, sprawling urban areas of today. But even if only a few dozen people populated the city, where did they all come from?

There is an eerie undertone in these questions that I have often asked myself. Something must have happened that the Bible does not directly address. Perhaps it is more of a suspicion than anything supported by tangible evidence, yet, I have often wondered if other people existed at that time besides Adam, Eve, and their offspring.

Why did Cain receive a mark to protect him from others—at a time when there is no Biblical record of anyone else? Who built and inhabited Cain's city? Who were the mysterious giant beings that dwelled on the Earth? These enigmas may imply that other humans (or other beings) were alive during the time of Adam and Eve.

If this suspicion is true, then another theory may be offered here. Perhaps human beings (or human-like beings) populated our world before Adam and Eve's creation. Those beings may have arisen through natural processes, or were created by God for some unknown purpose. Over time they dispersed into various regions of the world. God then selected one male member of that species and introduced a "spirit" into him. The new spirit-being—endowed by a spirit that was made in the image and likeness of God—was Adam, the first modern man.

If this theory is correct, then those ancient beings existed before modern man was created. God may have modeled His new creation—Adam—on their skeletal and genetic composition. In a sense, God created a new spirit-being based on a prior model.

The primary problem with this theory is that the Biblical description of Adam's creation does not in any way suggest that he was based on an existing "model." Even if other beings existed, the Bible records that Adam's creation was essentially unique, thereby rendering humanity a special, divine creation.

THE ENIGMA REMAINS

It is not known if any of these theories really provide legitimate solutions to the enigma of the Hominids. It is possible (and some might argue, probable) that none of these theories offer an accurate portrayal of the true course of events that led to the creation of modern man. Yet, these are some of the common proposals that attempt to explain the existence of the Hominids, based on Biblical text or religious-inspired theory. My personal belief is that the Bible never addresses the Hominids—much like it never mentions the dinosaurs.

Where did we come from? Which of the Hominids is our true ancestor? Has science provided us with definitive answers to either of these questions? The answer might be surprising to some. Even science does not know which of the *Homo Erectus* fossils are the remains of modern man's ancestors. At one time it was believed that Peking Man (a member of *Homo Erectus*) was an ancestor to the Asian population. Scientists claimed that they could actually "see" some of the traits of the modern Oriental race in the remains of *Peking Man's* skull. The most current theory, however, suggests that *Peking Man* probably went extinct, and that modern man originated somewhere in Africa, dispersed out into the world, and replaced the Hominids that previously lived there. This is commonly called the "Out of Africa" theory.

Many scientists still believe that they can "see" modern European features in the skulls of the *Neandertals*. They believe that these common features prove conclusively that the *Neandertals* hold a place in the ancestral line of many Europeans. However, genetic research on the DNA of one *Neandertal* skeleton reveals a different story. The research revealed that the *Neandertals* and *Homo Sapiens* did not interbreed, and that the *Neandertals* were not the ancestors of any modern day human beings.[10]

Genetic research may have removed the Neandertals from our ancestral lineage, and *Peking Man* (or *Homo Erectus*) may have been replaced by more modern Hominids. But neither of these current theories brings us any closer to understanding our origin. Both may be subject to revision; neither has been proven.

It is certainly intriguing that highly educated and respected men and women of science can sometimes "see" a particular characteristic on a fossil that may not actually exist. It appears that scientists, like everyone else, are sometimes more influenced by human emotions than reason. Perhaps, that is why I am skeptical of many of the numerous claims that they make about the Hominids.

It is possible that some disregarded theory about the Hominids will someday be embraced once again. But it is more likely that the correct theory of man's origin has yet to be developed. Even many scientists would agree that more research must be done before we will ever be able to clearly define the ancestral lineage of modern human beings.

I do not know if *Cro Magnon*, the Neandertals, *Homo Erectus*, or any of the Hominids are ancestors—or descendants—of Adam and Eve. I am also skeptical that a satisfactory Biblical explanation to this enigma exists. It may take many more years of scientific research and thousands of archaeological excavations before the definitive answer is found. But I believe that it is equally as likely that we will never know God's purpose in creating the Hominids.

Is the Biblical account of man's creation an inaccurate portrayal of what is widely accepted to be a natural process? Considering all of the aforementioned points that we have discussed, it would be imprudent to declare the Bible to be inaccurate. It is certainly preferable to allow scientists more time to uncover the truth of man's origins. We are now just beginning to develop the genetic research that may help us determine man's ancestral lineage. The DNA analysis of one *Neandertal* skeleton precludes it from being an ancestor to modern Europeans; that research was both surprising and very recent. More surprises are certainly to be expected with the DNA analyses of the more recent Hominids. We must remember that it was not until the twentieth century before we discovered that our universe is expanding, that time and space had a beginning, and that plate tectonics shape our continents. All of these recent discoveries have verified the claims of the Biblical Creation Story, however, it has taken mankind thousands of years to reach these conclusions. More research and more time may be needed before we can determine mankind's true origins.

THE BIBLICAL ZOOLOGICAL RECORD

The Fifth and Sixth Creation Days have come under considerable condemnation from critics of the Bible. The critics often cite the order of appearance of the animals as evidence of Biblical scientific inaccuracy. But a closer examination of the Biblical text, and reasonable interpretations (as we have demonstrated), have proven that the general order of animal-creation recorded in the Bible is correct.

Science has confirmed the following Biblical claims:

1. Animal life began in the sea (small aquatic animals came first; larger creatures came later).
2. Flying creatures followed.
3. Land mammals were created even later.
4. Modern man was God's most recent creation.

Even the Cambrian Explosion appears to be recorded for the sake of posterity in the Holy Scriptures. The scientific evidence has verified these Biblical claims, and should only serve to strengthen the believer's conviction of an inerrant Bible.

Some Creationists may be troubled by the fact that new species of plants and animals continued to appear for millions of years after their origin. While plants first appeared on the Third Day, flowering plants did not appear until the Fifth Day. Many Creationists would insist that all plant species appeared on the Third Day while all animal species appeared on the Fifth and Sixth Day.

A counter-argument to this reasoning involves the development of race and human beings. Whatever race Adam and Eve may have been they were certainly not a member of every race. They merely contained the genes that would eventually create the multiple races that exist within *Homo Sapiens*. The new races of humanity appeared later than the initial creation of the first human beings. This same principle can be extended to plants and animals. Many new species of plants and animals appeared much later than their initial creation.

CHAPTER TWENTY

▼

IN OUR IMAGE, IN OUR LIKENESS

Then God said, "Let us make man in our image, in our likeness,
and let them rule over the fish of the sea and the birds of the air,
over the livestock, over all the earth, and over all the creatures that
move along the ground."
So God created man in his own image, in the image of God he
created him; male and female he created them.

Gen. 1:26-27 (NIV)

The creation of mankind acquires special significance in the Creation Story. It is here where God creates a creature that is higher than the animals—a being possessing a special likeness to Him, and created in His very own image. It is this creation—God's final—that is the pinnacle of the Story. All six days discussed so far, and every creation event occurring within, has led up to this profound moment. For in humanity, God has developed a being that is capable of developing a personal, spiritual relationship with Him. And for the first time in the Bible, God directly communicates with mankind. He does this in Genesis 1:28 when, after blessing the first man and woman, He instructed them to *"Be fruitful and increase in number..."*

The personal relationship that spiritually bonds us with God is unique on our world. Plants, though certainly living entities, are incapable of thought. The animal world primarily consists of creatures that act on instinct. Some of the "higher" animals—mammals, such as dogs, apes, or monkeys—appear capable of intelligent thought, but do not form a spiritual relationship with God. In all of creation, we alone have been blessed with this wonderful ability and opportunity.

But what exactly does it mean to be made in God's image (the Hebrew word *tselem*[1]) and likeness (the Hebrew word *demut*[2])? Let us first examine these terms.

IMAGE AND LIKENESS

Some Biblical translators view these terms as synonymous. Yet, if their meanings are essentially identical, why would both words be included? *"Image"* and *"likeness"* are actually similar yet distinct terms. I believe they complement each other and better define what is meant by the passage.

You may also notice that *"image"* is mentioned three times in this passage. *"Likeness"* is mentioned only once. There does not appear to be any significance to this.

IMAGE

An image of something is duplicative in nature. Statues are made in the image of a person. On the term *"image,"* The Broadman Bible Commentary states:

> It describes an exact resemblance, like a son who is the very image of his father. Ancient kings would place such effigies of themselves in cities they ruled.[3]

LIKENESS

"*Likeness*" does not convey such preciseness as "*image*."[4] To be like someone means you possess many, but not all of the characteristics of that person. Obviously, man does not possess God's omnipotence, wisdom, righteousness, perfection, ability to create, and divineness.

EXAMPLES OF MAN'S IMAGE AND LIKENESS TO GOD

Now that we have a better understanding of the terms, let us examine the ways that we emulate God.

1. A SOUL

Human beings are similar to God—and the angels—in that we are spirit beings. Unlike the plants and animals, each of us possesses a unique soul. It is this soul that allows us to form a personal relationship with our Creator.

God reveals something about Himself by creating a creature capable of forming a relationship with Him. We consider it human nature to form relationships with others. We seem to possess a natural proclivity to form strong personal ties with members of our own family, and we continually attempt to extend the quantity of our personal relationships by forming bonds with friends. Yet, we have evidence here that God also possesses this very trait, as He seeks to deepen and add to the spiritual relationships that He has formed.

2. FREEDOM TO CHOOSE[5]

Each of us is capable of comparing the options before us, and are free to choose and make decisions. Like the angels, human beings possess free will. We may use this freedom to worship God or to curse Him. We may choose a path of righteousness or lead a life of iniquity. God tries to guide each of us in the proper direction, but He does not force His will upon us.

While God is always reaching out in an attempt to develop a relationship with us, it is we who must choose to accept His invitation. God's ability to forgive, and the unwavering patience He displays in waiting for us, far surpasses the patience and forgiveness that we display to our fellow man.

3. SOVEREIGNTY

We are like God in the sense that we have been given sovereignty over the entire Earth. God is responsible for the creation of the universe, and likewise, we are responsible for our world. This sovereignty, however, is not a birthright of ours. It is a sacred gift, given to us from God; it is a delegated responsibility. Just as God has created and formed our world to His liking, we are capable of changing it and managing it to our liking.

This responsibility that has been entrusted to us must not be taken for granted, because ultimately we are answerable to God for the conditions of planet Earth and the state of our fellow human beings.

4. WISDOM

None of us possess the wisdom of Almighty God, and few of us approach the legendary wisdom of Solomon. Yet, wisdom is a characteristic that both God and man possess. Only human beings, alone among all of God's Earthly creatures, possess the ability to understand right from wrong, the ability to reason, and the maturity to make intelligent choices without allowing selfish motives to consume us.

Throughout the centuries, mankind has searched the world for this desirable quality. We have climbed majestic mountains, trampled through thick rain forests, and have explored virtually every remote region of our world, seeking the ancient culture or the ancient writings that will reward us with wisdom. We have turned to the elderly, hoping their life's experiences have endowed them with wisdom. We have questioned the prophets, seeking their divine guidance in our search for wisdom. The intellectuals, the educated, and the philosophers have all been credited through the ages as having possessed some extraordinary wisdom. Adam and Eve ate fruit from the "*tree of the knowledge of good and evil.*" Many Biblical scholars believe the phrase, "*knowledge of good and evil*" is another way of saying "wisdom." It appears that even the earliest recorded human beings desired to expand their wisdom.

5. KNOWLEDGE[6]

Unlike the animals, human beings are capable of acquiring knowledge. The vast reservoir of knowledge that we have accumulated in the past century alone has expanded to a level that is virtually incomprehensible to the average man. Quantum physics, laser technology, virtual reality, nuclear fission, global communications, personal computers, jet engines, television, and supercomputers are all words and phrases that have become common in our society. We have landed astronauts on our satellite, the moon, and safely brought them home. We have landed space ships on Mars, and have sent probes beyond the limits of our solar system. We have discovered distant galaxies billions of light-years from Earth, and have developed microscopes that can see the most minute virus. We have unleashed the awesome power of the atom, and have developed computer microprocessing chips so efficient that they can perform billions of instructions every second.

Medical research has produced almost mind-boggling possibilities. We have cloned animals, transplanted internal organs, performed laser surgery, created workable prosthetics, and developed machines that take x-rays, resonance images, sonograms, and monitor the heart, the brain, and other organs. Dialysis cleanses our bodies, while heart bypasses and chemotherapy adds years to our already increasing life expectancy. Genetic research, new drugs, bio-research, and new medical treatments hold promise for an even greater future.

The explosion of knowledge in our modern technological society is an important development in the progression of our culture. In fact, it would be difficult to envision our technically dependent society without these advances. The progress that we have made has virtually transformed our planet into a global community. Even the remotest regions of the world will not remain isolated much longer.

With the advancements and the knowledge that we have acquired, mankind can no longer hide behind the pretense of ignorance. We are now fully aware of the consequences of our actions—whether it is recognizing our impact on the environment or the destructive capability of our weapons. It remains to be seen whether mankind's wisdom has kept pace with the technological advancements that we have made.

There is another type of knowledge that only mankind possesses. We are aware that life is only temporary, and that death is inevitable. We are also aware of an afterlife.[7] This knowledge of death and an afterlife may give us a sense of purpose, or the inclination to reflect upon our lives. While animals act mainly on instinct and the need to fulfill their immediate desires, we are capable of looking beyond our current situation. We are also aware that our actions today may have consequences later in life and beyond our Earthly departure.

6. LOVE AND COMPASSION

When we speak of love and compassion, we tend to think of these characteristics in human terms. However, we can also detect these very same traits among many mammals. It is difficult to know whether animals such as dogs, cats, and horses experience the same diversity and depth of emotions that we experience. But many animals do appear capable of love and compassion. We have all seen the mother cat cleaning her kittens, or ducklings swimming behind their mother. Elephants are weaned well into their teenage years, and puppies are nurtured and protected by their mother. In each of these cases, we witness some level of concern or affection between nonhuman creatures.

While it may be interesting that some animals exhibit the tender quality of love (and possibly compassion), there is at least one distinct difference between the love that animals and human beings are capable of displaying and sharing—only man has the ability to recognize, love, and worship God.[8]

7. MORALITY

Man is the only creature of God that understands the concept of morality. We have actually written morality and rules of conduct into the social-binding contracts that are contained in our laws. Human beings possess a conscience, which seems to be derived from our soul.[9] Perhaps our ability to comprehend what is right and wrong best exemplifies the way that we are most like God.

IN "OUR" IMAGE

The phrase, "*Let us make man in our image, in our likeness*" is a very curious statement. God appears to be addressing someone other than Himself. Who is being referenced in this statement? Who constitutes "*us*" and "*our*"? In the very next verse the reference mysteriously disappears, as God—and God alone—created man in "*His own image.*" The meaning of this enigmatic phrase has long been the subject of controversy. While there does not appear to be a conclusive answer, here are some of the possibilities.

1. OTHER GODS

Some scholars propose that this phrase was leftover from an earlier document that included in its text, references to multiple gods, or polytheism. Polytheism was pervasive at that time in man's history, so it was very likely that many Hebrews worshiped multiple gods. The inclusion of these gods in the Creation Story, it is argued, was an accident or an oversight by the author.

Such an oversight is highly unlikely, however. One of the primary underlying themes of the Creation Story is to establish the existence of only one, all-powerful God. The author was too deliberate in his writing to overlook any references to other deities.

2. THE ANGELS

If this is not a reference to other Gods, then perhaps it is an allusion to God's angels.[10] Long ago, the theory goes, God called together these spiritual creations of His to announce the creation of a new being—man. Man would be created in the image and likeness of God and the angels. This belief would indicate that the angels also possess many of the same characteristics of God and man—wisdom, being a spiritual being, sovereignty or responsibility over some of God's creations, the ability to choose, the ability to love, and knowledge.

3. THE TRINITY

Many Christians feel that this is an early Biblical allusion to the Holy Trinity, consisting of God the Father, God the Son, and God the Holy Spirit. Obviously, only Christian Theologians would embrace this interpretation, however, even many of them are disinclined to accept it.

4. A STATEMENT WITHOUT SIGNIFICANCE

It is possible that in this writing, the author did not attempt to accomplish anything special by using such an inclusive phrase. Perhaps after the passage of thousands of years, we are attempting to decipher a phrase that initially possessed no additional meaning when it was written, other than God's announcement to create man.

5. PLURAL OF MAJESTY

This interpretation suggests that God was acting like a King addressing His kingdom. Kings and Queens often use a plural noun such as "we" when speaking either to or for their countrymen. Presidents and Prime Ministers also use the word "we" when speaking to their nation or when formally replying to someone in the name of their nation. Many speakers use such a collective phrase when addressing a topic or an experience that they share with the audience. This interpretation renders the phrase a formal announcement issued only by someone of great power.

6. THE REMAINDER OF HIS CREATION

God may have been addressing either all of the creatures that He had created or all of creation in its entirety. This would also be a formal announcement indicating that the pinnacle of creation (mankind) was to follow.

7. DELIBERATION[11]

Some suggest that God is seen here deliberating before announcing the creation of man. This sets mankind apart from the rest of creation, heightening the special moment.

8. HIMSELF

It should be noted that the Hebrew word "*Elohim*" that is translated as "*God*" throughout the Creation Story, is a plural rather than a singular noun.[12] God may in fact, be doing nothing more than addressing Himself. Perhaps His announcement, "*Let us make man...*" would be similar to us saying to ourselves, "Let's do it!" or "Let's go!" In this scenario, no one else needs to be present for such a proclamation.

9. EXTRA-TERRESTRIALS

Despite the evidence produced by tabloids and other sources of dubious and questionable nature, few reputable Theologians support the hypothesis that God was discussing mankind's creation with sentient beings from other worlds.

MAN'S PLACE IN CREATION

Although we may never truly understand what is meant by the enigmatic references to "*us*" and "*our*" in this verse, the overall meaning of the passage is clear. In mankind, God has completed His final creation of the Creation Story. Consider what King David said of our creation and our special place among all of God's creations.

When I consider your heavens, the work of your fingers, the moon
and the stars, which you have set in place, what is man that you are
mindful of him, the son of man that you care for him?
You made him a little lower than the heavenly beings and crowned
him with glory and honor. You made him ruler over the works of your
hands; you put everything under his feet: all flocks and herds, and the
beasts of the field, the birds of the air, and the fish of the sea, all that
swim the paths of the seas.

Psalms 8:3-8 (NIV)

We have all been made in the image and likeness of God, and because of this, each of us is capable of determining our own destiny. Unlike the plants and animals, God has endowed us with the ability to form a relationship with Him, the ability to increase our knowledge and wisdom, and the responsibility of caring for the world that He has given us.

The fact that we are made in His image and likeness should inspire us with a sense of duty and purpose. As His primary creations, we are obligated to emulate and exhibit His divineness. We may find it complimentary that we have been made in His image, but all too often we have neglected the responsibilities that it entails. Above all of His Earthly creations, God has endowed each of us with a unique soul—making us accountable for all of our actions.

▼

CHAPTER TWENTY-ONE

MAN'S DOMINION

God blessed them and said to them, "Be fruitful and increase in number; fill the earth and subdue it. Rule over the fish of the sea and the birds of the air and over every living creature that moves on the ground."

Gen. 1:28 (NIV)

THE FIRST COMMAND

After God created the first man and woman, He commanded them to "*be fruitful and increase in number.*" God thus instructed mankind to procreate and expand our population. A large population is needed to achieve God's second request: "*Fill the earth and subdue it.*" This responsibility was reemphasized in a Psalm.

> *The highest heavens belong to the Lord, but the earth he has given to man.*
>
> Psalm 115:16 (NIV)

In the first several chapters of the Bible, it is evident that man obeyed God's first command and engaged in much procreation. But our hearts were soon consumed by wicked and evil inclinations, and God lamented over having created us. At that time, when mankind was enslaved by sin, only Noah was found to be righteous (Genesis 6). Noah and his family were saved from God's wrath by constructing an ark made of gopher wood—built to the specifications that God Himself gave to Noah. Noah and his family, along with the animals they brought on board, floated above the Great Flood that destroyed all of mankind. When the ark finally rested upon dry ground and the animals were released, God issued a very familiar command to Noah and his family:

> *"Be fruitful and increase in number and fill the Earth"*
>
> Gen. 9:1 (NIV)

This is the second time that God issued this command to mankind. We can imagine once again that man obeyed God and increased in number—human beings have never had a problem procreating. However, God also instructed us once again to fill the Earth. Did we obey Him the second time? By Genesis 11, we read of mankind yet again resisting God's instructions. In the story of Babel, we are told about the great tower that was being built, and we learn that humanity spoke only one language. It is also evident that the entire human race dwelled in only one region of the world—Mesopotamia. We can infer this centralization of the human population because it is revealed that before the tower was completed, God was compelled to intervene and scatter mankind across the Earth. God also limited man's ability to communicate by introducing numerous languages.

I will not endeavor to argue the facts of the story of Noah or the Tower of Babel. They have been included here to demonstrate that despite God's clear instructions to fill and subdue the Earth, mankind directly disobeyed God twice. Since that time, our inclination to procreate has certainly not diminished, however, it can be argued that we *have* filled the Earth—at least when we consider humanity's sphere of influence over the entire world.

It is regretful that our conquest of the Earth has not been more positive. God has given us the sacred and challenging responsibility to act as caretakers of our world. This is a special responsibility that only mankind received in the Creation Story. All of the birds of the air, the fish of the sea, and the animals that populate the land are our responsibility. We are the custodians of the oceans, the mountains, the rain forests, the prairies, and even the atmosphere. God has granted to us, in a way, the ability to act as God. The planet Earth is ours to govern. Whether we choose to rule it wisely or selfishly and foolishly depends on us.

WHAT IT MEANS TO RULE

Where the NIV uses the word "*rule*" in this passage, the King James Version uses the phrase, "*have dominion.*" "*Rule*" or "*have dominion*" is the translation of the Hebrew word "*Radah.*"[1] Of *Radah*, Bible scholar Bruce Vawter notes:

> Dominion is not a license to caprice and tyranny but, in its best sense, a challenge to responsibility and the duty to make right prevail. If Genesis is attended to carefully, we see that it gives every encouragement to the present-day ecologist who believes that the earth has been delivered into man's hands as a sacred trust that he can perpetuate in a nature-or God-given order which he had been given the capacity to learn and improve upon.[2]

If we consider the tremendous amount of pollution that we have unleashed upon the air, the water, and the land, it would be difficult to argue that we have not acted brashly and foolishly in our obligation. Land has been raped for its mineral wealth. Forests have been burned and cleared for roads and housing. We have senselessly slaughtered entire species of animals to the brink of extinction. Factory smokestacks and gas emissions from fossil-fuel engines continue to pollute the air. Oil tanker accidents release tons of poisonous crude oil into the seas. We continually produce toxic waste, nuclear waste, and other garbage—often without any concern for their safe disposal.

Mankind has fared little better acting upon its own kind. Slavery and caste systems have existed since the beginning of civilization. Civil wars and world wars are marking points on our historical record. Technological advancements have led to machine guns, tanks, fighter jets, submarines, battle ships, and guided missiles—all of which have contributed to our increasing ability to rapidly and effectively annihilate each other. Nuclear weapons and chemical weapons have already been unleashed upon humanity, and the future holds "promise" for even greater and more impressive technological weapons of mass destruction.

We have virtually failed in our duty as custodians or guardians of the planet Earth. We have acted imprudently and selfishly, and ignored our responsibilities, which were graciously granted to us by God. Far too often we have used the technology that we have developed in a negative or detrimental manner.

Technology itself possesses no moral inclination; technology is a morally neutral commodity. It is not nature, which was created by God, nor the technology developed by mankind, that has led us down this path of persistent historical destruction, and the future ecological disasters that are being predicted. The problem lies exclusively in the disobedient and avarice nature of mankind.

And that is something we must change if we are ever to fulfill the sacred responsibilities entrusted to us by God.

CHAPTER TWENTY-TWO

▼

THE GREEN PLANTS FOR FOOD

Then God said, "I give you every seed-bearing plant on the face of the whole earth and every tree that has fruit with seed in it. They will be yours for food. And to all the beasts of the earth and all the birds of the air and all the creatures that move on the ground— everything that has the breath of life in it—I give every green plant for food." And it was so.

God saw all that he had made, and it was very good. And there was evening, and there was morning—the sixth day.

Gen. 1:29-31 (NIV)

It is intriguing to notice that originally neither man nor the animals were given the right to eat flesh. They were intended to be vegetarians (vv. 29-30). This does not mean that the "law of tooth and claw" has not prevailed from the beginning, but that it has no place in the ultimate goal of history.[1]

The Broadman Bible Commentary

VEGETATION ONLY

From Genesis 1:29 through Genesis 8, God permitted mankind to eat only plants for food. That restriction was removed after the Flood, when God gave us permission to eat all that *"lives and moves"* (Gen. 9:3). Many readers point to this passage as evidence that human beings were initially vegetarians. However, such an assertion cannot be inferred from the Biblical text. Whether we obeyed the "vegetarian rule" is not mentioned in the Bible, but we can only surmise that meat was eaten, since man has always disobeyed God's commands. God has commanded us to abstain from all types of sin, including murder. That does not mean that murderers do not exist.

I have read and heard several theories that attempt to explain why God initially prohibited mankind from eating meat, but none of the explanations have ever completely satisfied me. Here are a few of them.

LONGER LIVES

Much has been made of the remarkably long lives of some of the early humans recorded in Genesis. Adam lived to be 930 years old, for example. Methuselah lived the longest of any person mentioned in the Bible—969 years. Even Noah lived for 950 years. After the Flood, the longevity of the people recorded in the Bible began to decline. This is also the time when God granted us permission to eat meat. Some have suggested that there might be a connection between the vegetarian diet and the longevity of the earliest humans. Dieticians would argue that a vegetarian diet, or a diet that minimizes the consumption of meat, is essentially healthier for human beings and may increase longevity. No one would suggest today, however, that such a diet would extend anyone's life to 900 years. Was there something special about the pre-Flood plants? The Bible does not say.

HARMONY

While animals may not attain the same lofty Biblical status as human beings, the taking of animal life—even for food—is still killing. Many scholars believe that had it not been for Adam and Eve's original sin, humans and animals would still be living together in harmony today, eating only the green plants for food. They believe that the Garden of Eden was a paradise where no animal would harm another, nor was any animal a threat to Adam or Eve. That peaceful coexistence was destroyed by sin.

While it is possible that there was no killing of any kind in the special enclave called Eden, it is not clear from a reading of the text that there was perfect harmony throughout the world as many experts claim.

CONDITIONS ON THE EARTH

There is some speculation that the conditions on planet Earth before the flood were dramatically different from the conditions that followed the flood (and continuing on through today). Because of those unique conditions (which remain unknown), human consumption of animals might have been somehow detrimental to our health. Consequently, a strict vegetarian diet was required for survival. This is similar to the "Longer Lives" argument.

DO NOT KILL

The most popular argument for the vegetarian diet is that God had intended for His creations to live in peace. Some point to a passage in Isaiah to support this belief.

> *The wolf will live with the lamb, the leopard will lie down with the goat, the calf and the lion and the yearling together; and a little child will lead them. The cow will feed with the bear, their young will lie down together, and the lion will eat straw like the ox. The infant will play near the hole of the cobra, and the young child put*

his hand into the viper's nest. They will neither harm nor destroy on
all my holy mountain, for the earth will be full of the knowledge of
the Lord as the waters cover the sea.

Isaiah 11:6-9 (NIV)

Perhaps this explanation is correct. God may have desired that all of His living creatures would coexist in peace and harmony—both humans and animals. However, it should be noted that carnivorous creatures have existed for hundreds of millions of years. If there was to be harmony among the animals, that harmony had been disrupted long before man had arrived on the scene. In addition, most Bible experts interpret Isaiah 11:6-9 as describing a future event—not something that has already happened. Harmony between man and the animals may be the intent or ultimate aspiration of God, but—for whatever reason—that state of harmony has yet to transpire.

IMPLICIT MEANINGS OF THE SIXTH DAY

I have marveled many times at the absolute brilliance of the Biblical Creation Story. It is cleverly written, and often reveals more when we read between the lines. The events of the Sixth Day are an excellent example.

You will notice that God created both the Sixth Day land animals (which were mammals) and human beings on the same day. In a sense, we appear to be relegated to the same status as the other mammals. That status is superior to the plants produced on the Third Day, and it is superior to the birds, the fish, and the other animals created on the Fifth Day. Each day and each passage leads us to a higher level of creation until God declared His Holy Day of rest.

While humans and the other mammals were created on the same day, we would be considered the higher creation, since our creation was subsequent to their creation. Our position was elevated when it was revealed that we were made in the image and likeness of God. That lofty status was further accentuated when God granted us dominion over all of the creatures of the Earth.

Yet, while we are considered to be God's highest creation, it is interesting that He gave us the green plants for food—the very same food that He gave the animals. So in a sense, we were reduced to the level of the other mammals once again.

The subtleties of what is being expressed here are intriguing. We are clearly the pinnacle of all of God's creations and are meant to have dominion over the entire world. Yet, it is hard not to notice our close ties to the land mammals, which were created the same day and were given the same food to eat. This could support the belief that animals and humans were meant to live together in harmony. But it also means that God expects us to rise above the animals and to conduct ourselves in a responsible manner, since we were given the responsibility to act as caretakers of the world.

▼

CHAPTER TWENTY-THREE

A DAY TO REST

Thus the heavens and the earth were completed in all their vast array.
By the seventh day God had finished the work he had been doing; so
on the seventh day he rested from all his work. And God blessed the
seventh day and made it holy, because on it he rested from all the
work of creating that he had done.
This is the account of the heavens and the earth when they were
created. When the Lord God made the earth and the heavens—

Gen. 2:1-4 (NIV)

THE SEVENTH DAY

For six days, God created all that exists in our universe. This includes everything that was recorded in the Bible during the first six Creation Days, and also anything else that He had created during that time. As I have previously explained, the Creation Story does not record all of God's creations—just the creations and actions that are most relevant to man.

Having completed all of His work, God rested (or as some would argue, "ceased to create"). This means that there have been no new creations since the end of the Sixth Day. God then blessed the day of rest that followed the previous six days of work, and declared it to be holy.

Here are some of the points about the Seventh Day that need to be addressed.

THE SEVEN-DAY CYCLE

The seven-day cycle that constitutes a week today is probably based on the pattern set forth by the Creation Week. Although the origin of the Sabbath is unknown, it is very likely that it was established from this Biblical precedent of the Seventh Day.

The Biblical days of creation are not 24-hour days. These consecutive periods of time are called "days" so that we may be able to better relate and understand God's period of activity. There is logic in this because God is setting a precedent. We have since emulated the seven-day cycle and established the week.

Even the youngest and strongest beasts of the field need time to rest and rejuvenate, and so God again set a precedent and chose one day in seven to desist from all work. God probably instituted this arrangement to make sure that each of us receives the proper physical rest our bodies require, while maximizing our ability to work. One day of rest in seven is probably the most efficient arrangement of time for human beings.

Since this is a day that God has declared to be holy, we have made it our day of worship—the Sabbath day. The fact that this day has been blessed by God should be of special importance to us, and each of us should observe it with proper reverence and respect.

THE SEVENTH DAY AND CLOSURE

Each of the first six days of creation is followed by the phrase "*evening was, morning was, the {number} day.*" This phrase declared the end of one Creation Day and anticipated the beginning of another. Yet, following the text of the Seventh Day this phrase is conspicuously and mysteriously missing.

Because this phrase was excluded, there are some that argue that the Seventh Day has never ended, and that each of us is currently living through this final day of creation. There is some merit to this argument, since the day was never officially closed in the Biblical text.

This would also strengthen the argument favoring long Creation Days. If we are still in the Seventh Day, then this final day of creation has continued for thousands of years. Consequently, if the Seventh Day is greater than twenty-four hours, it would seem very likely that the preceding days of creation were also long periods of time.

WHAT IT MEANS TO REST

Who but the God of the Bible could truly relax on the day that He declared to be holy? The gods created by other civilizations were always vigilant—forever fearful that their status and whatever realm they governed could come under attack at any moment by competing gods. Those gods often deceived each other and plotted against one another, sometimes using humans as pawns in their cunning games of perpetual conquest.

The Hebrew God knew of no such threat. His status as Supreme Being was never in peril by anyone or anything. The God of the Bible has no competition, for He is the Creator of all things. He is the only God capable of letting His guard down to the rest of the universe.

THE CLOSING PHRASE

This is the account of the heavens and the earth when they were created. When the Lord God made the earth and the heavens—
Gen. 2:4 (NIV)

These are the generations of the heavens and of the earth when they were created, in the day that the Lord God made the earth and the heavens,
Gen. 2:4 (KJV)

This closing verse is a phrase that would normally be used as a "heading" for the text that followed it.[1] However, in this case, most translators agree that this phrase is a summation of the events that had preceded it.[2]

"*Account*" or "*generations*" (the Hebrew word is "*toledot*"[3]) could also be translated as "chronicles" or "history". "*Account*" arguably gives the reader the best interpretation of what is being described.

The "*heavens and the earth*" would encompass all of God's creations—those that were included in the Creation Story, and those that were excluded. With this concluding phrase the Creation Story ends.

CHAPTER TWENTY-FOUR

▼

FULFILLMENT OF GOD'S COMMANDS AND HIS VERDICTS

GOD'S COMMANDS

It is both interesting and revealing that throughout the Creation Story, God's mere command produced a reaction. He created the universe, formed the Earth, initiated light, developed the atmosphere, and created plants, animals, and human beings. His mere desire both initiated and completed their creation.

The polytheistic cultures that existed in the ancient world wrote of their gods' abilities to bring rain, to cause fertility, to grow crops, to win wars, to induce love, to assure a safe journey, and much more. The gods of those cultures were frequently specialized—each possessing the ability to deliver a particular request or desire of man. Many of the ancient cultures also had a divine leader who acted as the head of the other gods. For example, the Greek's chief god was Zeus, while the Roman's head god was

Jupiter. While these divine leaders were very powerful, none matched the enormous power of the sole Hebrew God.

The power of the God of the Bible is unimaginable. How can any of us comprehend a Being that is able to create an entire universe and bring forth all manner of life with a mere command? In fact, God's power extends far beyond that—to the point where it is infinitely boundless. His words do not seem to merely evoke a reaction; His very words seem to *be* the action. If God wishes to create a universe, it is thus created—not by any strenuous actions, physical or otherwise by Him, but merely by His words. And since God's words are a reflection of His thoughts (assuming it is possible, or even reasonable, to distinguish between the two), then God's very thoughts will always be fulfilled and can never be denied. Since God's thoughts cannot be denied, then what He thinks *is* reality. Truly, God's words *are* truth. For God does not merely speak the truth as we do; His words are the truth, in the sense that it impossible to be otherwise.

Remarking on His complete sovereignty over His entire creation, the Lord says:

> *As the rain and the snow come down from heaven, and do not return to it without watering the earth and making it bud and flourish, so that it yields seed for the sower and bread for the eater, so is my word that goes out from my mouth: It will not return to me empty, but will accomplish what I desire and achieve the purpose for which I sent it."*
>
> Isaiah 55:10-11 (NIV)

If all of this seems incredible for us today, imagine how awesome the power of God must have seemed to the people that lived thousands of years ago, without the scientific knowledge that we possess today. This in itself, I believe, makes a strong case for the God of the Bible to be the One and only God—the true God. Polytheism was the general religious persuasion of that time. For the Hebrew people to have simply concocted such an omnipotent Being seems highly unlikely. It is understandable that creative storytellers of old could conjure up ancient tales of great wars between the gods, and gods engaged in titanic battles with colossal monsters of the sea. But how could any ancient author or authors possibly contrive a divine Being Whose very words—indeed, Whose very thoughts—are truth itself? This impossibility strongly suggests that the Scriptures are not merely the product of imaginative storytellers, but rather the inspired word of God.

GOD'S VERDICTS

God issued a verdict following many of His acts of creation. He found the following to be "*good*":

The light
The land and the sea
Vegetation
The sun, the moon, and the stars
The creatures of the Fifth Day
The animals of the Sixth Day

There was no verdict following the creation of man, nor was there any verdict on the Seventh Day. However, following the completion of the Sixth Day, God declared all that He had created to be "*very good*."

There seems to be a great deal of misunderstanding of what the Earth was like before the fall of man (Adam and Eve's original sin in the Garden of Eden). Many people of faith believe that the Earth was in a state of perfection, with peace and harmony existing between all of the various animals, and between the animals and human beings. They also believe that there was no physical death or sickness of any kind before man's fall.[1] Man's original sin is the reason that plants and animals die.

The universe and the Earth are wondrous, beautiful creations of God. The visual splendor of a starlit night, the breathtaking setting of the evening sun, the small stream that meanders through a thick, green forest, the colorful flowers that brighten a grassy meadow, and countless other works of nature have stirred the poet's heart, the artist's palette, and the writer's pen since the dawn of man. It is little wonder then that God was so pleased with His work that He declared it to be "*very good.*" I have reviewed all of the Biblical passages that are cited as evidence for a perfect world, and nowhere in the Bible does it pronounce the world to be "perfect" before the fall of man. The world is undeniably beautiful; it has just never been perfect. In addition, the Hebrew word for perfect, "*tamin,*" was not even used in the Creation Story.[2]

There are troubling aspects of nature that we prefer not to associate with God. They are the attributes of nature that compel us to ask "Why"? Why are the forces of nature often so violent and deadly? Floods, tornadoes, blizzards, electrical storms, earthquakes, and volcanoes wreak havoc on our world, sometimes killing thousands of unsuspecting, seemingly decent, moral people. Innocent babies and children who have barely tasted life, and are certainly too young to have committed any transgression against God, are often among the casualties of these great destructive forces.

Space is an incredibly hostile environment. Giant solar flares, dangerous radiation, and even fluctuations in the strength of our sun can cause detrimental effects on the Earth's climate and even to life itself. Comets, asteroids, meteors, and other great rocks that exist in space have been pummeling the Earth for billions of years—often annihilating entire species of plants and animals. We have witnessed super novas—gigantic, exploding stars that can virtually rip apart an entire solar system. And we have evidence for black holes—a collapsed area of space where the gravity is so great that not even light can escape its powerful grasp.

Lions, tigers, wild dogs, and other carnivorous creatures stalk their prey on land. Alligators, piranha, sharks, and other aquatic creatures stalk their prey in the waters. Wherever there is a herbivore grazing there is sure to be a carnivore waiting for an opening to attack. We cringe when we see a Preying Mantis slowly devouring the unsuspecting grasshopper in its clutches. We gasp when a snake lunges at its prey, a large cat rips apart an antelope, or a spider spins its deadly web around its next helpless victim. The sting of a scorpion and the bone crushing hold of a Boa Constrictor must be incredibly painful; imagine being their prey.

We see the atrocities committed my human beings upon each other and we wonder why God seemingly does nothing to prevent them. How could a good and loving God allow the Holocaust? Why does He permit wars that slaughter people by the tens of millions?

There are fanatical terrorists that bomb buildings, killing hundreds of innocent men, women, and children. There are tyrannical governments that torture their political prisoners and crush the people under them. Even today, human beings are still being sold into slavery in parts of the world—reducing these vessels of spirit created by God to mere merchandise to be bought and sold. In every instance, we wonder why God does not intercede.

Why didn't God create a world that was free from all of the violent forces of nature? Why are there terrible natural disasters? Why have animals been mercilessly preying on each other for hundreds of millions of years? How can God allow so much misery, pain, and suffering on our world?

Many people observe the world around us and refuse to believe that God could have created anything so cruel as nature. They attribute all of these atrocious killings, violent acts of nature, death, sickness, and imperfections in our world to man's original sin, and they believe that the world has suffered the consequences of that sin ever since.

This argument attempts to completely absolve God from all that we perceive to be cruel, violent, and senseless. Curiously, while we absolve God for anything that we judge to be bad, we still attribute to Him all that we perceive to be good. Critics of the Bible must be elated to have such contradictory convictions to feed their criticisms.

But is it the Bible that is contradictory? Or is it man's interpretation of the Bible, and our humanistic perspective of good and evil that is irrational? Naturally, we will attempt to examine these arguments in greater detail.

1. ANIMAL BLOODSHED

Millions of species of animals have existed on our world for hundreds of millions of years. Whether we believe that man first appeared only thousands of years ago, or millions of years ago, most species of animals went extinct before we had arrived. Consequently, to attribute all of these deaths to man's original sin makes little sense.

For the sake of argument, however, let us attribute all death in the animal world to man's original sin. I do not know how this can be reconciled with the evidence, but let us assume this anyway. Does this really solve our dilemma? Do we gain any consolation knowing that it was our disobedience in Eden that has caused animals to prey upon each other? Have we really absolved God from the problem? At this very moment, a hawk is hungrily swooping down upon its next victim, proceeding to shred it apart with its powerful beak and razor-sharp claws. Hungry bobcats are feasting on tiny field mice. Large fish receive nourishment by devouring smaller fish. Vultures are picking clean the carcass of some dead animal. Crocodiles, polar bears, hyenas, rattlesnakes, and leopards are all descending ferociously upon their unfortunate victims. Even under the misguided notion that all of this is man's fault, how is it any more comforting to know that God *allows* such violence and killing to occur? How can a kind and merciful God allow animals to suffer such agonizing deaths because of mankind's original sin?

If we accept the notion that death in the animal world is the result of our original sin, then the God of the Bible is certainly a curious Deity. He seems to punish one group of His creations for the actions of others. Is this justice? Is this logical or fair? If this is the type of God that we are describing, then few of us should rest easy at night—knowing that at any moment we may soon be punished for the sins of someone else.

Perhaps the dilemma of animal suffering should not be attributed to original sin—and certainly not with the illogical judgment of God—but rather in our perspective of the animal world.

It is interesting that most people who buy meat never seem to associate that purchase with the killing of an animal. In our industrialized, urban-based societies, few of us actually see the animal that is killed so that we may cook and eat its remains. Chickens, pigs, and cows are three common animals that most members of our society eat on a regular basis. Why is it more acceptable for us to kill these creatures in a bloody slaughterhouse than it is for a cheetah to stalk, outrun, and capture its prey? Why is it acceptable for humans to eat meat but when animals kill for food, we are uncomfortable and sometimes shocked to witness their cruelty?

Vegetarians may rise above meat eating, however, if their home is infested with roaches, termites, or ants they do not hesitate to exterminate these insects. Insects are also creatures of God. Why are their lives any less precious than a cow or a pig?

There are groups that protest the killing of dolphins, when dolphins are caught in nets that were designed to catch tuna. Mysteriously, we hear almost no protest over the killing of the tuna—just the dolphins. Laws have been passed that protect animals that are used in laboratory research. Many people feel that monkeys, rabbits, or rats should not be used at all for research—regardless of their benefits to man. Probably most people who are in favor of animal research regret the death of these animals, but feel that the overall health benefits that they provide for humanity is worth sacrificing these creatures. Yet, we think nothing of swatting a fly, stepping on an ant, or even killing a spider or a snake. Plants are also living things, created by God, and yet, so few of us lament when we eat a fresh salad.

There is one common denominator in all of these observations: the apprehension that we experience in the death of animals is largely focused on the fate of fellow mammals. We are all concerned with the slow depletion of fish in the world's oceans due to over-harvesting. We all share the concerns of environmentalists when we hear about the slashing and burning of the disappearing rainforests, and the loss of plant and insect life that dwells within them. But none of these deaths provoke the deep, personal anguish that we experience over the death of mammals. This is true both on the land

and in the sea. The fates of two sea creatures that particularly concern us are the whales and the dolphins—both mammals. We are seldom concerned with the deaths of sharks, jellyfish, crabs, or fish. We wince when a polar bear feeds on a baby seal, yet we consider it inconsequential to kill an alligator, destroy a beehive, or step on a caterpillar. This is because the baby seal was a cute mammal, and the other victims were non-mammals.

Our dilemma with death and cruelty in the animal world is primarily focused on the death of mammals, and not the suffering and death of all plants and animals. This is curious because, theoretically, we should be concerned with the pain and suffering of all creatures. Since we limit our compassion to one specific type of animal, then the real dilemma with animal death lies not with the killing of creatures in general, but our own personal cultural bias. We seem to perceive mammals as being different—or better—than other forms of life.

Yet even our compassion toward mammals is inconsistent. We are distressed when we witness a ferocious carnivore eating an antelope, a zebra, or a gazelle. To us, these victims are so helpless that we naturally develop sympathy for them. But where is the pity for the cow that we slice into steaks, the chicken that we barbecue at a family picnic, or the turkey that is the centerpiece of the Thanksgiving dinner? Apparently, even in the mammal world, we do not always extend our sympathy to all mammals. Cute, furry, baby mammals seem to draw our deepest compassion. That this is true reveals more about our inclination to favor adorable, little creatures than any coherent dogma that we have developed against animal bloodshed.

There is also a cultural bias in our apprehension toward animal suffering. Most of us would be horrified to eat the meat of a dog or a cat. We elevate these lovable animals to the status of family member when we make them our pets. Yet, many cultures around the world view these animals much as we view a cow or a pig—merely as food to be eaten.

Religions also place restrictions and regulations on what foods can or cannot be eaten and at what time. What a member of one religion may not eat is often a delicacy to a member of a different religion.

All of these factors point to one distinct fact. The anguish that we experience when we witness certain animals being killed and eaten is largely the consequence of our personal culture, and not a humanistic aversion to death. In general, we do not perceive the death of animals as necessarily an evil act, since what we deem as offensive depends on our culture, our religion, and our relationship to certain animals. If a hawk kills a cute puppy for breakfast we are horrified and perceive this as cruel. If the same hawk devours a rat for lunch we are relieved that there is one fewer rat in the neighborhood. The concept that animal bloodshed is evil is based purely on personal preferences and our perception of the animal being eaten.

Animals have been devouring each other for hundreds of millions of years. To find fault with the food chain and blame God or our original sin for their deaths makes little sense. Animals are not human beings; they may or may not possess some type of soul (this is a subject that has long been debated). However, even those who are inclined to grant some animals a soul would not compare the soul of an animal to the soul of a human being. The spirit that dwells within each of us has been made in the very image of God. No mention of such a divine spirit was ever associated with any animals in the Creation Story.

Animals have a role to fill here on Earth, but perhaps they play no part in God's Heavenly plans. God is certainly aware of each and every animal that He has created. But their deaths may be no more significant to Him in His grand design than the death of a garden weed is to us. Let us not forget that the entire world has been created for the purpose of mankind, and not the animals. If God claimed that all of His creation was "*very good*," then it must be so. To argue otherwise and perceive the death of animals to be evil is to impose our personal, cultural, and religious ideology on God. It is never acceptable to embrace such a conviction.

2. PHYSICAL OR SPIRITUAL DEATH?

And the Lord God commanded the man, "You are free to eat from any tree in the garden; but you must not eat from the tree of the knowledge of good and evil, for when you eat of it you will surely die."

Gen. 2:16-17 (NIV)

The Biblical passage above is often cited as evidence that physical death was brought into this world because of original sin.[3] The death being referenced in this passage, however, cannot be physical death. This is because Adam and Eve did *not* physically die after eating the fruit from the "*tree of the knowledge of good and evil.*" In fact, the Bible records that Adam lived to see the ripe old age of 930 years (Genesis 5:5), and Eve had several children. If Adam and Eve did not physically die after eating the forbidden fruit, then either the Lord lied to them or another type of death must have been referenced in this phrase. The Lord certainly does not lie, and the death that they suffered was death due to sin. This is a spiritual death, not a physical death.

Millions of plants and animals died before Adam and Eve sinned.[4] There were earthquakes, floods, meteor impacts, extinction of species, and many more natural disasters that occurred before the fall of man. What was new to our world was not death but sin. Mankind was responsible for introducing sin, and sin could not have been introduced any earlier, since plants and animals are not held to the same moral standards as human beings. Human beings are the only creatures capable of sinning.

Those who believe that physical death is being referenced here must explain why Adam and Eve did not immediately die after eating the fruit. The Bible certainly does not record it. Perhaps they also believe that God simply issued an empty threat or meant that "eventually" Adam and Eve would physically die. Since neither of these arguments is even remotely plausible, we must conclude that physical death is not being described here.

Still, let us not diminish the significance of Adam and Eve's transgression. Humanity had failed to achieve God's divine purpose, and spiritual death through sin had entered the world. This was a battle victory for Satan and the forces of evil. But God, of course, was merciful, and another plan for mankind's salvation was still to come.

3. HUMAN SUFFERING AND NATURAL DISASTERS

Theologians and philosophers have debated human suffering throughout the ages. It is not my primary purpose to answer the enigmatic questions that are raised by human suffering. However, I will briefly address the subject, since it is related to the topic that we are discussing—that being a perfect creation before man's sin. In the Creation Story, we are told that the Earth is mankind's dominion, and that we are responsible for all plant and animal life, and, consequently, the preservation of the world's resources. We are also responsible for each other.

Let us first examine the problem of starvation in our world. Each year, millions of men, women, and children experience horrible deaths due to starvation. We hear of their tortured existence, and see their emaciated bodies wasting away in some deserted region of the world. It is painful to even look upon their shriveled, skeletal bodies on the evening news. Imagine how painful it is to experience such a tragic demise.

Must these people die of starvation? Is the problem a shortage of food that is harvested in the world? I do not know what the future holds for agricultural production, but as of this moment, no person in our world should be dying of starvation. Most of the Western countries are producing surpluses of food each year. If there were a better way to distribute these surpluses, the world's population would be well fed and well nourished.

The problem lies not with the harvesting of food, but with the governments that sometimes prevent its proper distribution. The people living within the sphere of these governments' influence are often the victims of civil wars, poor government planning, and even deliberate starvation of the population. The lines that we draw on a map to divide the countries of the world are rather arbitrary. The Lord does not recognize such boundaries, and views each of us individually as His children. Unfortunately, some of His children are deliberately starving others. At this moment in time, starvation appears to be largely the direct result of contemptible actions by select people in powerful positions of leadership. God has graciously given us the ability to harvest enough food to feed the population of the world. Consequently, starvation is a tragedy precipitated by the actions of man.

A mass human atrocity such as the Holocaust was certainly the manifestation of evil in man. The Holocaust, the Cambodian Killing Fields, Stalin's forced famine in the Ukraine, Mao's Cultural Revolution, and other mass killings are literally attempts by one group of people to deliberately exterminate another group of people. The evil, virtually unimaginable actions of the perpetrators of these abominations are certainly not the fault of God.

We can expand this line of reasoning to include other enduring problems like war, murder, terrorism, oppression, and hatred. God did not cause either of the World Wars where tens of millions of people lost their lives, and tens of millions more suffered tremendous personal loss. He is not a proponent of the oppressors or bearers of hate. He is not a supporter of the terrorist or the murderer. All of these crimes against humanity are the result of human actions—not God.

Since God gave mankind dominion over the entire world, we can use that responsibility to assist one another or destroy one another. Perhaps that is one explanation for our persistent problems—we simply have not fulfilled the role that God has assigned to us.

And yet, can we simply excuse God from the abominations committed by man? Where was He when all of these atrocities were being committed? Did He answer the prayers of the victims? Does His apparent inaction make Him culpable in any of these tragedies?

It is difficult to answer any of these challenging and enduring questions. I am not sure that anyone can fully explain the tragic human atrocities or the natural disasters that threaten humanity. Maybe God is allowing us to decide our own fate—at least to a point. Perhaps God is active and we just do not recognize His actions or the mysterious ways He influences each of our lives. Whatever the reason may be, it appears that for the foreseeable future, human suffering will persist. And it will continue until God intervenes and saves us from our own shortcomings.

GOD'S BLESSING

> *The blessing is an important concept in the Old Testament. It is never merely a formal matter of words; it implies the transference from one person to another of power or vitality.*[5]
>   The Cambridge Bible Commentary

God granted His holy blessing several times in the Creation Story. His first blessing was bestowed upon the creatures of the Fifth Day. His next blessing was granted to men and women on the Sixth Day. Strangely, no blessing was given to the land animals that were created earlier on that day. God's final blessing was given to the Seventh Day; He also declared that day to be holy.

It is not completely clear what is all entailed in God's blessing. If we are to be guided only by the text in the Creation Story, the blessing seems to be mostly associated with reproductive capabilities. On the Fifth Day, God blessed all of His creatures and then instructed them to "*Be fruitful and increase in number.*" In the case of humanity, God blessed us and instructed us to reproduce. He also commanded us to subdue the Earth.

It is unclear why the animals of the Sixth Day were not blessed. Perhaps their exclusion is not significant, yet it is somewhat puzzling. Some have interpreted God's blessing of men and women at the end of the Sixth Day to include all of His creations for that day. That might be the only reasonable answer for their exclusion, however, it is never clearly stated in the text.

God's blessing is not limited to reproductive capabilities, as is evident by the Seventh Day. God's blessing seems to set the Seventh Day apart from the others, magnifying its importance.

GOD NAMES HIS CREATIONS

God named some of His creations in the Creation Story. He named:

The light:	"day"
The darkness:	"night"
The expanse:	"sky" or "heaven"
The dry land:	"earth"
The waters:	"seas"

Because God named these creations, it symbolizes His control or proprietorship over them.[6] It is interesting that God does not name any of the living creatures. Instead, in Genesis 2, God allowed Adam to name the animals. This symbolic action demonstrated man's dominion over the animals. It also strengthens the argument that the Creation Story and the story of Adam and Eve are not two different Creation stories, since the animals are created in one story and named in the other. On this point, the Creation Story tells us part of the account, while the story of Adam and Eve reveals the rest of the account.

In addition to naming the animals, Adam also named his new female partner "*woman*." This is intriguing, because if we follow the precedent set in the Creation Story, this means that Adam was given dominion over Eve. However, another precedent set in the Creation Story is one of ever-increasing importance. In the second chapter we learn that Eve was created after Adam. Consequently, Eve—or woman—was truly God's final and possibly highest creation on Earth.

But does the Bible grant men dominion over women? Or are women really God's highest creation—higher even than men?

The second chapter in Genesis seems to give conflicting signals on the importance of the two human sexes. Perhaps those signals have been overemphasized through the centuries—particularly men's dominance over women, which has resulted in women's subservient role.

It is just as significant that the creation of the first man and the first woman are mentioned together in the Creation Story. The author may have intentionally recorded their creation simultaneously to display that men and women are of equal importance to God. Certainly, the Creation Story does not raise either sex above the other. When God spoke to them, He did so as if they were one, representing all of humanity. The Creation Story appears to unite men and women, making God's final creation—human beings—the ultimate purpose in creation.

CHAPTER TWENTY-FIVE

▼

ACCORDING TO THEIR KINDS

The land produced vegetation: plants bearing seed according to their kinds and trees bearing fruit with seed in it according to their kinds...

Gen. 1:12 (NIV)

So God created the great creatures of the sea and every living and moving thing with which the water teems, according to their kinds, and every winged bird according to its kind.

Gen. 1:21 (NIV)

God made the wild animals according to their kinds, the livestock according to their kinds, and all the creatures that move along the ground according to their kinds.

Gen. 1:25 (NIV)

THE LIMITS OF REPRODUCTION

In the Creation Story, God gave living things the ability to reproduce *"according to their kinds."* This concept seems superfluous and insignificant today. Our modern society possesses a far greater understanding of the science involved in reproduction than the ancient cultures that existed in Biblical times. Today we know that an apple tree is only capable of producing another apple tree. Dogs breed and produce more dogs. Flies only reproduce more flies. This concept is recognized as a fundamental law of nature.

SPONTANEOUS GENERATION

It is difficult to comprehend today, but there was a time, not very long ago, when scientists believed that creatures could arise spontaneously from lifeless or rather arbitrary matter. This theory is called Spontaneous Generation.

For thousands of years, science was puzzled by the seemingly abrupt appearance of small animals and insects. Eventually, the scientific community embraced the concept that small creatures were being created from the very sources where they were found. Mud or straw produced mice; human sweat bred lice; dead animals or decaying meat generated maggots.

Through the centuries, some scientific experiments produced results that cast doubt on this theory, and there was considerable debate within the scientific community. The discovery of microscopic life only reinforced the belief in Spontaneous Generation. What other explanation was possible for the existence of bacteria?

In the 1860's, French scientist Louis Pasteur successfully and decisively disproved the theory of Spontaneous Generation in a famous experiment. Pasteur boiled broth in a special flask, which consisted of a long curved neck that allowed air to enter the flask but restricted airborne microorganisms from reaching the broth. The broth remained free of bacterial growth, proving that life could not be generated by Spontaneous Generation.

In retrospect, this experiment also affirmed the scientific validity of the phrase "*according to their kinds*" in the Creation Story. If life is only capable of reproducing "*according to their kinds*" then the reverse of this statement should also be true—life can only be produced from a similar form of life (or by divine intervention). If science had used this Biblical principle as a reference, scientists would have predicted that mice could not possibly be created from anything other than mice, insects can only be descendants of insects, and bacteria can be produced only from other bacteria. Today, our understanding of biological reproduction has confirmed the Biblical phrase, "*according to their kinds.*"

THE ORIGIN OF LIFE ON EARTH

The earliest evidence of life on planet Earth may date as far back as 3.85 billion years ago.[1] At that time the first simple, single-celled organisms called "prokaryotes" may have appeared. The exact scientific process that led to the creation of prokaryotic life still eludes scientists today. Whether these early organisms metabolized energy through the process of photosynthesis (utilizing light) or by another method, such as chemosynthesis (utilizing chemicals), is also unknown.

The origin of life on planet Earth has long baffled the scientific community. Although many theories have been proposed, there is no consensus as to how life first originated on the Earth. Science believes that the Earth's early atmosphere consisted of gasses such as methane, hydrogen, ammonia, and steam. These gasses may have combined with electrical discharge from lightning (other energy sources are also possible) to produce organic compounds. Organic compounds, which include amino acids, are recognized as the building-blocks of life.

Scientists acknowledge that even simple single-celled organisms are far more complex than the organic compounds that could have been formed from the pre-biotic conditions of ancient Earth. Yet, the origin of life is believed to have begun from some similar natural process and progressed through many steps over the span of millions of years, until the first sin-gled-celled life was created.

There are many scientific problems with this scenario, but the timing involved may prove most problematic. Before 3.8 billion years ago scientists believe that the Earth's surface was still in a state of considerable upheaval, as the last of the nebular debris bombarded the Earth. The appearance of life at that time is puzzling to many scientists, since it is not believed that the precursors of life could have survived such an inhospitable environment. Yet, life managed to make its appearance at the conclusion of that turbulent time and survive. This allows an almost a negligible time-frame for the building-blocks of life to progress naturally into living organisms.

The natural processes that scientists have theorized to explain the origin of life are far too complex to be explained here. But from a Biblical per-spective all of these theories contradict the Biblical Genesis. If life can only propagate *"according to their kinds"* as proclaimed by the Bible, it would be unacceptable to embrace the concept of life arising from non-living matter. Even if the change occurring within each individual step of the transforma-tion was so minuscule and so gradual that such steps could be argued as acceptable Biblical propagations, the overall transformation from lifeless matter to living creatures over time cannot be accepted.

We are seemingly in a contradiction between the Bible's claims and the theories of science. Science proclaims that life originated on our world through natural processes; the Bible declares that life can only originate from God. Although the contradiction between the two cannot be bridged by any other acceptable translation of the Creation Story, it must be noted that no scientific theory on the origin of life has proven conclusive, nor has any been accepted as a standard model.

This is not to suggest that the science offered on this subject is illegiti-mate. There are numerous problems when attempting to reconstruct the natural processes that initiated life. In many ways, this is very different from dating fossils or unlocking the secrets of plate tectonics. Fossils are tangible, and the process of dating their age is accepted science. Once the age of the fossil is determined, its place in the Earth's history is also known. And we can see plate tectonics in action today in many places in the world. The various fault lines visible on land, and the spreading of the sea floor along the mid-Atlantic ridge definitively support this theory. In contrast, merely duplicating the conditions of the early Earth is, in itself, significantly more complicated than either of the previous examples.

The problem is that the further back in time we travel into the Earth's history, the more alien our world becomes. The atmosphere and temperature of the Earth, the composition of the oceans, and even the energy received from the sun have all changed over time. Any attempt to recreate the processes that led to life must take into account those unique conditions. In addition, the chemistry and biology employed here is extremely complex, operating at the sub-cellular level. The functions and capabilities of amino acids and nucleic acids are only partially known to us. There is much to be learned about them even in the form they exist today; four billion years ago their structure and functions may have been greatly different. Even if most of the science were understood, there is always the possibility that some essential piece of the natural process is missing—forever lost in that ancient world. If that scenario is true—and there is a distinct possibility that it is—then the origin of life on Earth may never be duplicated in a laboratory or completely explained.

Although the origin of life remains a mystery, the slow transformation of non-living materials into simple life may still have transpired. Most scientists are convinced that some type of natural process—as opposed to a divine intervention—must still be accepted as factual, notwithstanding the lack of any standard model. Many believe that given enough time, more money, and additional research, the natural process that brought life to our world will someday be understood by science and, perhaps, duplicated by man. In any event, it would be wrong at this point for Creationists to reject the concept of a natural genesis; it has simply not been disproved.

Until such a natural process is proven conclusively, or at the very least, survives the scrutiny of the scientific method, we cannot reject a divine origin of life either. It is possible that the essential missing pieces of the natural-process puzzle are lost forever because they are of divine origin. Until we are able to prove otherwise, it is acceptable to believe that only the God of the Bible is capable of creating life.

CHAPTER TWENTY-SIX

▼

MORE BIBLICAL EVIDENCE FOR LONG CREATION DAYS

I have already explained that the Hebrew word for "day" (*yom*) possesses multiple definitions—all reflecting periods of time that must be determined by its context in the sentence or passage. While a flexible definition for "*yom*" allows for the possibility of long Creation Days, it is not the only Biblical evidence.

THE SEVENTH DAY

There is a curious attribute of the Creation Story that has puzzled countless readers, and has long been the subject of debate among scholars. Unlike the previous six days of Creation, the Seventh Day lacks any official closing phrase (*And there was evening, and there was morning—the {number} day*). Like many readers, when I first recognized the absence of any closure for the final day, I was uncertain how to interpret this mysterious omission. Other books of the Bible fail to provide the missing closure;

consequently, its absence is very real. Could the author simply have neglected to include the closing phrase? That scenario can be instantly dismissed, since the author appears to be too meticulous in his writing to make such an error. But if the omission was not accidental, then it is reasonable to assume that it was intentional. And if it was intentional, then its absence might be revealing something significant to its readers.

This dilemma creates an interesting challenge for Fundamentalists. If we are to interpret the Creation Story literally, then we must accept this absence for what it represents. If all seven Creation Days were initiated, but only the first six were completed, then we are required to accept that the Seventh Day has never ended. To merely assume that the Seventh Day was completed is to append something to the Scriptures that is clearly not there. If we are to accept the Bible at its word, then we cannot alter its meaning simply to have it conform to our personal views. A Fundamentalist has no alternative but to accept this conclusion.

For six days, God created the universe and the Earth, and all life that resides on the Earth—culminating in the creation of man. But on the final day, He ceased to create. This implies that God has created nothing new since Adam and Eve, and that the Seventh Day was a day of inactivity for God. When could such a day end? Even science would concede that the appearance of modern human beings was very recent. Essentially, we were among the last new species of life to appear on planet Earth. Since nothing new has been created since man's creation, it is logical to conclude that God's period of inactivity (in the creative sense) has persisted through today. What else has God been, if not creatively inactive, since man's creation? Consequently, it appears that we are all living in the Seventh Day of Creation.

This is another controversial interpretation that has been passionately debated through the years. However, this interpretation is not without additional Biblical support. Another piece of evidence appears in Psalm 95.

*For forty years I was angry with that generation; I said, "They are
a people whose hearts go astray, and they have not known my ways."
So I declared on oath in my anger, "They shall never enter my rest."*

Psalm 95:10-11 (NIV)

In the last two verses of Psalm 95, God declared that a generation of His people would never enter His "rest." For each individual man or woman, such an event would occur in the future, since physical death would have to take place first. The Creation Story already revealed to us that the Seventh Day was God's day of rest. Yet, in Psalm 95, God speaks of man entering His period of rest. The "rest" being referenced in this verse appears to lie either in the future or in the present—certainly not in the distant past. This period of "rest" in Psalm 95 only makes sense if it is a continuation of the "rest" that began at the beginning of the Seventh Day.

The exclusion of a closing phrase of the Seventh Day and the verses in Psalm 95 strengthens the argument that we are all currently living in the Seventh Day. It appears that God's rest has continued since the end of the Sixth Day.

THE FINAL YOM

*These are the generations of the heavens and of the earth when they
were created, in the day that the Lord God made the earth and the
heavens,*

Genesis 2:4 (KJV)

The Creation Story is continued in the second chapter of Genesis, and ends with the fourth verse, which is a title—or summation—verse. Many scholars recognize the entire fourth verse to be part of the Creation Story. Others believe that only the first part of that verse (designated as Genesis 2:4a) comprise the closing words.

I have included the King James Version of the entire verse above to demonstrate that the word "*day*" is found once again. "*In the day that the*

Lord God made the earth and the heavens," is designated as Genesis 2:4b. Many versions of the Bible do not use the word "*day*" in their translation of this sentence, despite the fact that the Hebrew word "*yom*" is included in the original text.[1]

This verse poses a dilemma for 24-hour Day Creationists, since the entire Creation Week is referenced as a "*day.*" If each Creation Day spanned twenty-four hours, then how can seven such days encompass a 24-hour period? There is simply no logic to this reasoning.

However, if the Creation Days are understood to be "Days of God," encompassing various lengths of unspecified time, then the text does appear consistent. In fact, this is the only interpretation that is rational. Consequently, the "Days of God" are best understood as "eras" or "periods of time." This final "*day*"—which represents the entire Creation Week—is also an unknown length of time. At the very least, the Creation Week—or the final "*day*"—would have to span a period of time that encompassed all seven days.

It should be noted once again that this evidence is only valid if Genesis 2:4b is included in the Creation Story, and is not the beginning of the next Biblical story, which is the story of Adam and Eve.

GENERATIONS

> *These are the generations of the heavens and of the earth when they were created, in the day that the Lord God made the earth and the heavens,*
>
> Genesis 2:4 (KJV)

The Hebrew word, *toledah*, is translated in Genesis 2:4 as "*generations.*"[2] A generation, in Biblical terms, does not possess an exact length of time. Generally, forty years is the time most often associated with a generation, however, it does vary depending on its usage. We may think of a Biblical generation as we still do today, with grandparents comprising one generation, parents comprising another, and the children comprising the youngest generation. However, *"generations"* is probably best understood as an indefinite time-period.[3]

Whatever length of time a single "generation" may represent, many scholars would agree that it is unacceptable to reduce its length to seven 24-hour days. In addition, the word used here is not singular but plural—indicating that the time spanned two or more generations. Unlike the preceding argument (the final *yom*), this phrase appears in Genesis 2:4a, which is widely accepted as being part of the Creation Story. The use of the word *"generations"* in this final phrase of the story is one of the more compelling pieces of evidence for long Creation Days.

THE ANCIENT EARTH

In several passages of the Bible, we are told of the ancientness of the Earth. The phrases used to describe the mountains, the hills, and the Earth itself are not phrases that support a young Earth or a recent creation. Six thousand years is not a very long period of time, especially when we consider that seven people in the Bible are said to have lived over 900 years (Adam, Seth, Enosh, Kenan, Jared, Methuselah, and Noah). It is impossible to determine the exact age of the Earth from these verses, but they strongly suggest that the Earth is quite ancient—certainly much older than a few thousand years.[4]

FINAL THOUGHTS ON LONG CREATION DAYS

Many scholars are convinced that a Creation Day must be twenty-four hours. Some attach great significance to this conviction, and contend that this is one of the fundamental beliefs required for salvation. The primary evidence and rationale behind 24-hour Creation Days is that one Earth day is twenty-four hours. But perhaps more than any other chapter or story in the Bible, the Creation Story is primarily reporting God's actions. While it is true that the creation of mankind is the pinnacle of the story, it is God's act of creating that is the main focus of the story. Throughout the first six days, God displays His infinite and incomprehensible power to create.

An Earth day is defined as one complete rotation of our planet on its axis. This may be seen as a wonderful gift from God—given to us to separate our time of work from our time of rest. But God is obviously not bound by human physical requirements such as sleep or rest, nor does He labor in our sense of the word. Consequently, an Earth "day" was designed to benefit mankind.

Perhaps the most convincing "evidence" of long Creation Days can be derived from this very concept. For while the day that is established by the Earth's rotation is clearly ours, the days of Creation clearly belong to God. They are the days that He labored—for lack of a better word—to complete His project. They were made for His purposes to fulfill His desires; the Creation Days are His and His alone. They were never given to mankind, nor were they created to benefit us. In fact, five full Creation Days had passed before we had even been created.

Many scholars, however, have unwisely accepted the antithesis of this concept. They maintain that Creation Days—which are the Lord's Days—must be twenty-four hours, since that is the length of an Earth day. This is essentially declaring that the days that the Lord labored must conform to the days that we labor. To engage in this type of argument is anthropocentric reasoning. God is certainly able to perform His tasks within our limited framework—that cannot be doubted. However, to restrict God's actions to conform to our time-frame is an interpretation that is neither mandated by the Scriptures nor accepted practice by Theologians. No honest Fundamentalist can accept such a heretical concept. We do not set the standard from which God operates; it is He Who is the designer of the standard.

The seven-day week and the concept of one day of rest in seven, were probably established from the Creation Story. In these examples, we have used the Lord's actions as a blueprint for our lives. Such an arrangement is mandated in the Scriptures (Exodus 20:8-11). It is only logical for us to embrace these examples set forth by God, since they are beneficial to human beings, and He is our Lord and Creator.

It is simply wrong to impose our concept of a "day" on the Lord. That reasonable philosophy should tell us that a Creation Day and our day probably spanned dissimilar lengths of time. The entire Creation Week belongs to God for His divine objectives, and it is best left to God to determine the length of the day that He chooses to work. It is inappropriate for us to impose our physical restrictions on Him.

If we combine the flexibility of the Hebrew word "*yom,*" the lack of closure of the Seventh Day, the use of the words "*day*" and "*generations*" to represent the entire Creation Week, the ancientness of the Earth as stated in various passages in the Bible, and the understanding that these are "Days of the Lord," we can conclude that no Creation Day should be limited to twenty-four hours. We also realize that long Creation Days are not only possible with a clearer understanding of the arguments, but that the Biblical text virtually mandates them.

CHAPTER TWENTY-SEVEN

▼

SCIENCE SUPPORTS SCRIPTURE

Each book of the Holy Bible is capable of standing alone in terms of spiritual theme and historical information. The lessons unveiled with each progressing passage remain as pertinent and inspiring in today's modern society as they did at the time of their writing. They are truly a timeless collection of God's inspired messengers.

While each of us may have a favorite book of the Bible, no book is capable of telling God's entire story or revealing His entire message.

We have just concluded a verse-by-verse analysis of the Creation Story, as written in Genesis 1:1—2:4. Much of the Bible's scientific information pertaining to nature, the creation of life on Earth, and man's origin is included within these verses.

They are not, however, the only source of Biblical scientific information. In various passages throughout the Bible, God reveals even more answers to the riddles of science. Each verse is yet another piece of the enigmatic Bible-science puzzle. Together they support each other, strengthen our argument for the existence of a divine Creator, and reveal that the Holy

Bible can still withstand the scrutiny of today's scientific challenges. The passages included below not only support a Biblical Creation, but they present the Bible as being scientifically accurate at a time when its authors had no knowledge of the scientific facts that we take for granted today. Here are some verses of Scripture that are supported by modern science.

THE EXPANDING UNIVERSE AND THE SPHERICAL EARTH

The following verses display two scientific facts that could not have been known at the time of their writing. The first verse, from Isaiah, declares that the Earth is round. All four verses reveal that the universe (the heavens) is expanding (or stretching). During the twentieth century it was discovered that our universe is indeed expanding—and has been expanding since the beginning of time.

> *He sits enthroned above the circle of the earth, and its people are like grasshoppers. He stretches out the heavens like a canopy, and spreads them out like a tent to live in.*
>
> Isaiah 40:22 (NIV)

> *He wraps himself in light as with a garment; he stretches out the heavens like a tent and lays the beams of his upper chambers on their waters. He makes the clouds his chariot and rides on the wings of the wind.*
>
> Psalms 104:2-3 (NIV)

> *This is what God the Lord says—he who created the heavens and stretched them out, who spread out the earth and all that comes out of it, who gives breath to its people, and life to those who walk on it.*
>
> Isaiah 42:5 (NIV)

(The Lord speaking)

> *"It is I who made the earth and created mankind upon it. My own hands stretched out the heavens; I marshaled their starry hosts."*
>
> Isaiah 45:12 (NIV)

THE EXISTENCE OF SPACE

In the Book of Job it is claimed that the Earth is suspended in emptiness, or space, which Job describes as "nothing."

"He spreads out the northern [skies] over empty space; he suspends the earth over nothing."

Job 26:7 (NIV)

THE HYDROLOGIC CYCLE

The basic stages of the water cycle are described in the following three verses. The third verse, from Ecclesiastes, may also indicate the sphericity of the Earth.

"He draws up the drops of water, which distill as rain to the streams; the clouds pour down their moisture and abundant showers fall on mankind."

Job 36:27-28 (NIV)

"He wraps up the waters in his clouds, yet the clouds do not burst under their weight."

Job 26:8 (NIV)

The wind blows to the south and turns to the north; round and round it goes, ever returning on its course. All streams flow into the sea, yet the sea is never full. To the place the streams come from, there they return again.

Ecclesiastes 1:6-7 (NIV)

THE ANTIQUITY OF THE EARTH

Many Creationists believe in a young or recently formed Earth—an Earth that may be only a few thousand years old. To those individuals, I recommend a careful reading of the following verses. These passages certainly appear to indicate that our world is very old. Note especially Psalm 90, the only Biblical passage credited to Moses outside of the first five books.

He stood, and shook the earth; he looked, and made the nations tremble. The ancient mountains crumbled and the age-old hills collapsed. His ways are eternal.

Habakkuk 3:6 (NIV)

A prayer of Moses the man of God.
Lord, you have been our dwelling place throughout all generations. Before the mountains were born or you brought forth the earth and the world, from everlasting to everlasting you are God. You turn men back to dust, saying, "Return to dust, O sons of men." For a thousand years in your sight are like a day that has just gone by, or like a watch in the night.

Psalm 90:1-4 (NIV)

Hear, O mountains, the Lord's accusation; listen, you everlasting foundations of the earth. For the Lord has a case against his people; he is lodging a charge against Israel.

Micah 6:2 (NIV)

"The Lord brought me forth as the first of his works, before his deeds of old; I was appointed from eternity, from the beginning, before the world began. When there were no oceans, I was given birth, when there were no springs abounding with water; before the mountains were settled in place, before the hills, I was given birth, before he made the earth or its fields or any of the dust of the world. I was there when he set the heavens in place, when he marked out the horizon on the face of the deep, when he established the clouds above and fixed securely the fountains of the deep, when he gave the sea its boundary so the waters would not overstep his command, and when he marked out the foundations of the earth."

Proverbs 8:22-29 (NIV)

I make known the end from the beginning, from ancient times, what is still to come. I say: My purpose will stand, and I will do all that I please.

Isaiah 46:10 (NIV)

What does man gain from all his labor at which he toils under the sun? Generations come and generations go, but the earth remains forever. The sun rises and the sun sets, and hurries back to where it rises. The wind blows to the south and turns to the north; round and round it goes, ever returning on its course. All streams flow into the sea, yet the sea is never full. To the place the streams come from, there they return again. All things are wearisome, more than one can say. The eye never has enough of seeing, nor the ear its fill of hearing. What has been will be again, what has been done will be done again; there is nothing new under the sun. Is there anything of which one can say, "Look! This is something new"? It was here already, long ago; it was here before our time. There is no remembrance of men of old, and even those who are yet to come will not be remembered by those who follow.

Ecclesiastes 1:3-11 (NIV)

THE COUNTLESS STARS

Gaze up into the sky on any starry night and you will witness only a minute fraction of God's creations. In our galaxy alone there are estimated to be over one hundred billion stars. And in our universe, there are hundreds of millions of galaxies. The stars in the universe then, would seem to be countless. But as you are gazing up into that starry night you might decide to count the stars anyway—and that might be possible. The average person is only capable of seeing a few thousand stars on any given night. Why then does the Bible speak of countless numbers of stars? How can a few thousand visible stars, which can surely be counted, be compared with the number of grains of sand on the seashore?—a number so vast that no one during Biblical times could even begin to estimate it.

Once again, the Bible seems to be revealing a scientific fact (the countless number of stars) that its authors could not have known nor ever have imagined. For the Bible to compare the number of stars and the number of grains of sand on the seashore, would indicate that the stars that exist in the heavens must far exceed that which is visible from the Earth. But how could the Bible's authors have known this without the inspirational knowledge from God?

This is what the Lord says:

> *"I will make the descendants of David my servant and the Levites who minister before me as countless as the stars of the sky and as measureless as the sand on the seashore."'*
>
> Jeremiah 33:22 (NIV)

The angel of the Lord called to Abraham:

> *"I will surely bless you and make your descendants as numerous as the stars in the sky and as the sand on the seashore. Your descendants will take possession of the cities of their enemies,"*
>
> Genesis 22:17 (NIV)

Jacob in a prayer to God:

> *But you have said, 'I will surely make you prosper and will make your descendants like the sand of the sea, which cannot be counted.'"*
>
> Genesis 32:12 (NIV)

The Lord to Abram:

> *He took him outside and said, "Look up at the heavens and count the stars—if indeed you can count them." Then he said to him, "So shall your offspring be."*
>
> Genesis 15:5 (NIV)

THE OCEAN FLOOR

Beneath the ocean's vast surface was a mysterious, unknown world that possessed wonders beyond the scope of ancient man's technology. The sailors of that age were no doubt skilled in the art of sea travel. Yet the murky depths of the seas they sailed were as mysterious to them as the distant galaxies of space are to us. It is little wonder then that the writers and storytellers of old conjured up horrifying tales of sea monsters and terrifying creatures of the deep. Man's imagination is most productive when he possesses the least amount of knowledge.

Even today, there is much about the ocean that remains mysterious and undiscovered. But the contour of the ocean floor is no longer a mystery. We now know that the bottom of the ocean is comprised of great mountain ranges, deep trenches, volcanoes, valleys, and plateaus. We take this knowledge for granted today, yet such information has only been verified in the past century, with the advent of sonar and satellites. How is it possible, then, that the Bible speaks of "valleys" existing beneath the sea?

The valleys of the sea were exposed and the foundations of the earth laid
bare at the rebuke of the Lord, at the blast of breath from his nostrils.
2 Samuel 22:16 (NIV)

THE BEGINNING OF TIME AND THE UNIVERSE

Lastly, let us return to the initial verse of the Bible. The revelations of this verse are often disregarded or greatly unappreciated, especially when we consider the level of scientific knowledge that existed at the time of its writing. It was not always known that time had a beginning. Many cultures believed that the universe existed in cycles or was eternal.

Yet, the very first verse of the Bible states, in simple terms, that both the universe and time did have a beginning. This is a fact that science has since verified. Whether this belief originated or was unique to the Hebrews is not as important as the fact that it was the correct belief. For once again, the Bible and science are in perfect harmony.

In the Beginning God created the heavens and the earth.
Genesis 1:1 (NIV)

CHAPTER TWENTY-EIGHT

▼

NATURAL PROCESSES AND ACTS OF GOD

NATURAL PROCESSES

It has long been assumed that whatever action God initiated on a particular Creation Day would be completed before the end of that day. This is a reasonable assumption since the Bible adds the phrase, *"and it was so,"* after most of God's creative actions. If we are to confine our research to only include the Scriptures, this belief may be justified.

Science has revealed to us a very different story. Many of the processes that I have described to explain the creations and actions of God did not happen immediately, but instead they persisted over the course of millions of years.

This does not necessarily contradict the Bible (unless of course, you subscribe to 24-hour Creation Days) but it may be troubling to some. The dilemma here lies not with the length of Creation Days but in our human expectations, and our misunderstanding of what God achieved in each of His actions. Even those who embrace the Day-Age theory may be troubled that God's commands were not instantly fulfilled, as we would expect from an omnipotent Being. But a more thoughtful analysis would suggest that these long processes should have been expected.

Let us examine the process of plate tectonics. The Bible states that on the Third Day, God brought forth the land from under the sea. I have interpreted this to be the beginning of tectonic plate development on our world. About four billion years ago, the entire Earth was virtually covered with water, as the land occupied only about one-tenth of its present size.[1] Plate tectonics began at that time, and for hundreds of millions of years landmass on planet Earth began to accumulate and grow. Over the course of time, some of that land would sink back into the water, while more land would rise to take its place. Some plates collided, pushing the land upward and forming large mountain chains. Sometimes entire continents collided and formed vast supercontinents. Today, land accounts for about three-tenths of the Earth's surface.

Since tectonic plate movement persists today, some may question whether the Lord's proclamation of bringing forth the land from under the sea on the Third Day was truly fulfilled. After all, this process does not appear ready to conclude any time soon. Other "natural" processes that God initiated also pose the same dilemma.

On the Sixth Day, God created a man and a woman—the origin of the human race. Men and women have successfully procreated ever since. Consequently, the process of creating more human beings continues today.

On the Fifth Day, God created the creatures of the sea and air. Since the initial moment of their creation, sea creatures and flying creatures have also successfully reproduced through today.

The hydrologic cycle (or water cycle) is a process that takes varying amounts of time to be completed. We are told that God created the hydrologic cycle on the Second Day, but this cycle is generally not something that is completed in a single day. The basic version of the hydrologic cycle includes the evaporation of water, its condensation, and its precipitation back into water. Water in the atmosphere may be renewed through this process in only a few days. Water in rivers or streams, however, may be renewed in a span measuring weeks. Other sources of water, such as glaciers or underground aquifers, may take dozens or even hundreds of years to be renewed. This process that God introduced on the Second Day also continues today.

In each of these examples, God began a process that has continued for thousands or millions of years. God *did* create birds on the Fifth Day—but He did not create *all* of the birds on that particular day. God created a man and a woman on the Sixth Day—but He did not create *every* man and woman on that particular day, either. We still attribute the creation of all living things to God, however, *none* of the living creatures that were created during the Creation Week are still alive today. Instead, God initiated a process whereby the continuation of His original actions or creations would endure beyond their inception or origin. We can apply this same reasoning to plate tectonics, plants, the land animals of the Sixth Day, or even the appearance of light on the Earth's surface.

If we wish to expand this concept, we could also include other creations of God that are not specifically mentioned in the Creation Story. God certainly created the planets, and all Creationists would acknowledge that He set them in motion around the sun. However, none of the planets complete their orbit in one day. Pluto, for instance, takes 247.7 years to complete one single revolution around the sun.[2] We recognize that God also set the Earth in motion to orbit the sun, but even that takes 365 days to be completed.

Perhaps our expectations are humanistic in nature. Our culture is obsessed with time, and a quick and instant completion to our endeavors. We are an impatient people, and would naturally assume that if God commanded something to be done it should be completed instantaneously. There is little doubt that God can do whatever He desires in any time-frame that He chooses. However, time is irrelevant for an omnipotent Being.

None of God's actions need to be achieved instantaneously to fulfill His commands. Whether it was to assure the continuation of life, the hydrologic cycle, the light from the sun, or plate tectonics, God did not merely create life or initiate a process and abandon it to die. Instead, we may understand God's commands as the inception of processes that persist today. Consequently, we can say with certainty that everything that God initiated with His mere words were fulfilled.

OVERLAPPING OF CREATION DAYS

Since we now understand that God's acts of creation actually initiated specific processes, we may conclude that the Creation Days did in fact overlap each other.

New life was still being introduced in the sea even after life had long been established on land. Plants were initially created on the Third Day, yet flowering plants did not appear until some time during the Fifth Day.

The fact that events in different Creation Days overlap each other is no threat to the credibility of the Bible. All of God's actions and creations should be expected to proceed right through today—and they do.

REPRODUCTION—GOD'S MECHANISM TO SUSTAIN LIFE

Many Creationists often disregard one of the most important processes initiated during the Creation Week. For at least 3.5 billion years, life of some form has existed on planet Earth. It has survived the passage of time, natural disasters, competition from other species, and the never-ending quest for sources of energy. To assure the survival of life, God introduced a mechanism that allows species to continue even after the death of one of its members. That mechanism is called reproduction.

There are many ways that animals can reproduce. Some, such as single-celled creatures, merely divide into two cells. Other organisms possess both pairs of sex organs. Human beings require one member from each sex to procreate. Reproduction not only allows life to continue, it also defines the type of life that is produced.

God's method of dealing with reproduction consists of two major concepts:

1. A member of one species can only reproduce with members of that same species (although there are a few exceptions).
2. Species propagate members of the same species.

The genes of any organism define its physical characteristics. Reproduction is essentially the successful continuation of those genes. After successful reproduction, the newly created organism will possess the genes of its predecessor(s). In this way, life will produce only similar life, assuring that the species that successfully procreates continues.

Today, we think of reproduction as a natural process. Everywhere that we look in nature, every species of life has found a way to continue to survive. Scientists believe that reproduction was something that simple life on ancient Earth had to achieve to continue to exist. It was nature's way of solving the problem of death and extinction. They theorize that many simple life-forms must have went extinct before, somehow, one of them finally possessed the ability to successfully reproduce (or replicate).

A clear understanding of the origin of life on planet Earth still eludes science—as does that early life's ability to successfully duplicate itself. Whatever scientific theories are proposed attempting to explain that first successful reproduction, the Bible states that reproduction of life was both a blessing and a command from God. This is an assertion that every Creationist embraces.

SPECIATION AND EXTINCTION

The phrase, "descent (of life) with modification," best describes the current scientific theory of how life has progressed on planet Earth. Beginning with the first recognizable forms of life that existed billions of years ago, life has continued to exist without cessation through today.

Variation among similar organisms, which is produced by differences in their genes, is the driving force behind "descent with modification." When any organism reproduces it passes its genes on to its offspring. However, the newly created life is seldom an exact duplicate of its parent or parents. The differing characteristics of the offspring may not be significant after only one generation. But after many generations the differences between the original parent and its descendants tend to increase. Current scientific theory believes that as these differences magnify over time, there is a point when an entirely new species may develop. This process whereby new species arise is called "speciation."

Many people who do not understand this process tend to exaggerate the claims made by science. No competent scientist today claims that after only a few generations, the descendants of some amphibian (such as a frog) will become reptiles. On the contrary, science believes that millions of years and millions of generations may pass before such a transformation is achieved.

Generally, two animals are considered to be different species if the dissimilarity in their genes is great enough to render them incapable of procreating. Human beings, horses, cats, and dogs are all separate species, and as such, the male sperm of one of them cannot fertilize the female eggs of any of the others. Through speciation, science theorizes that a descendant of an amphibian over time will be an amphibian-like creature that can only reproduce with other amphibian-like creatures. Eventually, the process of "descent with modification" renders the amphibian-like progeny incapable of reproducing with that original amphibian. Consequently, it is considered a new species.

Species may arise from a variety of scenarios. Some occur because of mutations. Others arise because some members of a species may have become geographically separated or isolated from other members of their species. Over time these separated creatures develop their own unique gene-pool and develop into different species. Environmental factors are believed to play a prominent role in speciation. Some members of the offspring may simply be better equipped to survive a change in the environment (such as a prolonged drought or an ice age). In this scenario, only the genes of the successful survivors are passed on, and the gene pool changes to produce creatures that best adapt to the new environment.

An example of this is the Arctic hare. During the winter months, their white fur blends in with the snow and ice, thereby providing them with a natural camouflage. Gray or brown-furred rabbits would be easily seen in the white Arctic terrain, and would be quickly eaten by predators. Consequently, their genes would not be successfully passed on while the genes of the camouflaged, white, Arctic hares would continue.

Creationists do not question the ability of species to adapt to their environment. It is indisputable that white-furred rabbits would succeed in the Arctic terrain, while darker-furred rabbits would eventually become extinct. In fact, the variation that exists within species that allows such adaptability is often recognized by Creationists as one of God's remarkable designs that yields successful propagation of life even under the most challenging environments.

Most Creationists would not even challenge the concept of speciation. It is difficult to find fault with the Bible if speciation produces two similar animals over time that technically belong to different species. The Bible tells us that life reproduces "*according to their kinds*," but it is not necessarily clear that "*kinds*" is equivalent to the modern scientific concept of "species." Ten distinct species of mice that live in some remote region of the Amazon jungle may be significant to scientists, but from a Biblical perspective, all ten species may simply be recognized as "mice."

Creationists will argue most vehemently against the scientific belief that "descent (of life) with modification" can begin with one animal, and over time result in an animal that is very different. Virtually all Creationists firmly maintain that human beings cannot be descendants of the apelike *Australopithecus*. And they are nearly unanimous in their conviction that all variations of plants and animals in the world today are not descendants of some primitive, single-celled, primordial life.[3]

The Cambrian Explosion might best illustrate how Day-Age Creationists believe that life has progressed on planet Earth over time.[4] I have already explained that virtually every animal Phyla that exists today has its origin in the ten million year time-frame that scientists call the

Cambrian Explosion.[5] That so many new species of animals could suddenly appear on our planet in such a short time may suggest that throughout the Earth's history, God introduced new species of life at predetermined times. When one species went extinct, God merely introduced a new species to replace it.

The recognized gaps in the fossil record may also provide evidence for this belief. Science will acknowledge that it does not possess a definitive, linear, fossil record whereby one species of animal is witnessed over time becoming an entirely new species. Instead, many species suddenly disappeared in the fossil record (due to extinction), and fossils of an entirely new species abruptly appeared. While science is convinced that many of these new species are descendants of the extinct species, what is often missing is the intermediate species' fossils that can prove the line of descent. Scientists attribute these gaps to a paucity of fossils from that time-period (in some cases this is probably true), and are convinced that many of these intermediate species' fossils will be found in the future.

While the Bible is not very specific about the time of creation for every species of life, it does reveal that for six days, God created. We already know that the days of Creation span long periods of time. And the Bible tells us that on the Third, Fifth, and Sixth Creation Days God created life. Therefore, it is reasonable to assume that God created life continuously throughout those Creation Days. In the case of the Fifth Day, which spanned nearly 500 million years, God may have continuously produced new life in the sea, air, and even the land. Once God introduced a new form of life it would continue to exist by reproduction, which God bestowed upon all living creatures.

A question must be asked at this time. Why did God continuously create new life? The answer is because virtually all life becomes extinct over time. But that only raises the issue of competence. Since God continuously introduced new creatures because His old creatures kept going extinct, what does this suggest about His competency?

That question will only be asked by someone who understands life from a humanistic perspective.

A Scientist-Creationist might explain that God may have been introducing particular forms of life at just the right moment in time to produce a particular result. Without the Cyanobacteria that lived during the Earth's early history, the abundance of oxygen in the atmosphere that we take for granted today might not exist. The coal and oil deposits that modern society requires for fuel are the product of millions of years of preexisting plant and animal life.

An Artist-Creationist may view the history of life on planet Earth as God's way of displaying and enjoying His creativity and artistry. God continuously introduced new forms of life because He liked to create, and He enjoyed the beauty of the nature that He made. That God declared His creations to be "*good*" in several places in the Creation Story reveals a God that enjoyed and appreciated the aesthetic beauty of that which He created. Dedicated human artists will continue to express their artistic abilities throughout their lifetimes. God may be understood here as an artist creating one life-form after another, and enjoying the very process.

But perhaps the most compelling explanation would come from the Theologian-Creationist. For God to have created life that would not eventually become extinct would run contrary to the very teachings of the Bible. All the fish in the sea, the birds in the air, and the animals that traverse the land are but temporary creations of God. No mountain range shall tower majestically forever; no forest shall remain thick and green and capable of sustaining an abundance of life. The waters that provide habitation for a multitude of marine life will inevitably evaporate; the barren dunes of an arid desert will some day host a myriad of plush life. Great empires rise upon the ashes of fallen empires, only to add another layer of ash in time. Stars radiate brilliantly for billions of years, yet their ultimate demise is assured the moment of their birth. No man can rise above his own mortality; to be born is to die, and to persist through life is to succumb to death. Even the universe had a beginning, and it too shall have an end. Throughout the teachings of the Holy Bible this theme is often repeated. Nothing shall survive eternity, for all that God creates is ephemeral, as only He has attained immortality.

THE SECOND LAW OF THERMODYNAMICS AND ENTROPY

There are some Creationists that attribute all physical death in our universe to Adam and Eve's original sin. They do not limit this absence of physical death to only human beings, but expand the concept to include all living creatures. Essentially, they believe that nothing died before Adam and Eve sinned. Generally, young-Earth Creationists embrace this belief, since all life on planet Earth could not possibly live without dying for millions of years before sin entered our universe.

Some Creationists even associate a scientific process to help explain the rationale for this claim. They believe that Adam and Eve's sin initiated the Second Law of Thermodynamics. Under this law, the concept of "entropy" was formed.

In the context that entropy is employed in this belief, what is being recognized is that all things tend to move from a state of "order" to a state of "disorder." Although this is neither the primary nor precise definition of entropy, it is an acceptable extrapolation of entropy's influence in nature. It is evident that virtually everything in nature does tend to "run down"; things do tend to move from a state of order to a state of disorder. All life on Earth ages over time; the sun is slowly burning up its fuel by radiating energy; the universe disperses its finite energy as it continues to expand. In a sense, these Creationists believe that when sin was introduced everything within our universe then began to move in a particular direction—that of increasing entropy (or "disorder") over time.

It is true that any natural process contained within a closed system will distribute its energy in such a manner that its entropy will increase over time. This is essentially what the Second Law of Thermodynamics attempts to define. However, what these Creationists are attempting to associate with entropy is overstating and incorrectly applying this accepted scientific process.

Entropy is a very difficult concept to understand. The most basic example of entropy is the transfer of heat from something that is hot to something that is cold. If we take a hot coal and place it in cold water, then the heat from the coal will transfer to the water and warm it. Eventually, the temperature of the coal and the water will reach equilibrium—the coal will be cooler and the water will be a bit warmer. In any natural system, energy always moves in such a direction—transferring heat from the hotter object to the cooler object. And in every case where this occurs, the entropy of the overall system will increase.

Entropy has been in existence since the beginning of time. It was not initiated by original sin and was not part of God's judgment on humanity. Energy or heat has always flowed to objects that are cooler. This is true everywhere in the universe, including planet Earth.

The simplest method to prove that the process of entropy existed before original sin is to observe what has been occurring each and every day since the sun first radiated its warmth to our planet. All Creationists, regardless of their interpretations, place the sun's creation before the creation of Adam and Eve. Whether they believe that the sun was created on the First Day or the Fourth Day, it is clear that the sun illuminated and heated the Earth since its creation–*before* mankind existed. This process illustrates the most basic concept of entropy in action. Since the hot sun heated the cold Earth before Adam and Eve were created, we can be sure that the natural process of entropy, and the Second Law of Thermodynamics, were in action before sin entered our universe. Without the fundamental principle of entropy, the heat and light radiating from the sun would not warm and illuminate the cold and dark Earth. Consequently, the Bible has confirmed that entropy existed long before sin had entered the universe, by placing the sun's creation before the creation of human beings.

CHAPTER TWENTY-NINE

▼

OTHER CREATIONIST CHALLENGES

THE STORY OF ADAM AND EVE

After the Creation Story ends at Genesis 2:4, the Bible begins another story that strangely appears to be a different account of creation. In the second story of the Bible, God formed a man from the ground at a time that seemed to precede any plants or animals. God gave life to the man by breathing the "*breath of life*" into his nostrils. He then created a garden, called Eden, where He placed the man. The animals were created so that the man could find a suitable helper. Each animal was brought before the man, and he determined an appropriate name for each of them, but no suitable helper was found among the animals. God placed the man in a deep sleep and removed something (not necessarily a rib) from the man's side. From this extracted part of the man, God formed a woman, and the man finally found a suitable mate.

Much has been made about the Bible containing separate, conflicting creation stories. However, many Theologians do not consider the story in

Genesis 2 to be a true creation story. In this account, the Earth, the sun, and the rest of the universe already existed before the story began.

The story of Adam and Eve focuses on man's creation, not the creation of the heavens and the Earth. In the Creation Story, highlights of each of the seven days of Creation are revealed. In the second story of the Bible— the story of Adam and Eve—the Bible returns to the Sixth Creation Day and reveals more details about the creation of mankind. In the Creation Story, both the first man and the first woman were created on the Sixth Day. In the story of Adam and Eve, Adam was formed first and Eve was created later. Since we were already told in the Creation Story that they were both created on the same day, we can logically conclude that it is the details of the Sixth Day that are being revealed. Consequently, all of the events occurring up to and including Eve's creation must have transpired on the Sixth Creation Day.

There is no conflict, then, about these two creation stories. The first story is an outline of the creation of all things, while the second story focuses on the details of the creation of mankind.

THE EARLY CHURCH GIANTS

Biblical readers might be interested in learning how the early leaders of the church interpreted the Creation Story. It is believed that those early giants of the faith, being historically closer to the actual events, held a greater understanding of the Bible. Consequently, their interpretations would be superior to any of the interpretations that are held with conviction today.

For the record, some of the early church leaders did believe that the Creation Days spanned long periods of time, and not the strict twenty-four hours that many Creationists embrace today. Modern scientific theories or discoveries did not influence those early leaders.

Perhaps an account of the early Day-Age church leaders, and their rationale for embracing such a conviction might prove informative. A point-by-point comparison of their arguments and the arguments of today's 24-hour Day church leaders might also be enlightening. However, I believe that such an account and such a comparison would prove inconsequential.

The church leaders of yesteryear were men and women of tremendous courage and faith. They shaped our understanding of science, philosophy, religion, and the Bible. Their written words and legendary actions still provide us with comfort, knowledge, wisdom, inspiration, and enlightenment today. But despite their faith and prominent stature in the church, their beliefs were not always accurate.

Whenever plagues or war ravaged a country or continent, many outspoken religious leaders would declare the end of the world to be near; many are still declaring it today. The Second Coming of Jesus has been predicted countless times over the centuries. Even the early disciples believed that His return was imminent, and the fall of the Roman Empire was in the foreseeable future. Instead, Christians are still awaiting Jesus' return, and the Roman Empire prospered, expanded, and survived for several additional centuries. While great prophets have lived and died, and many were recognized by religious leaders to be the Savior, the Jewish people are still awaiting their Messiah today.

At one time it was believed that the three continents of Europe, Africa, and Asia—the only known continents at that time—were symbolic of the three Godheads of the Holy Trinity. The discovery of additional continents proved that assumption to be inaccurate. Renowned scholars once believed that the world was both flat and at the center of the universe. They were mistaken. One of the most infamous examples of church error was the historical debacle between Galileo and the Catholic Church. In time, Galileo was proven to be correct.

The early church leaders possessed no greater understanding of the Bible than the church leaders of today. The early giants also argued and debated the Scriptures with great conviction and passion, and were just as divided in their contrasting interpretations. At the times of their deaths, they too, departed this world still puzzled by the many mysteries of the Bible, and the purpose and meaning of life itself.

We may turn to the written words and courageous lives of the early giants of our faiths for guidance, knowledge, and inspiration. But we must remember that no man and no woman has ever acquired all of the answers to the theological, philosophical, and Biblical questions that are still debated today.

THE FUNDAMENTALIST PERSPECTIVE

Many scholars insist that the Creation Story must be viewed from a literal or "fundamentalist" perspective. They believe that the story revealed in Genesis 1:1 through 2:4 is not an allegory, but a factual account of the actual order and events of Creation. I am in complete agreement with Fundamentalists on this point. The Creation Story does not in any way give the appearance of a fable or parable. It was written to be a chronological account of God's acts of creation.

Where I depart with some Fundamentalists is how they determine a "literal" interpretation. More often than not, they use the King James Version Bible to support their beliefs. There is nothing necessarily wrong with the King James Version. It is arguably the most poetic and wonderfully written of all of the versions of the Bible. However, it is only one of many available Bibles. All translations from one language to another—by their very nature—possess some imperfections. The Holy Bible and the King James Version are no exceptions.

The most common and divisive argument in a "literal" interpretation of the Creation Story centers on the word "day." Fundamentalists argue that since the word "day" was used, Creation Days are unquestionably twenty-four hours. We have already examined the meaning of the Hebrew word for "day" (*yom*) in the Creation Story, so there is no need to expound on that subject any further. But this is one example where something is lost in the translation of a language, and the precise interpretation was not properly conveyed.

Other interpretations pose similar dilemmas for the Fundamentalist. The events of the Fourth Day illustrate the conflict between logic and "literal" interpretation. Fundamentalists are convinced that the sun, the moon, and the stars were created on the Fourth Day. In their opinion, this is what the Biblical text clearly states. And yet, the very first verse of the Bible declares that "*God created the heavens and the earth.*" Traditionally, this verse has been understood to mean that God created the universe. If He did not create the stars until the Fourth Day, then what exactly was created on the First Day? Certainly, the stars would be included among the creation of the universe, since a significant percentage of the matter and energy in the universe is contained in the stars. If we were to exclude the stars from the creation of the universe, then the universe described in the first verse of the Bible is very different from the one that exists today.

Of course, stars are constantly being formed throughout the universe, and, technically, star-formation occurred every Creation Day. This is another of the "natural processes" that God has set in motion. But like the other natural processes, God reveals only the Creation Day that the process was initiated. Since it is virtually impossible to exclude the creation of stars from the First Day, then that day is the likely origin of their formation.

The creation of the sun and the moon on the Fourth Day—as many Fundamentalists claim is clearly stated—is also highly debatable. It is true that the NIV translation declares that "*God made two great lights,*" which represent the sun and the moon. But, as I have previously noted, Dr. Gleason L. Archer believes that this sentence is better translated as "*God had made…*"[1] Once again, the modern translations may not always convey the best meaning. This sentence could be understood to be describing an event that occurred in the distant past. It is difficult to understand the literal meaning of the Bible when the translation of a verse is of questionable quality or in error. Regardless of the translation, the sun was certainly the source of light on the First Day. Consequently, there is a conflict between logic and the traditional fundamentalist "literal" interpretation.

There are other problems with the King James Version. If we were only guided by the text of this popular version, then we would erroneously conclude that the only large sea creatures created on the Fifth Day (verse 21) were the whales. Other Bibles generally translate the text as "*great creatures of the sea*" or some similar general term which represents all of the large sea creatures. The general interpretations are superior to the more restrictive King James Version. It is interesting that many King James-reading Fundamentalists believe that the creation of whales *and* other large sea creatures are being described in this verse. This is a contradictory belief since the King James Bible says *nothing* of any other large sea creatures. How is it possible to interpret the Bible "literally" and then expand the meaning of the word "*whales*" to include other sea creatures that are clearly not being included? Is this a literal reading? Is this an appropriate interpretation for a Fundamentalist?

The King James Version also poses a problem on the Third Creation Day when it declares that "*grasses*" were created, as opposed to the more common translation, "*vegetation.*" I have read several attempts to corroborate the scientific record of grasses with the Bible. Others have actually expanded upon the meaning of the word "*grasses*" to include other vegetation. This is similar to what was done with the whales. Does a Fundamentalist believe that grasses, and only grasses, are being described? Or can the general term "*vegetation*" be used here? Those who base their evidence on the King James Version and believe in a strict literal interpretation of the Bible are obligated to believe that only the grasses were created. However, most Theologians would agree that the general term, *vegetation*, is a preferable translation.

The point in question—the literal interpretation of the Bible—should not be construed to be impossible to realize. I also believe in a literal interpretation of the Bible, unless the passage clearly allows or intends symbolism to be used. I am also in steadfast disagreement with those who believe that the Bible can be interpreted in any manner. That is clearly not true.

Fundamentalists must realize that any translation of the Bible must allow some latitude in its interpretation. I would never dissuade anyone from reading the King James Version, however, it must be recognized that other versions are available, and some offer translations that are preferable. This seems to be particularly true of the Creation Story.

There is one last point to be considered on this subject. We may turn to Theologians, translators, and other Biblical experts to guide us in our interpretation of the Scriptures. For the most part, their interpretations are reasonable—though sometimes they appear to be conflicting. However, the true message of any passage lies not with our interpretation of the text, but in the actual meaning of what the author was attempting to convey to the reader. When we study the Scriptures, we are attempting to determine the author's original intent. The vehicle used to relate that original meaning in the Creation Story is the Hebrew language. Unfortunately, ancient Hebrew, like any language, is somewhat limited. The Bible's true message—the message from God—can be very philo-sophical, with esoteric concepts that are not easily comprehended by the average reader. Can any language, no matter how unambiguously written, really capture the subtle philosophical inferences contained within the Holy Scriptures?

EVIDENCE FOR A RECENT CREATION (OR A YOUNG EARTH)

It is difficult to believe that I once embraced the concept of a recent creation. Like many people, I had heard some of the scientific facts and arguments that supposedly supported a creation event of 6,000 years ago. A recent creation clearly contradicts mainstream science, which estimates the universe and the Earth to be billions of years old.

When I began my research for this endeavor, I decided to focus my ini-tial investigation on this very question. I was determined to keep my mind open to all possibilities, and I spent months carefully examining each piece of evidence for a young Earth. I read arguments and counter-arguments on each subject, investigated numerous sources from both the scientific and religious perspectives of the arguments, and meticulously searched for any hints of disingenuous or bogus evidence. After several months of thorough investigation, I was left only with disappointment, and the dissatisfaction of wasting far too much time and energy on a subject that deserves no such attention. Despite all claims to the contrary, there is simply no compelling evidence to support a recent creation or a young Earth.

Some might suggest that my research was skewed by science and the prevailing scientific (or secular) culture that permeates all the resources of our society. Nothing could be further from the truth. In fact, not only did I not need an extensive science background to properly examine the evidence, but any objective person with the ability to reason would conclude that the arguments of the young-Earth Creationists hold no validity.

There are problems with all of the evidence that is purported to support a recent creation. Research and data that were formulated decades ago is often cited as proof today, despite the fact that more recent research has greatly improved, and sometimes altered, our scientific knowledge and theories. Quite often only one side of a scientific argument is submitted for proof of a young Earth, despite the fact that other relevant points— that have been ignored—are widely known. There is also the tendency to warmly accept scientific research or anomalies that appear to support a young Earth, while remaining suspicious of the scientific community when the research disproves a young Earth.

One example of evidence for a young Earth involves mountains and the process of erosion. The claim is made that the Earth's highest mountain ranges should erode away in only a few tens of millions of years, based on the rate of erosion of rock and soil. Since mountain ranges still exist, this demonstrates that the Earth must be less than tens of millions of years old. The problems with this scientific claim are numerous and typical of many of the young-Earth arguments, which is why I have selected it. The evidence used to support this belief focuses only on one portion of a known scientific process, that being erosion.

One old mountain range, the Appalachian Mountains, are a wonderful example of the effects that erosion has over long periods of time. Today, the

Appalachians are but a fraction of their former majestic size, due largely to erosive processes. This is visible evidence that supports the scientific belief that mountains erode over time. What is absent from the argument of a recent Creation is the fact that some mountain ranges are currently rising. The Himalayas are one mountain range that is still rising—due to the collision of tectonic plates. This is one reason why mountains still exist today and have not all eroded away in only a few million years.

Also missing from the young-Earth's argument is that land beneath the sea is being pushed upward in many parts of the world. We can even witness such growth of surface crust in real-time by observing the Hawaiian Islands. The Hawaiian Islands are currently growing as volcanic activity spews forth lava from beneath the sea, which cools and produces more land.

Even if we were to disregard rising mountain chains and the creation of land by volcanoes rising from the ocean floor, the young-Earth argument of mountain erosion would still not be valid evidence. Much of the rock that forms the continental crust today is sedimentary rock. This is rock that has been formed from sediments, which are produced by erosion. This means that the sediment that was produced millions of years ago has been recycled into newer rocks, forming much of the land today. So the very product of erosion—which is the catalyst cited as evidence for a recent Creation—is sediment, which has merely formed new rock. Ironically, this fact would tend to support a very old Earth, since it would take tens or possibly hundreds of millions of years for such a cycle to achieve equilibrium. Consequently, mountains and the process of erosion cannot be used to support a young Earth.

There are more scientific arguments and additional evidence that are used to support a young Earth, but most of them are based on faulty reasoning and misunderstanding of natural processes like the example that we have just examined.

Cosmic dust accumulation on the moon, the Earth's magnetic field, the existence of short-term and long-term comets, the salinity of the oceans, the amount of Helium in the atmosphere, and dozens of other scientific facts and processes are used as evidence to support a recent Creation. Many young-Earth proponents also maintain that radiometric dating is unreliable, that the universe is not as large as science believes, that the speed of light has diminished over time, and that the processes of coalification and the creation of the geologic column are not properly understood.

I will not attempt to refute every piece of evidence that is used to support a young Earth (that is worthy of an entire book). But many of the arguments use misunderstood processes, deal with anomalies that science is still debating, or use old or erroneous data. For example, some Creationists still claim that hundreds of thousands, or even millions, of tons of cosmic dust falls to the Earth each year–a figure that was popular decades ago. Today, science estimates the amount to be closer to 30,000 metric tons.[2] Like the erosion of mountains, some of the evidence for a young Earth fails to account for all of the scientific aspects involved in a process—choosing to state only one side or one part of a scientific process, while mysteriously failing to reference the rest of the known processes.

Even if every scientific principle that science has come to embrace through the centuries is false (which is not even a remote possibility), there is still one decisive piece of evidence that proves the Earth is older than 6,000 years: Core samples taken from the Greenland Ice Cap have been dated back to over 100,000 years ago.[3] We may question whether scientists understand how light travels through interstellar space, or if radiometric dating is completely reliable. But even the most unaccomplished professional scientist is certainly capable of counting layers of ice.

As the Bible has revealed to us, the Earth is a very ancient world.

CHAPTER THIRTY

▼

THE PREDICTIONS OF CREATION

If the Bible really does provide the evidence necessary to develop a Theory of Creation, then perhaps we should expect it to do more than simply agree with science. Throughout this endeavor, I have demonstrated that the Bible is in complete agreement with the accepted facts of science. In those examples, I presented the text of specific passages of Scripture, followed by the scientific facts that supports them. Thus far, our research has confirmed the accuracy and the legitimacy of the Bible. Now it is time to take the next step in our endeavor.

The Bible includes many statements concerning nature, the Earth, and the universe. Using the scientific knowledge that the Bible has revealed, it should be possible for us to develop predictions about science and nature. From this perspective, it is now the Bible that will be used to uncover the riddles of science. I have already discussed the harmonious agreement between the Bible and science in many of these predictions. In those cases, the predictions have already been proven to be accurate.

PREDICTIONS BASED ON THE CREATION STORY

1. The universe had a beginning. (Genesis 1:1)

2. Time had a beginning. (Genesis 1:1)

Analysis for 1 and 2: Verified. The Bible does not describe how the universe was created—whether it was by the Big Bang or some other method. But with discoveries made in the past century, it is now widely accepted that both the universe and time do have an origin. This was not always known.

3. The Earth was once covered by water. (Genesis 1:2)

Analysis: Verified. When the Earth cooled to the point where water could exist in its liquid state, the thick atmosphere unleashed torrential downpours onto the relatively smooth surface of the Earth. It is widely accepted that at some point, the Earth was virtually inundated by water.

4. The surface of the Earth was shrouded in darkness early in its creation. (Genesis 1:2)

Analysis: Verified. The lethal, young atmosphere of primordial Earth is believed to have been very thick, obstructing all sunlight.

5. Plant life was the first form of life. (Genesis 1:11)

Analysis: Verified. Fossil records demonstrate that plants appeared before animals in the sea and on the land.

6. "Spontaneous Generation" of higher forms of life is impossible. (life reproduces *"according to its kind"*)

Analysis: Verified. Spontaneous Generation was an accepted belief for centuries, yet the Creation Story clearly dictated that such a belief was false.

7. Animal life in the oceans preceded animal life on the land. (Genesis 1:20 and Genesis 1:24)

Analysis: Verified. The fossil record clearly shows that animal life in the oceans appeared hundreds of millions of years before animal life on the land.

8. Land mammals were among God's last creations. (Genesis 1:24)
Analysis: Verified. Multicellular life existed for hundreds of millions of years before mammals rose in prominence some 50 to 60 million years ago.

9. Man was God's final creation. (Genesis 1:27 and Genesis 2:2)
Analysis: Verified. Modern human beings appeared very late among the life-forms of planet Earth. No new creations should follow, since the Bible declares that God ceased to create after the Sixth Day.

PREDICTIONS BASED ON OTHER PASSAGES IN THE BIBLE

10. The stars in our universe are virtually countless. (Genesis 15:5, 22:17, and Jeremiah 33:22)
Analysis: Verified. Before the twentieth century it was not even known that other galaxies existed. Now we know that there are hundreds of millions of galaxies, each comprised of hundreds of billions of stars.

11. The Earth is suspended in nothing (or space). (Job 26:7)
Analysis: Verified. Ancient cultures held many erroneous beliefs about the Earth, but the Bible declared that the Earth was suspended in space.

12. The universe is expanding. (Isaiah 40:22, 42:5, 45:12, and Psalms 104:2)
Analysis: Verified. It was not known until the twentieth century that the universe is expanding. This is now an accepted fact of science.

13. The Earth is spherical. (Isaiah 40:22)
Analysis: Verified. Many ancient cultures believed that the Earth was flat. The Bible disagreed and was proven to be accurate.

PREDICTIONS BASED ON BIBLICAL ASSUMPTIONS

14. Since there is only one God, there is only one Creator. This may suggest some type of common design by that Creator.

Analysis: Verified. If it is acceptable to assume that a single Creator would probably use some type of common design in His creations, then this prediction has been verified. All living creatures contain DNA. This was also not known until the twentieth century.

15. Man is a distinct species, unrelated to any of the Hominids. This is based on the Biblical presentation of man's creation, which appears to be unique and separate from all of the other animals.

Analysis: Undetermined. Science has concluded that human beings must have descended from at least one of the known Hominids. However, this belief cannot be known conclusively until the genes of the various Hominids are compared to modern man. One such comparison of genes has shown that the Neandertals were not the ancestors of *Homo Sapiens*.[1] This surprising discovery supports man's special creation—at least until further research is done. With the science of genetic research still in its infancy, this debate is now just beginning.

16. The origin of life on planet Earth cannot be of a natural origin.

Analysis: Undetermined. This prediction is a bit more complicated. The theory of Spontaneous Generation can quickly be dismissed based on Biblical text, since higher life-forms can only reproduce "*according to their kinds.*" The first forms of life on planet Earth were probably simple, single-celled creatures. Before that time, the building-blocks of life are believed to have existed in the primordial oceans. If the scientific theory of life's origin is accepted, the building-blocks of life appeared first, then later somehow developed into simple cells. At what point in that process do we recognize the product of any of those intermediate steps to be life? Would this be covered by the Bible's restriction on reproducing only "*according to their kinds*"?

It is interesting that the Bible also states that plants reproduce "*according to their kinds*," since the ancient Hebrews did not consider plants to be alive. Because that restriction is also applied to plants, it could be argued that the law of reproducing "*according to their kinds*" is applicable to anything that is capable of reproduction. This should include microscopic life, such as the simple, single-celled creatures (prokaryotes) of early Earth. If prokaryotes can only produce other prokaryotes, then the reverse may also be true: prokaryotes can only descend from prokaryotes. To say that the first recognizable life descended from, or was produced by, non-living matter appears to be unacceptable under this Biblical principle.

While this Biblical belief contradicts modern scientific thought, science would acknowledge that the exact processes that initiated life on planet Earth have yet to be discovered.

17. One day of rest in seven is probably the most efficient arrangement for human beings and animals—maximizing their productivity, while supplying the necessary physical and mental rest. (Genesis 2:2-3 and Exodus 20:8-11)

Analysis: Unknown. Research will have to be conducted on this Biblical principal before it can be verified.

▼

CHAPTER THIRTY-ONE

THE THEORY OF CREATION

THE FIRST DAY

The first verse of the Holy Bible, "*In the beginning God created the Heavens and the Earth,*" reveals the origin of our universe and the beginning of time. This revolutionary statement was issued at a time when it was not known that our universe, and time itself, had a beginning. The Bible neither explains nor describes the creation event; it only declares that it was achieved by the will of God.

Today, the scientific community widely embraces the concept of a birth to our universe. It is believed that between ten and twenty billion years ago the universe exploded into existence from a single point of infinite space-time density, in an enormous explosion known as the Big Bang. This initial explosion was of unparalleled magnitude, and it contained such a tremendous reservoir of energy that it would produce the entire universe (the pure energy that existed in those initial seconds would eventually cool into matter). The universe continues to expand today because of that explosion.

Our solar system's formation began about five billion years ago. It formed from a nebular cloud that was the remains of a super nova. The sun is thus considered a "second generation" star because it was produced from the dust and gas of an earlier star. When the solar system first began to form, most of the matter from the nebular cloud collapsed inward because of gravity, and created the sun. The planets, moons, comets, and asteroids were composed of the remaining matter.

The Earth was formed by a process called "accretion." Matter that revolved around the young sun soon began to accumulate into a distinct body. As the Earth's mass slowly grew its gravity increased, and it attracted the smaller matter that remained from the nebular cloud. Meteors, comets, asteroids, and small planetesimals pummeled our turbulent world. The constant bombardment by the nebular debris, and the radioactivity released from the Earth's core, produced a planet that was a fiery ball of molten metals. Volcanoes exploded everywhere, spewing forth lava, steam, and toxic gasses. About 4.5 billion years ago, our world finally became a distinct planet; it was also uninhabitable.

The primordial Earth had a hot, dense, toxic atmosphere, that was produced primarily by outgassing and the introduction of gasses that were contained in the extraterrestrial debris that battered our world. Carbon dioxide, hydrogen sulfide, methane, and ammonia were some of the gasses that comprised our atmosphere. The impenetrable atmosphere blanketed the Earth, enveloping the planet in prolonged darkness and trapping the heat from the sun via the Green House effect.

The Bible describes the early conditions of the Earth as "*formless and empty*" of life. This is a description that we now know to be accurate, for no life could exist in such hostile conditions.

Around four billion years ago, the Earth cooled to the point where steam could liquify. This precipitated a great deluge.[1] For millions of years, torrential rains poured down upon the surface of the Earth, eroding the volcanic mountains and cutting valleys. Stable mountain ranges as we recognize them today did not exist at that time, because the process of plate tectonics had not yet begun. The surface of the Earth was relatively smooth, and was soon covered by a global ocean.[2] The Bible's depiction of a young Earth shrouded in darkness, and engulfed by water (*"darkness was over the surface of the deep"*) has been confirmed.

The precursors to life—and maybe the first simple life—appeared at about that time, possibly extending as far back as 3.85 billion years ago.[3] Science has been unable to duplicate the natural mechanisms that initiated life on our world. The Bible, however, may provide us with some clues. The enigmatic phrase *"and the Spirit of God was hovering over the waters"* may be the author's subtle way of providing an answer to the puzzle of life's origin. Here, God is described as intermingling or providing energy to the waters at about the time that life first appeared on our world. Although the definitive interpretation of this mysterious verse remains elusive, the time of the event parallels the scientific time-frame that life originated. This may give some credibility to the belief that it was God that initiated life on planet Earth.

As the torrential rains continued to fall upon the Earth, the atmosphere slowly dissipated, and light reached the watery surface of our world for the first time. Without the light from the sun, our planet would be a barren ball of rock and ice, and life as we know it could not be sustained. This important event was highlighted in the Bible, when God spoke His first recorded words: *"Let there be light."* With that command, the Earth's surface received illumination from the sun. God declared the light to be good, and named the light *"day"* and the darkness *"night."* It was His final act of the First Day.

The Hebrew word that is translated as *"created"* in Genesis 1:1 is *"bara."*[4] What is being conveyed here is not the customary definition of the word "create." In the true sense of the word, mankind does not actually "create"— we merely manipulate matter that already exists. Only God can truly create (*bara*) something from nothing.[5] It is this particular usage of the word *"create"* that is being expressed in the Bible. Before the Big Bang, matter, energy, space, and time did not yet exist. After the Big Bang, the entire universe appeared and time began to move forward. Such a creation from nothing is referred to as "Creation Ex Nihilo."

The author of the Creation Story lived thousands of years ago when scientific knowledge was minuscule and in its infancy. Yet, consider what he declared:

1. The universe had a beginning.
2. Time had a beginning.
3. The young Earth was desolate and void of life.
4. The surface of the Earth was blanketed in darkness.
5. The Earth was covered by water.
6. Light finally illuminated the surface of the Earth, but only after all of the above had occurred.

The scientific validity of all of these statements has been confirmed. If we were to disregard divine inspiration, we could not begin to explain how an author living so long ago could have acquired such knowledge.

A CREATION DAY

Science has learned that the creation of the universe, and the formation and development of life on planet Earth, was not confined to six 24-hour days. Even the events described on the First Day of Creation spanned the passage of billions of years—from the explosive birth of the universe to the dissipation of the Earth's primordial atmosphere. Because of this scientific knowledge, it is tempting to dismiss the Biblical account of creation. This rejection primarily centers around one point of contention. After an initial reading of Genesis 1:1 through 2:4, most readers are convinced that the Biblical Creation Days were twenty-four hours.

The length of the Creation Day has long been the principal dispute between the many factions of Creationism. And yet, once we rise above the emotions generated from our personal dogmas, and we gain a clearer understanding of the Biblical verses, it should be difficult to find reasons to argue. None of the days of the Creation Story should be confused with the days that human beings experience on Earth; our day is determined by the rotation of our planet.

1. EVENING AND MORNING

The Biblical First Day ends with the phrase "*And there was evening, and there was morning—the first day.*" The words "*evening,*" "*morning,*" and "*day,*" are used throughout the Creation Story, and are considered by many to be conclusive evidence that the days of Creation spanned twenty-four hours. But even in the English language, the words "evening" and "morning" (and possible metaphors) are not limited to specific periods in a 24-hour day. Consider such terms as "The dawn of the Roman Empire," "Morning in America," "Our twilight years," and "The dawn of man." There are many phrases in the English language that contain the words "morning," "dawn," "twilight," and "evening." Like the previous examples, many of these phrases denote the beginning or ending of an unspecified period of time, and are not restricted to a standard 24-hour day.

There are some logistical problems with the standard interpretation of this phrase that may indicate something unconventional is taking place here. When and where does dawn arrive on a planet that is in constant rotation? Where is the reference point on the Earth to experience the rising sun? At any time during a 24-hour day, the sun is both rising and setting somewhere on our planet. As experienced from the barren world of the First Day, without any reference point, how is it possible to differentiate between evening and morning? Both events are occurring simultaneously somewhere on our world all of the time. The problem is that these terms can only possess traditional meanings if we are located at a particular place on the Earth. Since no such place is mentioned anywhere in the Creation Story, and the only stated reference point is the entire planet, these terms— as understood by the general reader—are illogical. The entire Earth cannot experience a morning or an evening.

This is the most compelling reason that I believe we should abandon the most common and popular definitions of "*evening*" and "*morning*" in this story. The word "*evening*" is not describing the setting of the sun, which is followed by twilight and then darkness. And "*morning*" is not the introduction of dawn, followed by a rising sun. Neither would make sense in this passage since the world experiences both events simultaneously, all of the time. Since the primary definitions produce illogical results, it is necessary to turn to secondary meanings. "*Evening*" then, can be thought of as an "end" or an "ending" to a period of creativity, while "*morning*" can be perceived as the "beginning" of another period of creativity.[6]

2. A DAY

The word "*day*" in the Creation Story is the translation of the Hebrew word "*yom*."[7] Like "evening," "morning," and virtually every word in the English language, "day" possesses more than one definition. The Hebrew word "*yom*" is actually similar to the English word "day" in the ways it may be used. Here are some of its meanings.

A. TWENTY-FOUR HOURS

Twenty-four consecutive hours is the most common understanding of the word "day," both in the Bible and in the English language. The translation of "yom" in the Bible is overwhelming meant to depict a 24-hour period. The frequency of this interpretation is often cited as evidence for a 24-hour day. Despite the prevalence of this usage of the word, this should not preclude us from seeking alternative definitions. There is nothing particularly special about a 24-hour Earth day that would compel God to limit His creative activity to accommodate that time-frame. An Earth day is the time it takes for the spinning Earth to complete one full rotation. This may be important to human beings and animals, however, no animals appeared until the Fifth Day, and human beings were created on the Sixth Day. Why would God be constrained by the rotation of a planet that contained no animal life until the Fifth Day? On such a lifeless world it would be pointless for God to complete His work in a manmade time-frame.

B. DAYLIGHT

The first time the word "*yom*" is used in the Bible is when God named the light "*day*" (Gen. 1:5).[8] In this instance, "day" only refers to the daylight portion of the day. This varies in length but may average from ten to fourteen hours. An interesting point can be made about this definition. Above the Arctic Circle or below the Antarctic Circle, "daylight" and "night" extend for several consecutive months of the year. Twilight also lasts longer in the Polar Regions.

The length of "day" in this example is relative to the position on planet Earth where the measurement is made.

C. AN ERA

A "day" may also refer to an era. Some examples of this are found in the expressions: "The day of the automobile" or "The day of the Lord." We often hear older people say, "Back in my day..." In these examples, the period of time that is encompassed in a "day" may be years or even decades.

The use of the word "day" in this circumstance almost never represents twenty-four hours. It can designate a period of time that may span weeks, months, or even years. In these examples, a "day" represents a period of time (an "era") that is generally not recognized by specific chronological boundaries, but by the activity that it contains.[9]

D. A UNIT OF WORK

The final usage of "day" is in a unit of work or activity.[10] Before this era of rapid transportation, people would often think of distance in terms of "days" of travel: "Three days distance by horse" or "Two days march to the enemy fort."[11] The word "day" in these examples does not actually represent twenty-four hours of continuous activity. Instead, it represents the time to complete a designated task—traveling a particular distance. While the distance remains constant, the time to traverse the distance is dependent on the form of travel.[12]

In today's modern office, it is not uncommon for employees to refer to the completion time for projects as "a few days of work" or "a whole day of work." People of all employment today often put in a "full day of work" at their jobs. In these modern examples, a "day" is actually referring to an eight-hour workday and not the entire day. In addition, it is assumed that for those employed from Monday through Friday, weekends and Holidays are not factored into any assessment of project completion. Consequently, entire "days" are excluded.

In all of these examples, a "day" is a measurement of the time involved to complete a task, and not the passage of twenty-four consecutive hours.

E. CONCLUSION

The Hebrew word "*yom*" represents a period of time, the length of which is determined by its context in the sentence. While it is most often interpreted as a 24-hour day, the previous examples demonstrate that the word "day" need not be restricted to exactly twenty-four hours. It may be no less than the daylight portion of a day, but it may span many years. While this does not substantiate the passage of millions or billions of years required for scientific corroboration, the flexibility of "*yom*" does allow us some latitude in our interpretation of the Creation Story.[13]

3. OTHER BIBLICAL EVIDENCE FOR LONG CREATION DAYS

A flexible definition for "*yom*" allows us to interpret the Creation Days to be longer than twenty-four hours, however, this is not the only Biblical evidence for long days. Other verses in the Creation Story and other books of the Holy Bible offer considerable evidence to confirm that Creation Days span long periods of time.

A. THE SEVENTH DAY

Each of the first six days of Creation conclude with the phrase *"there was evening, and there was morning…"* followed by the number of the day. The seventh and final day, however, mysteriously excludes a formal closing.

Some might suggest that the omission was an oversight, however, the author of the Creation Story appears to be too meticulous in his writing to make such an egregious error. In addition, other books of the Bible fail to provide the missing closure; consequently, its absence is very real.

But if the omission was not accidental, then it is reasonable to assume that it was intentional. If it was intentional, then its absence might be revealing something significant.

The Seventh Day's lack of closure creates an interesting dilemma. If we are to embrace a literal interpretation of the Creation Story, then we must accept this absence for what it represents. If all seven Creation Days are initiated, but only the first six are completed, then we are required to accept that the Seventh Day has never ended. To merely assume that the Seventh Day has concluded is to append something to the Bible that is clearly absent. We simply cannot alter the meaning of the Scriptures to have them conform to our personal views.

There is another piece of Biblical evidence that supports this belief. It is found in the 95th Psalm.

> *For forty years I was angry with that generation; I said, "They are*
> *a people whose hearts go astray, and they have not known my ways."*
> *So I declared on oath in my anger, "They shall never enter my rest."*
> Psalm 95:10-11 (NIV)

In the last two verses of Psalm 95, God declared that a generation of His people would never enter His *"rest."* For every man or woman, such an event would occur in the future, since physical death would have to take place first. God already revealed that the Seventh Day was a day of rest for Him, and yet in Psalm 95 He spoke of mankind entering His period of rest. The "rest" being referenced in this verse appears to lie either in the future or in the present—certainly not in the distant past. This "rest" in Psalm 95 makes the most sense if it is a continuation of the rest that began at the beginning of the Seventh Day.

For six days, God created the universe and the Earth, and all life that resides here. On the seventh and final day, He ceased to create. This concept means that God has created nothing new since Adam and Eve. Everything that we perceive as being "new" is simply the product of a continuing process that God had already initiated, such as new life through reproduction. The Seventh Day is a day of inactivity for God. When could such a day end? God's creative inactivity has persisted through today. What else has God been, if not creatively inactive since man's creation?

If we combine the exclusion of a closing phrase for the Seventh Day with the verses in Psalm 95, then the argument that the Seventh Day continues through today is strengthened. In both pieces of evidence, it appears that God's period of rest has continued since the end of the Sixth Day.

B. THE FINAL YOM

The Creation Story is continued in the second chapter of Genesis, and ends with the fourth verse, which is a title—or summation—verse. In the King James Version (which offers us a better translation for this example), the final verse of the Creation Story, Genesis 2:4, supplies us with two more pieces of evidence.

> These are the generations of the heavens and of the earth when they were created, in the day that the Lord God made the earth and the heavens—
>
> Gen. 2:4 (KJV)

In this concluding verse the entire Creation Week is referred to as a "*day.*" Many versions of the Bible do not use the word "*day*" in their translation of this sentence, despite the fact that the Hebrew word "*yom*" is included in the original text.[14]

If we declare that each Creation Day is twenty-four hours, then how can seven such days be referenced as a 24-hour period? There is simply no logic to this reasoning. However, if the Creation Days are understood to be "Days of God," encompassing various lengths of unspecified time, then the text does appear consistent. In fact, this is the only interpretation that is rational. This evidence demonstrates that the Creation Days are "Days of God," and are best recognized as "eras" or "periods of time." This final "*day*"—which represents the Creation Week—is also an unknown length of time. The Creation Week—or the final "*day*"—would have to span a period of time that encompassed all seven days.

It must be noted that this evidence is only valid if Genesis 2:4b is included in the Creation Story, and is not the beginning of the next Biblical story, which is the story of Adam and Eve.

C. GENERATIONS

The second piece of evidence in Genesis 2:4 is the Hebrew word, *toledah*, which is translated as "*generations.*"[15] A generation, in Biblical terms, does not possess an exact length of time. It is sometimes associated with a span of forty years, however, it does vary depending on its usage. We may think of a Biblical generation as we still do today, with grandparents forming one generation, parents comprising another, and the children constituting the youngest generation. However, "*generations*" is probably best understood as an indefinite time-period.[16]

Whatever length of time a single "generation" may represent, many scholars would agree that it is unacceptable to reduce "*generations*" to a time-span as brief as seven 24-hour days. In addition, the word used here is not singular but plural—indicating that the time encompassed spans two or more generations. The use of the Hebrew word *toledah*—or "*generations*"—in this final verse of the story is one of the more compelling pieces of evidence for long Creation Days.

D. THE ANCIENT EARTH

In several verses of the Bible, we are told of the ancientness of the Earth.[17] The phrases used to describe the mountains, the hills, and planet Earth are not phrases that support a young Earth or a recent creation. Six thousand years is not a significant passage of time, especially when we consider that seven people in the Bible are said to have lived over 900 years (Adam, Seth, Enosh, Kenan, Jared, Methuselah, and Noah). It is impossible to determine the exact age of the Earth from these verses, however, these verses only possess significance if the Earth and the mountains are very old—perhaps in the millions or billions of years.

E. DAYS OF THE LORD

While no one argument for long Creation Days is conclusive, the accumulation of evidence strongly suggests that the days of Creation are actually long periods of time. The evidence also demonstrates that the days of the Creation Week are best understood as "Days of the Lord." These are His days and His workweek. The entire Creation Week belongs to God for His divine objectives, and it is best left to God to determine the length of the day that He chooses to work. It is inappropriate for us to assume that He would subscribe to our methodology for determining the length of a day. His days are not bound by the Earth's rotation, for the God of the Bible cannot be governed by His own creations. A 24-hour day may be appropriate for human beings, with our physical limitations and our requirement for sleep, but the Lord does not possess such limitations.

Although the Hebrew word *yom* is interpreted to be a standard 24-hour day in the majority of its uses in the Bible, the Creation Story is one of the few places in the Bible where the days in question are not referring to human days. While it is true that the creation of mankind is the pinnacle of the story, it is God's creation of the entire universe that is the main focus of the story. In fact, the first man and woman were not even created until the Sixth Day.

This concept—that the days in question are "days of the Lord," and have no relation to our limited 24-hour concept of the term "day"—is the final argument for long Creation Days.

THE SECOND DAY

On the Second Day, God created "*an expanse between the waters to separate water from water.*" He named the expanse "*sky.*" The NIV translates the Hebrew word "*rakia*" as an "*expanse.*"[18] Many people have misinterpreted the events of the Second Day, and believe that the author was describing a thin, hammered-out, metal canopy that ancient people believed was suspended over the Earth. This metal canopy was thought to store a repository of water that was the source of rainwater.

If this were the only definition of *rakia* then the passage would clearly contradict established science. It is our atmosphere that separates us and protects us from space, not a metal canopy. However, *rakia* also possesses other meanings that do not necessarily imply a stretched-out, metallic substance. It can also mean "an expanse" or "thinned out."[19,20]

The "*expanse*" or "*firmament*" (the word used in the KJV) is the area between the surface of the Earth (water under the expanse) and the clouds (the water above it). This is an area of the atmosphere that we call the troposphere. It supplies the air that we breathe, and the clouds that yield the rain.

The author has also indirectly revealed to us that on the Second Day God created the hydrologic cycle (or water cycle). The sun is the catalyst of the hydrologic cycle, and light was finally visible on the surface of the Earth when the Second Day began. Since the deluge of the First Day, water existed in both its liquid and gaseous states. Science tells us that a stable water cycle began at that time.

SUMMARY OF THE FIRST AND SECOND DAYS

The first two Creation Days consist of several highlights. God initially created an entire universe from nothing. From an unformed, barren world, He brought forth a planet that received light. He also created the sun, which provided the energy needed to maintain the life that He would create. A stable atmosphere and the hydrologic cycle were formed out of the Earth's turbulent beginnings.

With each passing verse and with each passing day, we learn that God created order from that which previously had no order. Each of His actions brought greater stability to the Earth, and virtually all of His creations were dependent on His prior creations.

There were no other gods present at the beginning of time, as other ancient cultures believed. The Bible tells us of no great battles between gods seeking supremacy. Instead, the Bible departed from the common cultures of that time and declared that there was only one omnipotent God, and He created all that we see around us.

THE THIRD DAY

On the Third Day, God called forth the land to rise from beneath the oceans (*"let dry ground appear"*). God named the dry ground *"land"* and He called the waters *"seas."*

Around the same time that light first reached the Earth's watery surface, and the hydrologic cycle was just beginning, the reign of bombardment from small planetesimals, meteors, and comets was coming to an end.[21] In addition, the interior of our world—which had consisted of thick, swirling, molten metals—was slowly cooling. It was also around this time that tectonic plates began to form.

About four billion years ago the continents were only about one-tenth of their size today.[22] The cornerstones of the continents, granitic rock called "cratons," began to buoy out of the water at that time.[23] While the seafloor mostly consists of dark, heavy, basaltic rock, the land is composed of lighter, granitic rock, which tends to rise above sea level like an object floating on water.[24] Initially, the young Earth was too turbulent to support the horizontal process that we recognize as plate tectonics. The interior of the Earth was still very hot and the process was more vertical and more violent. As more cratons formed, they were thrust violently upward and moved quickly and freely above the Earth's watery surface. The moving cratons often collided, merged, and formed large landmasses. Eventually, the Earth's interior cooled and the craton's vertical movement subsided. It was then, some 2.5 billion years ago, that the horizontal, or sliding, process we understand as plate tectonics truly began, and the continents began to form.[25]

The Bible does not explain how the dry land formed. It only reveals the land's subterranean origin. In fact, even science did not understand the basic process of tectonic plate formation until the last few decades. Today, science is convinced that the origin of land on this planet came from beneath the sea. This is something that the Bible had explicitly claimed thousands of years ago.

PLANT LIFE OF THE THIRD DAY

Although the ancient Hebrews did not recognize plants as life (they do not possess souls[26]), the Bible declares that God's next creation was *vegetation*. Two types of vegetation were described: "*plants bearing seed*" and "*trees bearing fruit*." The Bible appears to say that plants first appeared on dry land ("*the land produced vegetation*"), yet it must have been evident to the author that plants certainly existed in the seas. This is not necessarily an omission—deliberate or otherwise—by the author. The Hebrew word for "*land*" generally refers to dry land, which may encompass a region, kingdom, something equivalent to a country, or simply the dry surface where man resides.[27] However, this word may also represent land of all sizes, including the entire Earth. The Hebrew word used here, *ha'arets*, was also used in Genesis 1:1, and was translated as "*Earth*."[28] The author is revealing here that plants in general were God's next creation.

Plants in the seas had been established long before animals appeared there. Evidence of seaweed and planktonic algae in the oceans dates back tens of millions of years before sea dwelling animals appeared.[29] This was hundreds of millions of years before life of any type appeared on land.

The earliest that we are able to date any rudimentary plant life on land may be 476 million years ago.[30] However, plants probably did not achieve prodigious success on land until the Devonian Period.[31] This was a period that extended from 412 to 354 million years ago.[32] Soon after, animals followed the lead of the plants and also appeared on the land. In the seas and on the land, science has established that plants preceded animals.

Most readers would assume that the plants created on the Third Day consisted of complex vegetation, such as apple trees, flowers, and herbs. Such an interpretation is not necessarily mandated. It is acceptable to understand the Biblical references to vegetation as very primitive forms of plants.[33]

Plants may not have been considered living things at the time the Creation Story was written, but the ancient people must have recognized that plants occupied an integral position on the food chain. Without plants, animal life could not be sustained. It is here on the Third Day, that we begin to see logic in the order of life that God created. Each living creation of God was generally of greater intelligence than prior living creatures. Each creature generally held a higher place on the food chain than those before it. Finally, each creature became increasingly important to man, to the point where we are able to actually form relationships with the last "higher" animals created just before us. God continued to increase order and complexity with each passing day.

REPRODUCTION

Plants may not possess a soul but it is evident that plants do reproduce. Reproduction is indirectly referenced for the first time on the Third Day when God commanded plants to procreate *"according to their various kinds."*

Life on our world has existed without cessation for billions of years. God may have devised a multitude of methods to achieve continuous existence of life, but the method He chose was reproduction. Without the ability to procreate and pass genetic information to the offspring, life would have ceased after the first generation of life had expired. There are numerous methods of reproduction on our world. God has granted appropriate and sometimes unique methods for every species. Single-celled creatures, plants, amphibians, reptiles, and human beings all have different techniques for reproducing.

Yet, the phrase *"according to their various kinds,"* reveals a limitation to reproduction. The fact that human beings can only produce another human being is an example of this limitation. The reason for this restriction is in the genes. An organism's genes are what determines its physical characteristics. It defines an organism's individual uniqueness and makes it part of a unique species. Members of a species may only reproduce with each other (although, there are some exceptions). Since the offspring carries the genes from its parents—who are members of the same species—it must also be a member of that same unique species.

THE FOURTH DAY

The Fourth Day has caused tremendous confusion among many Biblical readers. This was the day that the sun, the moon, and the stars were believed to have been created. Yet simple reasoning provides us with an argument against such an interpretation. The very first verse of the Bible tells us that the universe was created, and that light from the sun appeared on our world during the First Day. Since the creation of the universe would certainly include the creation of the stars and galaxies, and the sun was shining light upon the Earth on the First Day, we have our first clues that these celestial bodies were not created on the Fourth Day.[34]

The Hebrew word for *"created"* that we find in the first verse of the Bible was not used on the Fourth Day.[35] Instead, we are told that *"God made two great lights"*—the *"greater light"* being the sun, and the *"lesser light"* representing the moon. Although most translations of the Bible are satisfactory for the casual reader, the translation of this phrase is inadequate for a scientific investigation. It has been argued that a preferable translation of this verse should be: "God *had* made two great lights."[36] This is additional evidence that these heavenly bodies were made sometime in the past, and not on the day in question.

But if God was not creating these astronomical bodies, what was being accomplished on the Fourth Day?

One scientific possibility lies in the formation of our atmosphere. Although light may have first illuminated the Earth's surface during the First Day, the current theory of our planet's formation tells us that the early atmosphere was still murky and translucent. The first light may not have been direct light from the sun, but reflected, scattered light that passed through our heavy atmosphere. Over time, the atmosphere slowly dissipated, until at some point the sun, the moon, and the stars were all visible from the Earth's surface. There is some Biblical logic to this theory. Since these heavenly bodies are all mentioned together in the same verse, it does appear as if they are all suddenly visible at the same time. A clear atmosphere like we have today would make that possible.

Yet the primary purpose of the Fourth Day probably lies in the practical and theological implications it presents. These celestial bodies were to *"serve as signs to mark seasons and days and years."* God gave us the sun, the moon, and the stars for calendrical purposes. The time to plant, the time to harvest, the seasons, and many religious holidays are still determined by these heavenly bodies.[37,38]

These celestial bodies have also aided navigation. The position of the sun during the day, or even during the year, has directed mankind for thousands of years. Travelers at night, such as sailors and nomads, have been safely guided by the markers in the night sky.[39]

An implicit purpose of the Fourth Day can be discerned by the names that the author used for the sun and the moon. Here they are only referenced as *"greater light"* and *"lesser light."* Many ancient cultures worshiped the sun and the moon, believing they possessed some divine powers. But the author purposely did not address them by their proper names, so as not to grant them any unearthly power that they certainly did not possess.[40] These lights were creations of God, created for the expressed purpose of aiding mankind. They were meant to serve humanity and not to rule over anyone. It is implied here once again, that no other gods exist except the God of the Bible.

THE FIFTH DAY

With plants established on the Third Day, it was time for the animals to follow. The Bible tells us that the seas were the first place that God created living creatures (*"so God created the great creatures of the sea and every living and moving thing with which the water teems"*). Science agrees that animals first appeared in the seas and not the land. Sometime between one and two billion years ago the first multicellular organisms appeared. By 600 million years ago multicellular creatures were flourishing in the seas, but no life of any kind had appeared on the land. The Bible gives us a general description of the types of creatures that were created during the Fifth Day. This included creatures that lived in swarms, flying creatures, and the *"great creatures of the sea."*

Some readers believe, mistakenly, that birds were the only flying creatures created during the Fifth Day. In fact, the Hebrew word that is used does not make such a distinction, and any creature capable of flight could be included.[41] This group might consist of birds, flying insects, bats, and even the extinct Pterosaurs.

The *"great creatures"* would include any of the large creatures that have ever dwelled in the Earth's waters. The King James Version specifically states that *"whales"* were created, but that is much too restrictive of an interpretation. Whales, sharks, large fish, and extinct creatures such as the Plesiosaurs, Ichthyosaurs, and the giant Mesosaurs might all fall under the title *"great creatures of the sea."*

Despite the fact that the Fifth Day seems to focus on sea life, we may also infer that life on the land was not excluded. The author was certainly aware that birds are primarily land creatures. This opens the possibility of expanding the types of life that were created.

Amphibians are animals that begin their lives in the water but when they mature they may live exclusively on the land. Frogs are amphibian creatures. Baby frogs are called tadpoles, and are confined to life in the water. They are only capable of dwelling on the land after they mature and become frogs. Since amphibians are associated with water, they might be included with life on the Fifth Day.

Single-celled organisms have existed on our planet for billions of years. Today, they form an essential foundation for the food chain. Their home throughout much of this time was in the oceans. One of the earliest forms of life on the Earth was Cyanobacteria (also called "blue-green algae"). Cyanobacteria are believed to have played a prominent role in altering the atmosphere of the planet. These microscopic, ancient life-forms first appeared on our world some 3.5 billion years ago. They were probably photosynthetic and used the light from the sun to produce the energy needed to sustain their lives and reproduce. Oxygen was a by-product of their metabolic processes, and was essentially waste material. The success of Cyanobacteria meant that an increasing amount of oxygen was continuously released into the atmosphere. Eventually, Cyanobacteria greatly altered the atmosphere of the Earth, providing us with much of the oxygen that we require to breathe today.

It is tempting to place photosynthetic, single-celled organisms with the creation of the plants on the Third Day. But what day would the Bible place the creation of other single-celled organisms? Would they be among the creatures of the Fifth Day? Or is their origin alluded to on the First Day, with the puzzling phrase *"and the Spirit of God was hovering over the waters"*? It does not appear that microscopic organisms are ever addressed in the Creation Story. Certain days may provide us with indirect evidence to associate that day with the origin of these creatures, but the overall evidence is inconclusive.

Insects are creatures that are not specifically mentioned in the Creation Story. The creation of land insects, which were among the earliest land animals, is sometimes placed on the Sixth Day. However, it is arguably more logical to group them with the "swarming" creatures of the Fifth Day.[42] As previously stated, flying insects could probably be included with the other flying creatures.

Dinosaurs and other reptiles are popular animals that the Bible does not specifically address. Some scholars place them with the land animals of the Sixth Day; other scholars group them with the great creatures of the Fifth Day. Once again, there is no consensus.

THE FIFTH DAY ZOOLOGICAL RECORD

There is an intriguing declaration in the Biblical text of the Fifth Day that may present us with additional evidence for scientific corroboration. God proclaimed: *"Let the water teem with living creatures"* and *"Be fruitful and increase in number and fill the water in the seas."* God commanded His creations to multiply and to fill the seas by reproducing. Such a command implies a great surge in the diversity and multitude of life in the seas. This description may be the Biblical recording of a unique and pivotal period in the Earth's history. Around 540 million years ago, there was a sudden and prodigious explosion of diverse marine life that science has named the Cambrian Explosion. Over the course of ten million years, every animal phyla that exists today abruptly appeared in the Earth's waters.[43] This tremendous eruption of life filled the seas with all manner of living creatures.

As the Bible correctly states, animal life began in the seas. The Cambrian Explosion introduced a tremendous diversity of life on our planet— although life was still confined to the water. By 530 million years ago, the seas literally teemed with all manner of life. The extinct trilobites were the most prevalent species of life that existed at that time, but primitive clams and snails had also appeared.[44] By 520 million years ago, the first vertebrates made their appearance.[45] Jawless fish soon followed by the Ordovician Period—about 500 million years ago.[46] Jawed fish arrived by 460 million years ago.[47] Around 400 million years ago, larger marine creatures such as sharks followed them.[48] Amphibians would venture onto dry land during the Devonian Period (between 412 and 354 million years ago)[49,50] The Mesozoic Era—or the "Age of Dinosaurs" (250 million to 65 million years ago)—saw the rise of enormous marine creatures such as the Ichthyosaurs, Plesiosaurs, Mesosaurs, and giant crocodiles.[51]

In the air, flying insects were the first to appear, about 300 million years ago.[52] The reptilian Pterosaurs filled the skies during the "Age of Dinosaurs," while birds finally appeared some 150 million years ago. By the time the first bird took to the air, the creatures of the sea had increased in number and filled the waters—just as God had commanded. Soon the birds flourished and filled the sky.

The Fifth Day spanned nearly 500 million years—beginning with the Cambrian Explosion and ending, approximately, with the demise of the dinosaurs. By the time the dinosaurs went extinct, some sixty-five millions years ago, all of God's commands for the Fifth Day had been fulfilled. The seas were literally teeming with life and the birds were the kings of the air.

It may seem to some readers that the swarming creatures, the flying creatures, and the great sea creatures were all created at the same moment in time. The Biblical text certainly does not reveal any lapse of time between their creations. We now know, however, that the Fifth Day spanned hundreds of millions of years before its completion. It would serve little purpose to acknowledge any passage of time between these creations. Consequently, the author deliberately spared us countless pages of pointless text by limiting and summarizing the events of that day. The Biblical text that describes the creations of the Fifth Day can be thought of as a summation of work completed on a particular day in the distant past—and does not necessarily indicate simultaneous creations.

It is significant that for the first time, God gave His blessing during the Fifth Day. Following the blessing of His creations, He commanded them to "*Be fruitful and increase in number.*" God's blessing in this situation was associated with reproduction.

THE SIXTH DAY

On the Sixth Day, God turned His attention to the land, and created the "*living creatures.*" These animals would be considered a higher order of creature, since their creation occurred later than any other animal, and just prior to man. They possessed superior intelligence to God's previous creations, were exclusively mammalian, and were endowed with a living "soul"—which is not to be confused with the living spirit that God has bestowed to man. God created three types of "*living creatures*": "*livestock,*" "*creatures that move along the ground,*" and the "*wild animals.*"

There is general consensus that "*livestock*" were the domesticated animals.[53] This group included cattle, goats, sheep, oxen, pigs, horses, donkeys, mules, camels, and possibly dogs. These are animals that can be controlled by man, and some are capable of forming relationships with man. In the animal kingdom, mammals are generally the only animals that are capable of domestication.

The "*wild animals*" were probably the large mammals that are wild in nature but cannot generally be controlled by man.[54] This group included lions, elephants, leopards, tigers, hippopotamuses, bears, and other large animals. Some scholars place the dinosaurs with this group. However, it is not clear that dinosaurs are ever mentioned in the Creation Story or the Bible.

The "*creatures that move along the ground*" is the most debated of the three categories. Reptiles and insects are often included in this group, however, these inclusions are probably inaccurate. Reptiles are a modern scientific classification, and it is not clear that we could group such a diverse class with these Biblical creatures. Snakes, lizards, crocodiles, and even turtles might meet the Biblical text criteria, since they do seem to crawl along the ground. However, it is not clear that these animals would be of a "higher order" like the mammals in the first category. If we were determined to classify the insects, then a Fifth Day origin would be preferable—flying insects with the flying creatures, and non-flying insects with the swarming creatures. It is arguably better not to speculate the Creation Day origin of reptiles and insects, since they are not specifically addressed in the Bible, and they exist in such diverse types on our planet.

Consistency must also play a role in our analysis. We have already determined that the *"livestock"* was comprised exclusively of mammals, and mammals probably dominated the category called *"wild animals."* Consequently, the *"creatures that move along the ground"* were also probably mammalian. Mice, rats, shrews, moles, and other rodents are small mammals that appear to fit the criteria, both thematically and theologically.[55] Despite the fact that only mammals may meet the criteria for the first category (*livestock*), it isn't always best to group Biblical animals with modern scientific classifications—such as mammals. This uncertainty provides critics with (they believe) their best arguments against the validity of a Biblical creation.

It is particularly challenging to translate the animals mentioned in the Bible. Thousands of years have passed since the writing of the Old Testament, and many of the animals mentioned no longer inhabit the areas in which they were once found.[56] In addition, some of the terms used to describe animals can possess multiple meanings (as many as ten in some cases[57]). When we view the Bible from this perspective, the challenge of deciphering the precise animal, or animals, described in the text is magnified. Many of the animals named in today's Biblical translations are no more than educated guesses, and in some cases, the meaning of the animal names have been lost through the passage of time.[58] While there is occasional agreement on some animals—such as the *"livestock"*—more often there is tremendous disagreement in interpreting phrases such as *"creatures that move along the ground."*

Some Creationists may be troubled by the fact that new species of plants and animals continued to appear for millions of years after their origin. While plants first appeared on the Third Day, flowering plants did not appear until the Fifth Day. Many Creationists would insist that all plant species appeared on the Third Day while all animal species appeared on the Fifth and Sixth Day.

A counter-argument to this reasoning involves the development of race and human beings. Whatever race Adam and Eve may have been they were certainly not a member of every race. They merely contained the genes that would eventually create the multiple races that exist within *Homo Sapiens*. The new races of humanity appeared later than the initial creation of the first human beings. This same principle can be extended to plants and animals. Many new species of plants and animals appeared much later than their initial creation.

THE CREATION OF MAN

After nearly six days of preparation, the Earth was finally ready for the pinnacle of the Creation Story—the creation of man. The Biblical concept of man's importance is a radical departure from other ancient religions. The prevalent view in the ancient world was that men and women were beasts of burden, sexual toys, and playthings for the whimsical gods that human beings created. The gods were believed to control the wind, the rain, the sun, the moon, fertility, war, love, hunting, fishing, farming, the sea, and much more. Natural disasters such as drought, earthquakes, and floods were all attributed to the anger of the gods. But in the Hebrew Bible there is only one preeminent God that created the entire universe. And the God of the Bible created human beings not for the purpose of subservience or sexual favors, but with the intention of forming a personal relationship with us.

Both the first man and the first woman were created on the Sixth Day ("*male and female He created them*"). Since representatives of both sexes were created at that time there is some confusion with the Creation Story and the story of Adam and Eve, which begins in Genesis 2. Many people cite a conflict between these two stories, or at least an inexplicable repetition of humanity's creation. The issue of contradiction or reiteration is simply one of misunderstanding. The Creation Story contains a summary of the creation of human beings. It reveals that the first man and woman were created during the Sixth Day. In Genesis 2, the Bible returns to the Sixth Day and provides us with the details of that day, in the story of Adam and Eve. Humanity was not created twice, and a careful analysis of the two stories reveals that they do not contradict each other.

Some people believe that the lateness of our creation diminishes our importance, however, it might also be considered an honor that all of creation was completed and ready for us when we were created.[59]

HIS IMAGE AND LIKENESS

In the Creation Story, we are told that all of humanity was made in God's "*image*" and "*likeness*." Mankind's creation is highly regarded in the Bible. Psalm 8 declares that we were made only "*a little lower than the heavenly beings,*" which were probably the angels.

There are many ways in which human beings resemble God. Unlike the animals, human beings are essentially spirit beings. After our physical demise, we will continue to exist in a spiritual form. This spirit allows each of us to recognize and form a relationship with our Creator.[60] It is also because of this spirit that man, above all creatures, understands the concept of morality. Human beings possess a conscience, and are able to recognize right from wrong.[61] Perhaps this ability best exemplifies the way that we are most like God.

Man also possesses the ability and freedom to choose.[62] While animals seem to act primarily on instinct, human beings are capable of making decisions and are free to enact those decisions. We are able to increase our knowledge and develop wisdom. Since these traits distinguish us from the rest of creation, we are that much more responsible and accountable for our own actions. We are free to choose a life of righteousness or pursue a path of iniquity. We may use our knowledge to better the world or carelessly destroy it. The fate of mankind resides in the path that we choose to follow.

MAN'S DOMINION

Mankind was instructed to "*rule over the fish of the sea, and the birds of the air, over the livestock, over all the earth, and over all the creatures that move along the ground.*" God entrusted man with the responsibility of managing the world. This is another example where man has the ability to embody the "*image*" and "*likeness*" of God—that being sovereignty. God may be controlling the forces of nature and the processes of the universe, but on planet Earth, it is humanity that will decide the ultimate fate of our world.

God gave man "*every seed-bearing plant*" and every "*tree that has fruit with seed in it*" for food. This meant that mankind was originally required to adhere to a vegetarian diet. It was not until Noah's ark rested on dry land that God permitted man to eat meat. Although God's instruction is clear, we are never told whether man strayed from the vegetarian diet. Perhaps it wasn't necessary. There isn't a commandment anywhere in the Bible that human beings haven't transgressed, so there is little doubt that there were meat-eaters during those early years.

HOMO SAPIENS AND THE SCIENTIFIC RECORD

Perhaps the most enigmatic and pertinent omission from the Biblical Creation is the absence of the Hominids.

Science theorizes that modern man is a descendant of primitive ape-like creatures called Hominids that date back millions of years. From the scientific perspective, human beings are just another animal that has descended from the same common ancestor as all other life on planet Earth.

The Bible is mysteriously silent on the subject of the Hominids. These creatures should have been created on the Sixth Day, just prior to man. Instead, the order of creation on the Sixth Day moves directly from the higher order of mammals to human beings. Mankind is recorded as God's final and most important creation.

The omission of the Hominids might be no more significant than the exclusion of many creatures in the Creation Story. It is simply pointless for the Bible to record every animal that has ever existed on our world. However, these ape-like creatures have certainly added an intriguing element to the debates between religion and science during the past century. The religious community has been baffled by the existence of these creatures, particularly since science is convinced that they are man's ancestors—something that clearly contradicts our Biblical origin. Yet, it just may be that the Bible did not include the Hominids because their existence is inconsequential to man. Whether the Bible purposely excluded these creatures is unknown, but certainly the existence of the Hominids in the distant past plays no role in man's current attempts to attain eternal salvation. If the Hominids were merely additional creatures that were not part of man's special creation, then they would not have been created in the image of God; consequently, they were not spirit beings and their existence holds no special theological relevance.

Science and the Bible are in agreement on one fundamental aspect of man's creation. Modern man made a very late appearance on planet Earth. Hundreds of millions of years, and countless millions of creatures of the air, land, and sea would come and go, before man—*Homo Sapiens*—finally arrived. This Biblical fact should not be minimized. This is the one claim that the Bible made about man's creation that can be scientifically verified—and it has been confirmed.

THE SEVENTH DAY

The Seventh Day stands apart from the previous six days of Creation. On the Seventh Day, God "*rested from all his work.*" We should not think of God as actually resting or sleeping during this time; God does not require physical rejuvenation. It is preferable to understand the verse to mean that He had "ceased" to work.[63] God "*blessed the seventh day and made it holy."* Perhaps this was done because it was the final day or because no work was done. But just as likely, God blessed the final day to set an example for mankind. The Sabbath day probably owes its origin to the Seventh Day. God set three precedents with this final day: the seven-day week, one day of rest in seven, and the Holy Day or Sabbath Day. All three of these traditions continue today.

The final phrase of the Creation Story, *"This is the account of the heavens and the earth when they were created"* is generally regarded as a heading or title for the entire story preceding it, rather than a summary or concluding phrase that we would expect.[64] *"Heavens and earth"* is a phrase that encompasses all of God's creations, including everything that was not recorded in the story.

FINAL THOUGHTS

The Creation Story is a carefully crafted, organized account of the creation of the universe, the Earth, and the life that exists here. There is an abundance of duality contained in its passages: day and night, light and darkness, dry land and the sea, water above the expanse and water below the expanse, male and female, and the greater light (the sun) and the lesser light (the moon). There is also increasing order and complexity with each passing day. A universe was created from what was once nothing. The Earth was transformed from a fiery ball of molten materials into a planet capable of sustaining life. Life arose from lifelessness. Simple organisms appeared at first but over time organisms became more complex. The foundation of the food chain was created first; the pinnacle of the food chain was created last. Light illuminated the Earth before plants took root. Plants appeared before animals. Life in the sea flourished long before there was life on the land. The higher mammals were among the last creatures created, followed only by human beings, which were God's final creation. Intelligence, design, and purpose are all evident and increasing with each passage.

Within its verses also exist many implied or subtle inferences. There is only one God in the Creation Story (and the Hebrew Bible). His existence is assumed, His power is infinite, His life is eternal, His authority is unchallenged, His creativity is boundless, and His wisdom and knowledge are immeasurable. The author was careful not to indirectly reference other deities that were believed to exist at that time—even referencing the sun and the moon as "*the greater light*" and "*the lesser light*."

Natural processes, such as the sun's production of light, the hydrologic cycle, plate tectonics, the Cambrian Explosion, and the reproduction of life all owe their origin to God. The initiation of these processes were captured for posterity in the Creation Story, and continue in some form today.

The Bible may not be very specific or explanatory in its scientific statements. It may not satisfy the demands of science in its explanations, its reasoning, or its methodology. This is because the Bible's primary objective is to reveal God's message to humanity, and not to answer the riddles of science. The Bible is not a scientific textbook, although it does contain many verses that are scientific in nature. Its mission is primarily spiritual salvation, and not scientific conjecture or solutions. This makes the science of the Bible very difficult to assess and discern. And yet, throughout the Creation Story the theme is indisputable. Every natural process, every natural system, every law of science, and all life, matter, and energy that exists within our universe today are derived from one, omnipotent source—and that is the Hebrew God of the Holy Bible. Not even modern science has been able to repudiate this scientific statement, which is the very foundation of the Biblical Creation.

▼

CHAPTER THIRTY-TWO

THE MEANING OF CREATION

OUR ELUSIVE CREATOR

Any critical analysis of the Bible will undoubtedly inspire a multitude of interpretations and opinions. The countless denominations that exist under the umbrella of Christianity are a testament to those differences. Despite the quest for a perfect interpretation, the deciding factors that shape our religious convictions do not always reside in the text that we read. In general, the opinions that we acquire from reading the Scriptures are derived from our personal experiences. Our fellowships, social and marital status, personal liberties and freedoms, age, maturity, wisdom, the quality of our education, and our Biblical instructors and mentors are among the factors that influence our perspectives on religion and life.

In addition, it is our personal experiences that determine what we aspire to obtain from a religion. The impoverished, the oppressed, mourners, and the handicapped may all seek eternal salvation, but what they hope to acquire from the Bible for their time here on Earth would certainly differ.

The oppressed would focus on Biblical passages that spoke of freedom and overcoming persecution. The impoverished might find solace in verses that describe the heavenly riches that await them. People that mourn the death of a loved one might be comforted knowing that their dearly departed has been freed of pain and affliction, and is now at peace with God. Whether we are in love, are wrongfully accused, bitter, lonely, sorrowful, angry, or simply confused, we turn to the Bible seeking answers, guidance, and reassurance for whatever emotion is predominant in our lives. For every occasion and every emotion, the Bible seems to have something meaningful and relevant to contribute to our lives. It addresses virtually every aspect of human nature, through which each of us seeks its message, personally embraces it, and then interprets it in a manner that best quenches our spiritual thirst and our emotional needs. Perhaps, that is why it is as relevant today as it was during the time it was written.

The Creation Story is just one of hundreds of stories and themes that the Bible addresses. We have thoroughly analyzed it, seeking both its theological implications and its scientific validity. We may disagree over the proper interpretation of the story, but there is general agreement that the Bible is revealing something important to us on the subject of creation.

Even if we have been successful in our endeavors, and have eloquently demonstrated that the Creation Story has withstood the scrutiny of the most current theories of science, there is one aspect of the story that has remained an enigma through the ages, and is still inexplicable today.

The Creation Story assumes the existence of God.

That God exists and was the architect of our creation is the one presupposition in the story. His creation and existence is never explained, but He was there when the story of our universe began.

The God of the Bible is shrouded in mystery. We can only pretend to understand His personality through our own understanding of ourselves. This endows us with an infinitesimally minute perception of what it means to be an omnipotent Being. It also leaves us with the realization that God's thoughts and actions are incomparable and simply beyond our comprehension. Because we are made of flesh, and are only capable of accepting that which we can see or understand, the existence of God has long been fervently debated.

Can God's existence be proven? Or can we only believe in that which we can comprehend? Theologians have engaged in endless arguments on the subject through the ages. And while most human beings do claim some belief in a divine Being, there are many that do not acknowledge His existence.

MATERIALISM AND MAN

The cosmos is all that is or ever was or ever will be.[1]

Carl Sagan
Cosmos

When the sun rises above the eastern horizon each day, few of us take time to reflect on its appearance. It is the dawn of yet another day on our part of the world. The sun, which gives us the energy to sustain life here, has appeared at dawn for billions of years. The massive, fiery ball of thermonuclear reactions lies ninety-three million miles away from Earth. Perhaps, it is more accurate to state that we lie ninety-three million miles away from the sun. The sun is our nearest star and the nucleus of our solar system. The Earth is just one of nine known planets, hundreds of satellites, and thousands of chunks of ice and rock that orbit the engine of our solar system.

There does not appear to be anything unique about our nearest star. It is not the largest star in the universe, it does not radiate any unusual energy, and it does not reside at the center of anything special in space. The sun lies on the edge of a group of over 100 billion stars that comprise our galaxy, the Milky Way.

If we were able to travel at the speed of light (which is an incredible 186,000 miles per second) it would still take us over four years to reach our nearest star. When we consider the tremendous distances between the stars in our galaxy, and then consider the number of stars in our galaxy, the amount of space that the Milky Way encompasses staggers the imagination. Consider also that our galaxy is but one of hundreds of millions of galaxies that exist in the universe. The distance between neighboring galaxies may span millions of lights years—and the universe continues to expand, increasing the amazing distances between galaxies.

The universe was created in the Big Bang some ten to twenty billion years ago. The physical matter around us owes its existence to that initial explosion of incomprehensible energy. Our sun was not among the first stars that formed. As I have previously explained, it is believed that billions of years ago a very large star that had come to the end of its nuclear fusion cycle, collapsed, and then exploded into a supernova. Our solar system, including the Earth, was probably formed from the remains of such a star. Four and a half billion years after our planet's birth, human beings finally appeared.

Nothing then seems very special about our existence. We are but one planet of perhaps thousands or millions of planets in an ordinary galaxy. We cannot claim to be among the primary creations in our universe—just organized debris that was the remnants of some ancient, exploding star. Man is seemingly insignificant when compared to the vastness of space, and less than a blip on the clock of universal time.

To magnify our irrelevance, it has even been theorized that our universe is just one of many universes that may exist all within a super-universe. It has also been speculated that universes may have been bursting into existence for hundreds of billions, trillions, or even quadrillions of years. Some may have dissipated away over time, while gravity may have ended the existence of others in a "big crunch." Maybe our universe is not unique. Perhaps, universes have always existed, and sentient beings much like ourselves, living trillions of years ago in some other distant universe, questioned their purpose and existence, and the Being that created them.

Even on our own world, scientists tell us that we owe our existence primarily to randomness and chance. A multitude of various creatures stalked the land for hundreds of millions of years before *Homo Sapiens* appeared. Had the dinosaurs avoided extinction, it is speculated that we would probably not exist today. Mammals might have remained scurrying little creatures that dodged the mighty, reptilian rulers of the world. If one of our ancestors had not walked upright four million years ago, we might still be swinging in the forests of Africa, along with the chimpanzees. If our forefathers had never thought, or had the need, to use stone tools 2.5 million years ago, the great civilizations of history might have never existed.

Any number of species might have risen to dominance in our place. Today, the Earth could have been ruled by dinosaurs, giant birds, insects, or even chimpanzees, if the factors that favored their successful ascension, or the randomness of chance, had fallen in their favor.

In this entire universe, after the passage of billions of years, it appears there is virtually nothing to support the belief that our existence is significant. And if we are but the product of billions of years of randomness and chance, what place then does that leave for God?

THE QUESTION OF DESIGN

> Human existence is possible because the constants of physics and the parameters of the universe and Earth lie within certain highly restricted ranges…. The "coincidental" values of the constants of physics and the parameters of the universe point, rather, to a designer who transcends the dimensions and limits of the physical universe.[2]
>
> Hugh Ross
> The Fingerprint of God

In the past two centuries, it seems that the more we have learned about the world and the universe around us, the more inconsequential we have become in the grand design of the cosmos. If we were important to God, then why weren't we among His initial creations? Instead, we are creatures that did not appear until billions of years after the Earth's formation. If we are the only significant life-form in the universe, then why is the universe so vast and why does it contain so many other galaxies, stars, and—undoubtedly—planets? Why isn't the Earth the center of our solar system? Why isn't our solar system the nucleus of our galaxy?

Because these questions cannot be properly addressed without understanding the mind of God, many agnostics do not recognize the significance of our creation. Since our very existence was just as likely generated from natural processes (as most scientists claim), there does not appear to be any real purpose in accepting the existence of a Supreme Being.

And yet, where is the Bible wrong in any of its claims about humanity? The Creation Story clearly states that God created all of creation before He made us on the Sixth Day. We were said to be last among God's creations, not among the first—a fact that science has since verified. Nowhere in the Bible does it ever claim that the Earth resides at the center of our solar system, with the sun, the planets, and the rest of the universe revolving around our world. Human beings may have claimed these beliefs to be true, but the Scriptures never corroborated with any of them.

Today, scientists and non-scientists agree that the Earth does not appear to be located at the center of anything. What was once heresy—the discovery that our Earth revolved around the sun—is now accepted fact. At that time, it appeared that God and the holy words of the Bible were being seriously challenged by scientific knowledge. Today, it is clear that the Bible has withstood that discovery.

Perhaps a similar scientific challenge is being mounted today in the form of time. Science has determined that our universe is billions of years old. Millions of stars lived and died before our sun had ever emitted a single spark of light. In addition, over 4.5 billion years have passed since our Earth was created. To many believers, such a tremendous passage of time is unacceptable; consequently, they refute the science that has determined this. Our obsession with time today compels us to think in much shorter terms than billions of years. Some believers feel that it makes little sense for God to wait so long before creating His most important creation.

Hundreds of years ago, it might have been heresy to believe that billions of years had passed before man was created—much as the heliocentric system was considered heresy. But as our endeavor has demonstrated, the passage of such enormous amounts of time does not threaten the credibility of the Bible or the Creation Story. The exact date of the creation event is never given in the Scriptures, and long Creation Days is not only acceptable but also a preferable interpretation.

Human beings are more fixated with impertinent matters like the physical location of the Earth, and the time that has passed since the initial moment of the Big Bang. Neither of these scientific discoveries diminishes our creation. If God desired to make a fully operable universe in one hour, He could have achieved just that. But if God wishes to wait a million years, a billion years, or even a trillion years, why does that trouble us? How is time relevant to an omnipotent Being? What is important is not the passage of time but man's special creation, and the possibility of establishing a personal relationship with God.

As I have demonstrated throughout this endeavor, many scientific discoveries of the twentieth century have supported and validated the Creation Story. The Big Bang, plate tectonics, and our growing understanding of the Earth's formation have all proven the accuracy of the first chapter of the Bible.

As science continues to unlock the secrets of our universe, it might have been anticipated that the God of the Bible would be proven away for all eternity—much like the multitude of myths and legends of ancient man. This would certainly be expected considering the size and age of our universe. But as science resolves and understands more of the mysteries of nature, something else is occurring. The evidence for a Designer or Creator of our universe is now growing.

While science and our secular culture might not have anticipated "finding" God in their eternal quest for truth and knowledge, such a discovery would only serve to confirm that which Biblical readers already knew. The wonder and complexity of nature itself reveals God's works, and thus His existence. Two Biblical passages that speak of nature as evidence are:

> *The heavens declare the glory of God; the skies proclaim the work of his hands. Day after day they pour forth speech; night after night they display knowledge.*
>
> Psalms 19:1-2 (NIV)

> *"But ask the animals, and they will teach you, or the birds of the air, and they will tell you; or speak to the earth, and it will teach you, or let the fish of the sea inform you. Which of all these does not know that the hand of the LORD has done this?"*
>
> Job 12:7-9 (NIV)

We have all heard scientists proclaim that there must be millions or even billions of Earth-like planets in our universe. If there are so many worlds that are comparable to ours, then the probability that life exists elsewhere is greatly magnified. In fact, many scientists will declare unequivocally that life does exist somewhere besides planet Earth. But is their confidence supported by the evidence?

When we think of an Earth-like planet we envision a world that contains a breathable atmosphere, possesses fresh water, and is capable of supporting plants and animals. Perhaps our "exposure" to the alien worlds that we witness in science fiction movies and television simplifies the factors involved to sustain human life. In reality, the ability of any planet—or even the universe—to produce and sustain intelligent life is far more complicated than most non-scientists would expect.

The Earth's gravity, magnetic field (protects us from stellar radiation), axial tilt (moderates surface temperature), ozone layer (protects us from UV radiation), and atmospheric composition are all significant factors in maintaining life on our planet.[3] If these conditions varied greatly or did not exist, life on planet Earth might not be sustainable.

The Earth-moon system is unique among the planets in our solar system. The size of the moon in comparison to the Earth is considerably higher than any other satellite in our solar system (the Pluto-Charon system might be the one exception). Because of the moon's size, it exhibits a far greater gravitational pull on the Earth than any other planet receives from its satellite(s). The gravitational pull of the moon produces the tides on the Earth. The tides deposit water (and its nutrients) over greater areas of land, while cleansing coastal areas. It is also believed that the moon has stabilized the Earth's rotational spin over time, preventing it from wobbling excessively and threatening any life that existed here. The moon's ability to reflect light from the sun has aided mankind through the centuries, softly illuminating the otherwise dark and dangerous night. The existence of our satellite is either a serendipitous stroke of fate or a blessing from a Creator that possessed both intelligence and foresight.

Water, which is essential for life, possesses the unique and unexpected property of becoming lighter in its solid form (ice). Without this remarkable property, bodies of water would begin to freeze upward until becoming completely solid. That a simple molecule formed of hydrogen and oxygen could attain this extraordinary characteristic is either highly fortuitous for mankind or a carefully contrived achievement of a master Designer.

On a larger scale, life on our planet would be greatly threatened if our solar system was a binary or multiple star system. The mass and age of our sun, the sun's distance from the center of our galaxy, the Earth's distance from the sun, and even the age of the universe are all factors in determining the type of life that is able to exist on Earth.[4]

The Big Bang theory, and the discovery that our universe had a beginning, has done more than just augment our ever-expanding scientific knowledge. It also allows for the existence of a Creator. If the universe had always existed—as many had believed through the centuries—there would not have been a need for someone to create it. Yet this relatively recent discovery begs the question: If the universe had an origin, who or what created it? Ironically, with the scientific discovery of the Big Bang and our universe's origin came the rational acknowledgment that the existence of a Creator could no longer be dismissed.

Even subatomic processes do not escape the appearance of a divine Creator. In "*God: The Evidence*", Patrick Glynn observes:

> Even the most minor tinkering with the value of the fundamental forces of physics—gravity, electromagnetism, the nuclear strong force, or the nuclear weak force—would have resulted in an unrecognizable universe: a universe consisting entirely of helium, a universe without protons or atoms, a universe without stars, or a universe that collapsed back in upon itself before the first moments of its existence were up. Changing the precise ratios of the masses of subatomic particles in relation to one another would have similar effects.[5]

The failure of scientists to duplicate the origin of life on planet Earth allows for yet another possibility for God's existence. Only a few decades ago, science eagerly anticipated the imminent discovery of the "natural" mechanisms that led to the origin of life on our planet. Today, they would acknowledge that such mechanisms are far more complicated than they had originally anticipated. While many interesting and potentially plausible scenarios have been proposed and considered today, the process that once initiated life continues to elude the best scientific minds on our world. If such a natural process remains undiscovered and inexplicable in the future, can we continue to dismiss the possibility of a Creator and a divine origin?

All of these factors demonstrate that our universe—and our planet—have been "fine-tuned" by a master Designer to accommodate life on planet Earth. They also suggest that God had a reason, or purpose, in His creation. Perhaps, we are discovering evidence of His design through nature.

In the book of Isaiah, it is revealed that God did have a purpose when He created the Earth.

For this is what the LORD says—he who created the heavens, he is God; he who fashioned and made the earth, he founded it; he did not create it to be empty, but formed it to be inhabited—he says: "I am the LORD, and there is no other."

Isaiah 45:18 (NIV)

As science forges ahead in its quest to understand our universe, it may come to realize that the numerous parameters and conditions that we have come to accept as "natural" have actually been specifically designed by God. It would be ironic, indeed, if those seeking natural solutions to the enigmas of the universe stumbled upon the inescapable conclusion that there must be a Designer or a God. They may conclude that the universe does not just aimlessly exist with no real plan or purpose. Instead, the universe is actually a highly complex creation designed by a Deity that endowed us with the very abilities that we use to reason, comprehend, and learn about His creations. If mankind ever stumbled upon the existence of God it would certainly be our greatest discovery.

But could such a scenario really come to pass? Could our search for truth really lead us to the incontrovertible recognition of a Designer? Some may demonstrate the countless cosmological parameters that must be satisfied for human beings to exist. The evidence they offer might be compelling when we consider that without these conditions we might not even be here to ponder our very existence. More than likely, however, many in science will offer a greatly different interpretation: The conditions and physical constants of our universe were not designed for the sake of man, but rather, man was the product of the conditions and physical constants of our universe. Even if the evidence was overwhelming, there are too many in the scientific community that will simply not embrace any theory or indirect evidence that establishes a Creator. Consequently, it is difficult to envision a time when man's search for truth will discover the existence of God.

WHEREFORE ART THOU GOD?

Scientific evidence alone will probably not confirm the existence of God. There will always be alternative scientific explanations to counter any evidence that may be offered. Without endorsement from the scientific community, many in our science-dependent, technical societies will not accept the existence of a Supreme Being.

But for others, it is not so much the lack of evidence that brings them to question God's existence, but their self-aggrandizing nature. Consider what an individual "loses" by accepting God's role in their creation: The talents and intelligence that they possess can no longer be attributed to anything that they have done, but are instead gifts from God. Many people of exceptional talent and superior intellect, in particular, seem to resist attributing these traits to anything or anyone other than themselves. Perhaps, to acknowledge that they are beneficiaries of God's gifts is to render them indebted to God. Human beings generally do not wish to be indebted to anyone.

There is an arrogant side of human nature—a tendency to consider ourselves superior in at least some way to others. People often manufacture ways to "separate" themselves from what they perceive to be the "mindless masses." There are always individuals who root against the local sports teams, or disdain the popular television show or hit movie. They will always vote against the popular candidate, and only read the most obscure magazines and books. These individuals generally reject whatever is popular, and by doing so believe that they have in someway elevated themselves above the common man. In their mind, this is how they achieve superiority. Quite often, and by the same reasoning, it is these types of people that frequently reject the existence of God. In virtually every culture in the world there is a predominant belief in some type of deity. Consequently, to accept the existence of God is to "diminish" these individuals to the level of the average person—which is the one position that they are not willing to accept.

A small percentage of the human population will always refuse to acknowledge the existence of God. For the purposes of our quest, their continued existence is something that we must learn to accept.

The real problem still lies with the requirements of science and the theory that I have proposed. Any legitimate scientific theory can only assume that which has been verified or has been widely embraced by mainstream science. While many claim to "see" God in the works of nature, or feel His presence in their life, it cannot be denied that His existence has not been proven. Consequently, the Biblical assumption that a Supreme Creator exists would probably not withstand a scientific challenge. Science does not assume anything without some evidence that can be verified.

But if science cannot discover God's existence in nature, and it prevents us from assuming His existence, how then can the Theory of Creation be embraced as a legitimate scientific theory?

THE AUTHOR OF THE BIBLE

Anyone that has been raised in a Christian or Jewish culture is aware that God has been credited as the actual author of the Bible. While it is true that each book of the Bible was transcribed by a human being, it is acknowledged that God ultimately inspired those human authors. This then is our first piece of evidence to prove God's existence. No one that is alive today has ever met Plato; consequently, it is impossible to directly prove his existence. However, the very fact that "The Republic" has been attributed to him is indirect evidence of his existence. That the Bible exists and is ultimately attributable to God is part of the evidence.

Critics will naturally challenge this divine authorship. That the Bible exists is proof that someone originally wrote the many books that comprise it. It does not require God to write religious manuscripts—human beings have been doing that for thousands of years. The critic's argument would be valid if the Bible was any ordinary human-derived work of literature. But what the Bible proclaims—particularly in the first eleven chapters of

Genesis—would be beyond the scope of any human author's imagination, if it were verified.

The Creation Story is only one story in the Bible. Yet it is one of the few that reveals information about the past that can be considered scientific in nature. We have already reviewed the Creation Story verse by verse and argument by argument. While many questions remain unanswered, it cannot be denied that what the Bible claims is scientifically accurate. Here is a general outline of the Biblical Creation events that can be analyzed and verified by science:

1. The universe had a beginning.
2. Time had a beginning.
3. Initially, the primordial Earth was desolate and void of life.
4. The surface of the Earth was blanketed in darkness.
5. The young Earth was covered by a global ocean.
6. Light finally illuminated the surface of the Earth, but only after everything above had occurred.
7. A stable water cycle began between the clouds and the sea, in an area called the "sky" (or atmosphere).
8. Dry land originally emerged from beneath the global sea.
9. Plants were the first life introduced on the Earth.
10. Animal life began in the sea.
11. Flying creatures were subsequently created.
12. The land mammals were created near the end of creation.
13. Man was God's final creation, and the last new life to appear on planet Earth.

This list is an abbreviated scientific interpretation of the Creation Story. While it has been produced with caution and a careful, conservative reading of the Biblical text, it can still generate some questions.

Many scholars will insist that the plants created on the Third Day were restricted to the land. Such an interpretation would cast the Creation Story into error. Yet, I believe that it is just as acceptable (and possibly preferable) to interpret the events of the Third Day as the beginning of plant life in general on planet Earth. While the arguments for my interpretation are compelling, they are certainly not conclusive.

The animals described on the Fifth and Sixth Creation Days have long been the subject of controversy. But by obtaining a better understanding of the Hebrew words used, and making reasonable assumptions as we have done, it is hard to find fault with the Biblical order of the creation of animals. It is to be expected, however, that many scholars will continue to debate the types and order of the animals created. The primary reason for this zoological debate is the inherent difficulty in translating the names of animals in the Bible.

Although the fossil remains of the Hominids have brought into question man's origin, it must be noted that the Bible never mentions the Hominids. Its only scientific claim in reference to man is that human beings were God's final creation on planet Earth. Science concurs that modern man has appeared very recently, when compared to the other living creatures. Consequently, what the Bible states about *Homo Sapiens* does not contradict current scientific knowledge.

We must once again realize that the Bible is not presenting a detailed, species-by-species account of the history of life on planet Earth. In fact, such a comprehensive account would be overwhelming and pointless since the Bible is not a scientific textbook. The Creation Story is simply a general chronology of the major creation events on our world (and the universe). A more constructive scientific analysis of the Bible would be to determine if the events of creation that were included are in the correct scientific order. This is a standard that the Bible satisfies.

Even if we were to disregard the challenging and controversial classification of the animals completely—deciding that it is too difficult to interpret—the remainder of the Biblical order of creation—and the claims that it makes—are in virtual agreement with science. The critics that attribute the writing of the Creation Story to some ancient human author—and not God—must explain how any human being that lived thousands of years ago could possibly conjure up a story of creation that so closely compares to the scientific record.

The Bible's supporters claim that it is the inerrant word of God. God, then, is the ultimate author of the Bible, since it was through His inspiration that it was written. If the Bible can be shown to be factual, and its statements that can be verified by science do in fact withstand scientific scrutiny, then we can only come to one inescapable conclusion.

Our scientific validation of the Biblical Creation Story has taken us one step closer to achieving one of man's ultimate aspirations—proving the existence of God.

CONCLUDING THOUGHTS

Philosophers, Theologians, and men and women of renowned intellectual ability have debated the purpose of our existence since the beginning of time. We have pondered the pervasiveness of human suffering and natural catastrophes, and the inevitability of death. We can not comprehend why God waited for billions of years before He created the stated primary purpose of creation—mankind. We even question why He created in the manner that He did.

Where is God? Why does He remain silent? Has He said all that we need to hear? Has He allowed mankind to determine our own fate? Or does He intervene at predetermined times in answer to prayers? What is man's purpose? If God's existence is in such doubt why does He not proclaim His existence to the entire world?

The list of unanswered questions could continue for hundreds of pages. And yet, what if God were to respond to our questions? Could any of us even begin to comprehend the wisdom, methodology, and thoughts of an omnipotent Creator? To stress this very point, the Lord says in Isaiah:

> For my thoughts are not your thoughts, neither are your ways my ways,"
> declares the Lord. "As the heavens are higher than the Earth, so are my
> ways higher than your ways and my thoughts than your thoughts."
>
> Isaiah 55:8-9 (NIV)

The explicit purpose of man's creation in the Creation Story is to act at custodians of our world. This is something that one person could influence, yet it would take the cooperation of the entire world to achieve. This explicit purpose is important in that it is a goal that can only be realized by working together—something that God certainly expects from humanity.

Many will argue that science and the Bible cannot be reconciled since each understands the world around us from unique and exclusive perspectives. Science strives to ascertain the natural processes and order of our universe. The Bible's primary focus is something that science can neither measure nor understand—and that is the human soul.

It is the soul that is the focus of the implicit purpose of our creation–a purpose that only an individual can achieve. Mankind was not merely created to rule over God's creations. All of us were created with the intent of forming a personal relationship with our Creator. It is the spirit, or soul, that dwells in each of us that separates us and elevates us above the rest of creation. Consequently, it is the soul that must be the primary focus of our personal lives. Each of us must take the soul that God gave us, spiritually nourish it, grow with it, and strive to improve upon it. The condition of our soul at the moment of our demise will be our personal evidence that will be presented before Him.

No human being is capable of fully understanding or answering the endless, enduring questions that are raised by a divine Creation. Perhaps, we are not supposed to know, or perhaps in time, God's ultimate purpose will be revealed to us. But until then we may be comforted in knowing that His eternal presence endures in the wonders of nature, the sacred words of the Scriptures, and in the hearts and minds of each of us.

The Theory of Creation has successfully withstood the scrutiny of a rigorous scientific analysis. But despite this prodigious achievement—which many will gratefully embrace and use to support their faith—men and women of unwavering conviction and deep religious faith need not turn to science to justify their devotion to their Creator and His Holy words. The God of the Bible transcends any scientific theory that mankind proposes, for He is eternal—He existed at the beginning of time and will survive its end. His words will endure the test of time and the achievements of His creations—for His words are His very thoughts, His message to humanity, His declaration of morality and iniquity, and mankind's sole opportunity for eternal life and salvation.

In this, the ancient Hebrew account of Creation, mankind has been elevated above the animals, freed from the bondage of whimsical, imaginary gods, given dominion over the entire Earth, and spiritually heightened to the point where a relationship with our very Creator is within our reach.

The Theory of Creation, then, is not merely the Bible's profound answers to the probing questions of science. It is, instead, a solid foundation and a promising, rewarding beginning to guide us on life's challenging journey toward eternal life with God. From the moment of our creation, God's almighty hand has been extended to all of mankind; all that remains for each of us is to recognize His gracious offer and embrace it.

NOTES

---▼---

CHAPTER 1: THE ORIGIN OF GENESIS

1. Charles M. Laymon, ed., *The Interpreter's One-Volume Commentary on the Bible* (New York and Nashville: Abingdon Press, and Nashville: Parthenon Press, printed and bound, 1971), p.1
2. Ibid., p.3
3. Ibid., p.3
4. Bruce Vawter, *On Genesis: A New Reading* (Garden City, New York: Doubleday & Company, 1977), p.22
5. Powel Mills Dawley, "Ussher, James", *The Encyclopedia Americana, International Edition*, 1997, Vol.27, p.822

CHAPTER 2: IN THE BEGINNING, GOD CREATED

1. "NIV" stands for the New International Version Bible. In other chapters the popular King James Version will also be referenced, and will be represented by "KJV."
2. Robert Jamieson, A.R. Fausset, and David Brown, *A Commentary Critical and Explanatory on the Whole Bible* (New York: Richard R. Smith, Inc., 1930), p.17

3. Stephen W. Hawking, *A Brief History of Time* (New York: Bantam Books, 1988), p.8

4. Henry M. Morris, *The Genesis Record* (Grand Rapids, Michigan: Baker Book House, 1976), p.41

5. *Torah Portions*, World Ort Union, "Navigating the Bible", 1996, April 16, 1997 <HTTP://BIBLE.ORT.ORG> The various Bible Commentaries that I quote often have different spellings for the original Hebrew words. I will only use this particular reference when I cite the original Hebrew text.

6. Harry M. Orlinsky, ed., *Notes on the New Translation of The Torah* (Philadelphia: The Jewish Publication Society of America, 1969), p.49

7. Adam Clarke, *Commentary on the Holy Bible*, One-Volume Edition, Abridged from original six-volume work by Ralph Earl (Grand Rapids, Michigan: Baker Book House, 1967), p.16

8. Charles M. Laymon, ed., *The Interpreter's One-Volume Commentary on the Bible* (New York and Nashville: Abingdon Press, and Nashville: Parthenon Press, printed and bound, 1971), p.3

9. Frederick Carl Eiselen, Edwin Lewis, and David G. Downey, eds., *The Abingdon Bible Commentary* (New York and Nashville: Abingdon-Cokesbury Press, 1929), pp.220-221

10. Adam Clarke, Commentary on the Holy Bible, One-Volume Edition, Abridged from original six-volume work by Ralph Earl (Grand Rapids, Michigan: Baker Book House, 1967), p.16

11. Henry M. Morris, *The Genesis Record* (Grand Rapids, Michigan: Baker Book House, 1976), p.39

12. Adam Clarke, *Commentary on the Holy Bible*, One-Volume Edition, Abridged from original six-volume work by Ralph Earl (Grand Rapids, Michigan: Baker Book House, 1967), p.16

13. Nathaniel Kravitz, *Genesis: A New Interpretation of the First Three Chapters* (New York: Philosophical Library, 1967), p.19

CHAPTER 4: UNFORMED AND VOID

1. *Torah Portions*, World Ort Union, "Navigating the Bible", 1996, April 16, 1997 <HTTP://BIBLE.ORT.ORG>
2. P.R. Ackroyd, A.R.C.Leaney, and J.W.Packer, eds., *The Cambridge Bible Commentary: Genesis 1-11* (Cambridge: At The University Press, 1973), p.15

CHAPTER 5: DARKNESS ENVELOPS THE EARTH

1. Jon Erickson, *"Plate Tectonics: Unraveling the Mysteries of the Earth"*, The Changing Earth Series (New York, Oxford: Facts on File, Inc., 1992), p.124
2. R. Monastersky, "Speedy spin kept early Earth from freezing," *Science News*, June 12, 1993, p.373. Four billion years ago the young sun only radiated about 70% of the energy that it radiates today.
3. James B. Pollack, "Venus", *McGraw-Hill Encyclopedia of Science and Technology*, 8th Ed., 1997, Vol.19, p.212

CHAPTER 6: A WATERY WORLD

1. I have read some accounts where this water is believed to be the water from Noah and the Great Flood. Although water from that mighty flood is said to have covered the globe, the water mentioned in these early verses is clearly from a period of time that preceded Noah. Nearly all Biblical scholars accept this interpretation.
2. R. Monastersky, "Water Flowed Early in the Solar System," *Science News*, Feb 24, 1996, p.117
3. Jon Erickson, *"Plate Tectonics: Unraveling the Mysteries of the Earth"*, The Changing Earth Series (New York, Oxford: Facts on File, Inc., 1992), p.125
4. Ibid.
5. Ibid.

CHAPTER 7: GOD HOVERS OVER THE WATERS

1. Bernard Orchard, Edmund F. Sutcliffe, Reginald C. Fuller, and Ralph Russel, eds., *A Catholic Commentary on Holy Scripture* (London: Thomas Nelson and Sons Ltd, 1953), p.182

2. I say "probably" since science may find that life had begun and failed several times before it was able to maintain itself. However, such a scenario would not seem likely in the context of this chapter.

3. Harry M. Orlinsky, ed., *Notes on the New Translation of The Torah* (Philadelphia: The Jewish Publication Society of America, 1969), p.52

4. Ibid.

5. *The Broadman Bible Commentary*, Vol.1 (Nashville: Broadman Press, 1973), p.122

6. Bernard Orchard, Edmund F. Sutcliffe, Reginald C. Fuller, and Ralph Russel, eds., *A Catholic Commentary on Holy Scripture* (London: Thomas Nelson and Sons Ltd, 1953), p.182

7. P.R. Ackroyd, A.R.C.Leaney, and J.W.Packer, eds., *The Cambridge Bible Commentary: Genesis 1-11* (Cambridge: At The University Press, 1973), p.16

8. Adam Clarke, *Commentary on the Holy Bible*, One-Volume Edition, abridged from original six-volume work by Ralph Earl (Grand Rapids, Michigan: Baker Book House, 1967), p.16

9. *Torah Portions*, World Ort Union, "Navigating the Bible", 1996, April 16, 1997 <HTTP://BIBLE.ORT.ORG>

10. J.H. Hertz, ed., 2nd Ed. *The Pentateuch and Haftorahs* (London: Soncino Press, 1960), p.2

11. Ibid.

12. Bernard Orchard, Edmund F. Sutcliffe, Reginald C. Fuller, and Ralph Russel, eds., *A Catholic Commentary on Holy Scripture* (London: Thomas Nelson and Sons Ltd, 1953), p.182

CHAPTER 8: LIGHT!

1. Robert Jamieson, A.R. Fausset, and David Brown, *A Commentary Critical and Explanatory on the Whole Bible* (New York: Richard R. Smith, Inc., 1930), p.17

CHAPTER 9: THE EVENING AND THE MORNING

1. Hugh Ross, *Genesis One: A Scientific Perspective,* Rev. Ed. (Pasadena, CA: Reasons To Believe, 1983), p.17
2. Ibid.
3. Gleason L. Archer, *Encyclopedia of Bible Difficulties,* (Grand Rapids, Michigan: Zondervan Publishing House, 1982), pp.60-61
4. The Earth's rotation has not always been twenty-four hours (actually, it is currently closer to 23 hours and 56 minutes). When the Earth first formed, it rotated much faster than it does today. The gravitational pull of the moon is the principal source of the Earth's diminishing speed. Even today, the Earth's rotation continues to slow because of our large satellite. The fact that the Earth rotated faster billions of years ago means that a day at that time was shorter than today. We are then left with the dilemma that the first Creation "Day" (or any of the early Creation Days) was not even long enough to encompass what we would now consider to be a full "day"—that being twenty-four hours. This scientific fact provides further evidence against a strict 24-hour day interpretation.
5. Gleason L. Archer, *Encyclopedia of Bible Difficulties,* (Grand Rapids, Michigan: Zondervan Publishing House, 1982), p.61
6. *Torah Portions*, World Ort Union, "Navigating the Bible", 1996, April 16, 1997 <HTTP://BIBLE.ORT.ORG>
7. Gleason L. Archer, *Encyclopedia of Bible Difficulties,* (Grand Rapids, Michigan: Zondervan Publishing House, 1982), p.61

CHAPTER 10: WHAT IS A DAY?

1. J.H. Hertz, ed., 2nd Ed. *The Pentateuch and Haftorahs* (London: Soncino Press, 1960), p.3
2. Harry M. Orlinsky, ed., *Notes on the New Translation of The Torah* (Philadelphia: The Jewish Publication Society of America, 1969), p.56
3. *Torah Portions*, World Ort Union, "Navigating the Bible", 1996, April 16, 1997 <HTTP://BIBLE.ORT.ORG>
4. John D. Davies, *Beginning Now* (Philadelphia: Fortress Press, 1971), p.45
5. Ibid., p.46
6. Ibid., p.46
7. Hugh Ross, *Genesis One: A Scientific Perspective,* Rev. Ed. (Pasadena, CA: Reasons To Believe, 1983), p.17
8. Herbert Lockyer, Sr., ed., *Nelson's Illustrated Bible Dictionary*, (New York: Thomas Nelson Publishers, 1986), p.262

CHAPTER 11: THE FIRST ACT OF GOD

1. Harry M. Orlinsky, ed., *Notes on the New Translation of The Torah* (Philadelphia: The Jewish Publication Society of America, 1969), p.49
2. The Jewish Publications Society of America, *The Torah: The Five Books of Moses*, 2nd Ed. (Philadelphia: The Jewish Publication Society of America, 1967), p.3
3. Ibid.

CHAPTER 12: GOD CALLED THE EXPANSE "SKY"

1. Adam Clarke, *Commentary on the Holy Bible*, One-Volume Edition, Abridged from original six-volume work by Ralph Earl (Grand Rapids, Michigan: Baker Book House, 1967), p.17
2. *The Broadman Bible Commentary*, Vol.1 (Nashville: Broadman Press, 1973), p.123
3. Nathaniel Kravitz, *Genesis: A New Interpretation of the First Three Chapters* (New York: Philosophical Library, 1967), p.27

CHAPTER 13: LAND EMERGES FROM THE SEA

1. Michael Balter, "*Looking for Clues to the Mystery of Life on Earth*," Science, Aug 16, 1996, p.870
2. Jon Erickson, "*Plate Tectonics: Unraveling the Mysteries of the Earth*", The Changing Earth Series (New York, Oxford: Facts on File, Inc., 1992), p.19
3. Ibid., p.23
4. Ibid., p.23
5. S. Ross Taylor and Scott M. McLennan, "*The Evolution of Continental Crust*," Scientific American, Jan 1996, p.79
6. Jon Erickson, "*Plate Tectonics: Unraveling the Mysteries of the Earth*", The Changing Earth Series (New York, Oxford: Facts on File, Inc., 1992), p.19
7. Ibid.
8. Ibid., p.11
9. Carl Zimmer, "In Times of Ur," *Discover*, January 1997, p.18. It is believed that one billion years ago the continents came together to form one large landmass called Rodinia. Five hundred million years before that, a prior super landmass (though smaller than Rodinia) called Nena may have formed.

CHAPTER 14: VEGETATION–THE FIRST LIFE

1. *Torah Portions*, World Ort Union, "Navigating the Bible", 1996, April 16, 1997 <HTTP://BIBLE.ORT.ORG>
2. J.H. Hertz, ed., 2nd Ed. *The Pentateuch and Haftorahs* (London: Soncino Press, 1960), p.3
3. *Torah Portions*, World Ort Union, "Navigating the Bible", 1996, April 16, 1997 <HTTP://BIBLE.ORT.ORG>
4. Frederick Carl Eiselen, Edwin Lewis, and David G. Downey, eds., *The Abingdon Bible Commentary* (New York and Nashville: Abingdon-Cokesbury Press, 1929), p.220

5. Wade Roush, "Probing Flowers' Genetic Past," *Science*, Sept 6, 1996, p.1339

6. William B.N. Berry, "Silurian", *McGraw-Hill Encyclopedia of Science and Technology*, 8th Ed., 1997, Vol.16, p.466

7. Ibid., p.464

8. J.G. Johnson and P.H. Heckel, "Devonian*", McGraw-Hill Encyclopedia of Science and Technology*, 8th Edition, 1997, Vol.5, p.197

9. Ibid., p.192

10. Paul Kenrick and Peter R. Crane, "The Origin and early evolution of plants on land," *Nature*, Sept 4, 1997, p.33

11. Hugh Ross, *Genesis One: A Scientific Perspective,* Rev. Ed. (Pasadena, CA: Reasons To Believe, 1983), p.9

12. Adam Clarke, *Commentary on the Holy Bible*, One-Volume Edition, Abridged from original six-volume work by Ralph Earl (Grand Rapids, Michigan: Baker Book House, 1967), p.17

13. Geerat J. Vermeij, "Animal Origins," *Science*, Oct 25, 1996, p.525

CHAPTER 15: THE LIGHTS IN THE SKY ABOVE

1. Bruce Vawter, *On Genesis: A New Reading* (Garden City, New York: Doubleday & Company, 1977), p.48

2. Robert Jamieson, A.R. Fausset, and David Brown, *A Commentary Critical and Explanatory on the Whole Bible* (New York: Richard R. Smith, Inc., 1930), p.17

3. *Torah Portions*, World Ort Union, "Navigating the Bible", 1996, April 16, 1997 <HTTP://BIBLE.ORT.ORG>

4. Gleason L. Archer, *Encyclopedia of Bible Difficulties* (Grand Rapids, Michigan: Zondervan Publishing House, 1982), p.61

5. Ibid.

6. Nathaniel Kravitz, *Genesis: A New Interpretation of the First Three Chapters* (New York: Philosophical Library, 1967), p.35

7. Robert Jamieson, A.R. Fausset, and David Brown, *A Commentary Critical and Explanatory on the Whole Bible* (New York: Richard R. Smith, Inc., 1930), p.17

8. J.H. Hertz, ed., 2nd Ed. *The Pentateuch and Haftorahs* (London: Soncino Press, 1960), p.4

9. P.R. Ackroyd, A.R.C.Leaney, and J.W.Packer, eds., *The Cambridge Bible Commentary: Genesis 1-11* (Cambridge: At The University Press, 1973), p.21

10. Bernard Orchard, Edmund F. Sutcliffe, Reginald C. Fuller, and Ralph Russel, eds., *A Catholic Commentary on Holy Scripture* (London: Thomas Nelson and Sons Ltd, 1953), p.182

11. P.R. Ackroyd, A.R.C.Leaney, and J.W.Packer, eds., *The Cambridge Bible Commentary: Genesis 1-11* (Cambridge: At The University Press, 1973), p.21

12. Keith C. Seele, "Ancient Egypt", *The Encyclopedia Americana, International Edition*, 1997, Vol.10, p.44

13. P.R. Coleman-Norton, "Helios", *The Encyclopedia Americana, International Edition*, 1997, Vol.14, p.66

14. "Sol", *The Encyclopedia Americana, International Edition*, 1997, Vol.25, p.187

15. "Luna", *The Encyclopedia Americana, International Edition*, 1997, Vol.17, p.851

16. Ibid.

CHAPTER 16: LIFE FLOURISHES IN THE SEA AND AIR

1. *The Broadman Bible Commentary*, Vol.1 (Nashville: Broadman Press, 1973), p.124

2. *Torah Portions*, World Ort Union, "Navigating the Bible", 1996, April 16, 1997 <HTTP://BIBLE.ORT.ORG>

3. J.H. Hertz, ed., 2nd Ed. *The Pentateuch and Haftorahs* (London: Soncino Press, 1960), p.4

4. Ibid.
5. Hugh Ross, *Genesis One: A Scientific Perspective,* Rev. Ed. (Pasadena, CA: Reasons To Believe, 1983), p.12
6. Henry M. Morris, *The Genesis Record* (Grand Rapids, Michigan: Baker Book House, 1976), p.69
7. Robert Jamieson, A.R. Fausset, and David Brown, *A Commentary Critical and Explanatory on the Whole Bible* (New York: Richard R. Smith, Inc., 1930), p.17
8. Karl F. Koopman, "Chiroptera", *McGraw-Hill Encyclopedia of Science and Technology,* 8th Ed., 1997, Vol.3, p.622
9. Henry M. Morris, *The Genesis Record* (Grand Rapids, Michigan: Baker Book House, 1976), p.69
10. Richard Harrison and M. M. Bryden, eds., *Whales Dolphins and Porpoises,* (New York and Oxford, England: Facts on File Publications, 1990), p.16
11. Henry M. Morris, *The Genesis Record* (Grand Rapids, Michigan: Baker Book House, 1976), p.69
12. P.R. Ackroyd, A.R.C.Leaney, and J.W.Packer, eds., *The Cambridge Bible Commentary: Genesis 1-11* (Cambridge: At The University Press, 1973), p.22
13. Matthew Henry, *Matthew Henry's Commentary on the Whole Bible,* Vol.I., (New York, London, and Edinburgh: Fleming H. Revell Company, n.d.), p.8
14. Henry M. Morris, *The Genesis Record* (Grand Rapids, Michigan: Baker Book House, 1976), p.69
15. J.H. Hertz, ed., 2nd Ed. *The Pentateuch and Haftorahs* (London: Soncino Press, 1960), p.4
16. Stephen Jay Gould, "Of it, not above it," *Nature,* Oct 26, 1995, p.681
17. Allison R. Palmer, "Cambrian", *McGraw-Hill Encyclopedia of Science and Technology,* 8th Edition, 1997, Vol.3, p.186
18. Carl Zimmer, "An Explosion Defused," *Discover,* December 1996, Vol.17, p.52. It must be noted that the Cambrian Explosion primarily

gave rise to sea creatures with shells. Before that time, most invertebrates did not possess a shell; consequently, their soft remains left little fossil evidence. The Discover magazine article that I reference questions whether all of the animal phyla that exists today first appeared during the Cambrian Explosion, or actually existed in abundance before that event—as soft, shell-less invertebrates that left behind no tangible, fossil evidence of their existence. In either scenario, the Cambrian Explosion saw a tremendous change in the life-forms of planet Earth, and the Biblical recording of such an event is not diminished.

19. Allison R. Palmer, "Cambrian", *McGraw-Hill Encyclopedia of Science and Technology*, 8th Edition, 1997, Vol.3, p.186

20. Carl Zimmer, "Breathe Before You Bite," *Discover*, March 1996, p.34

21. Tom Waters, "First Fish," *Discover*, January 1997, p.59

22. Carl Zimmer, "Breathe Before You Bite," *Discover*, March 1996, p.34

23. Victor G. Springer and Joy P. Gold, *Sharks in Question: The Smithsonian Answer Book* (Washington D.C., London: Smithsonian Institution Press, 1989), p.30

24. J.G. Johnson and P.H. Heckel, "Devonian", *McGraw-Hill Encyclopedia of Science and Technology*, 8th Ed., 1997, Vol.5, p.192

25. Alfred S. Romer and Everett C. Olson, "Amphibia", *McGraw-Hill Encyclopedia of Science and Technology*, 8th Ed., 1997, Vol.1, p.582

26. Alan J. Charig, "Reptilia", *McGraw-Hill Encyclopedia of Science and Technology*, 8th Ed., 1997, Vol.15, p.422

27. Frank M. Carpenter, "Insecta", *McGraw-Hill Encyclopedia of Science and Technology*, 8th Ed., 1997, Vol.9, p.236

CHAPTER 18: THE LAND ANIMALS OF THE SIXTH DAY

1. *The Broadman Bible Commentary*, Vol.1 (Nashville: Broadman Press, 1973), p.125

2. Adam Clarke, *Commentary on the Holy Bible*, One-Volume Edition, Abridged from original six-volume work by Ralph Earl (Grand Rapids, Michigan: Baker Book House, 1967), p.18

3. J.H. Hertz, ed., 2nd Ed. *The Pentateuch and Haftorahs* (London: Soncino Press, 1960), p.4

4. Adam Clarke, *Commentary on the Holy Bible*, One-Volume Edition, Abridged from original six-volume work by Ralph Earl (Grand Rapids, Michigan: Baker Book House, 1967), p.18

5. E.A.Speiser, ed., *The Anchor Bible: Genesis,* 1st Ed., (Garden City, NY: Doubleday & Company, Inc. 1964), pp.6-7

6. Robert Jamieson, A.R. Fausset, and David Brown, *A Commentary Critical and Explanatory on the Whole Bible* (New York: Richard R. Smith, Inc., 1930), p.18

7. Jerry Falwell, Exec ed., *Liberty Bible Commentary,* (Nashville: Thomas Nelson, Inc. 1983), p.13

8. J.H. Hertz, ed., 2nd Ed. *The Pentateuch and Haftorahs* (London: Soncino Press, 1960), p.4

9. Hugh Ross, *Genesis One: A Scientific Perspective,* Rev. Ed. (Pasadena, CA: Reasons To Believe, 1983), p.12

10. Adam Clarke, *Commentary on the Holy Bible*, One-Volume Edition, Abridged from original six-volume work by Ralph Earl (Grand Rapids, Michigan: Baker Book House, 1967), p.18

11. Hugh Ross, *Genesis One: A Scientific Perspective,* Rev. Ed. (Pasadena, CA: Reasons To Believe, 1983), p.12

12. Ibid.

13. Herbert Lockyer, Sr., ed., *Nelson's Illustrated Bible Dictionary,* (New York: Thomas Nelson Publishers, 1986), p.49

14. Ibid.

15. Ibid., p.48

16. Richard A. Kerr, "Biggest Extinction Looks Catastrophic," *Science*, May 15, 1998, p.1007. The largest known mass extinction actually occurred at the end of the Permian Period of the Paleozoic Era, some 250 million years ago. It is believed that as much as 85% of marine species and 70% of land vertebrates went extinct at that time. The cause for that mass extinction is still unknown.

17. There are many other less violent causes that also may have triggered such an extinction. Some of the possibilities include disease, a dramatic change in climate, and even the rise of flowers (or pollinated plants). Currently, science accepts the scenario that the Earth was struck by a meteor, an asteroid, or a comet.

18. This common title arguably does not best describe the Cenozoic Era. The past sixty-five million years has also seen a great expansion and diversification of birds and flowers. Thus, it would be just as appropriate to nickname the Cenozoic Era "The Age of Flowers" or "The Age of Birds."

19. Bilal U. Haq, "Paleocene", *McGraw-Hill Encyclopedia of Science and Technology*, 8th Ed., 1997, Vol.13, p.30

20. Frederick S. Szalay, "Artiodactyla", *McGraw-Hill Encyclopedia of Science and Technology*, 8th Ed., 1997, Vol.2, p.154

21. Donald R. Prothero, "Perissodactyla", *McGraw-Hill Encyclopedia of Science and Technology*, 8th Ed., 1997, Vol.13, p.254

22. Richard H. Tedford, "Carnivora", *McGraw-Hill Encyclopedia of Science and Technology*, 8th Ed., 1997, Vol.3, p.293

23. Frederick S. Szalay, "Proboscidea", *McGraw-Hill Encyclopedia of Science and Technology*, 8th Ed., 1997, Vol.14, p.410

24. Donald R. Prothero, "Perissodactyla", *McGraw-Hill Encyclopedia of Science and Technology*, 8th Ed., 1997, Vol.13, p.254

25. Albert E. Wood, "Rodentia", *McGraw-Hill Encyclopedia of Science and Technology*, 8th Ed., 1997, Vol.15, p.643

CHAPTER 19: THE CREATION OF MAN

1. J.H. Hertz, ed., 2nd Ed. *The Pentateuch and Haftorahs* (London: Soncino Press, 1960), p.5

2. Matthew Henry, *Matthew Henry's Commentary on the Whole Bible*, Vol.I. (New York, London, and Edinburgh: Fleming H. Revell Company, n.d.), p.9

3. All dates listed for the existence of the Hominids are approximate.

4. This may also prove to be impossible since DNA degenerates over time. It is not known how long DNA can be preserved, but a limit of 100,000 years has been suggested.

5 *The Neandertals* are also classified by some as *Homo Neanderthalensis*. This classification allows us to designate modern man as *Homo Sapiens*—which is a distinct, separate species.

6. Jerry Falwell, Exec ed., *Liberty Bible Commentary* (Nashville: Thomas Nelson, Inc. 1983), p.4

7. Hugh Ross, *The Fingerprint of God*, 2nd Ed. (Orange, California: Promise Publishing Company, 1991), p.159

8. Jerry Falwell, Exec ed., *Liberty Bible Commentary* (Nashville: Thomas Nelson, Inc. 1983), p.1587

9. John Kappelman, "They might be giants," *Nature*, May 8, 1997, p.126

10. B. Bower, "Neandertals make big splash in gene pool," *Science News*, July 19, 1997, p.37

CHAPTER 20: IN OUR IMAGE, IN OUR LIKENESS

1. P.R. Ackroyd, A.R.C.Leaney, and J.W.Packer, eds., *The Cambridge Bible Commentary: Genesis 1-11* (Cambridge: At The University Press, 1973), pp.24-25

2. Ibid.

3. *The Broadman Bible Commentary*, Vol.1 (Nashville: Broadman Press, 1973), p.125

4. Ibid.

5. William Neil, *Harper's Bible Commentary*, (New York and Evanston: Harper & Row, Publishers, 1962), p.16

6. Matthew Henry, *Matthew Henry's Commentary on the Whole Bible*, Vol.I. (New York, London, and Edinburgh: Fleming H. Revell Company, n.d.), p.10

7. Hugh Ross, *Genesis One: A Scientific Perspective*, Rev. Ed. (Pasadena, CA: Reasons To Believe, 1983), p.13

8. Henry M. Morris, *The Genesis Record* (Grand Rapids, Michigan: Baker Book House, 1976), p.74
9. Hugh Ross, *Genesis One: A Scientific Perspective,* Rev. Ed. (Pasadena, CA: Reasons To Believe, 1983), p.13
10. Harry M. Orlinsky, ed., *Notes on the New Translation of The Torah* (Philadelphia: The Jewish Publication Society of America, 1969), p.58
11. J.H. Hertz, ed., 2nd Ed. *The Pentateuch and Haftorahs* (London: Soncino Press, 1960), p.5
12. Ibid., p.2

CHAPTER 21: MAN'S DOMINION

1. Bruce Vawter, *On Genesis: A New Reading* (Garden City, New York: Doubleday & Company, 1977), pp.57-58
2. Ibid., p.59

CHAPTER 22: THE GREEN PLANTS FOR FOOD

1. *The Broadman Bible Commentary*, Vol.1 (Nashville: Broadman Press, 1973), p.125

CHAPTER 23: A DAY TO REST

1. The final sentence of this passage is sometimes recognized as the beginning of the next story in the Bible.
2. Harry M. Orlinsky, ed., *Notes on the New Translation of The Torah* (Philadelphia: The Jewish Publication Society of America, 1969), p.59
3. *Torah Portions*, World Ort Union, "Navigating the Bible", 1996, April 16, 1997 <HTTP://BIBLE.ORT.ORG>

CHAPTER 24: FULFILLMENT OF GOD'S COMMANDS AND HIS VERDICTS

1. Some Creationists acknowledge that lower forms of life such as bacteria or virus may have died before the fall of man. However, they will

not extend physical death to the higher forms of life that we interact with each day, such as plants and animals.

2. Gleason L. Archer, *Encyclopedia of Bible Difficulties* (Grand Rapids, Michigan: Zondervan Publishing House, 1982), p.65   .

3. Other Scriptural passages that are often cited for evidence of a perfect, death-free Earth are: Genesis 3:14-19, Genesis 3:21, Genesis 9:3, Isaiah 11:6-9, Acts 3:21, Romans 5:12, Romans 8:20-22, 1 Corinthians 15:21-22, Hebrews 9:22, Revelation 21:4-5, and Revelation 22:3. I welcome you to read through these verses and come to your own con-clusions. I maintain that nowhere in the Bible does it declare that the world was in a state of perfection and free of all physical death before man's sin.

4. Many Creationists that believe in 24-hour Creation Days also contend that the sun, the moon, and the stars were created on the Fourth Day. Plants, as we all agree, were part of the Third Day's creations. If phys-ical death had not entered the world until Adam and Eve, how do we prevent plants from dying without the sun (which these Creationists believe was created a full day later)? Without the warmth from the sun, the temperature of the Earth would plummet to near Absolute Zero. No plant life could have sprouted, let alone survive for a full day.

5. P.R. Ackroyd, A.R.C.Leaney, and J.W.Packer, eds., *The Cambridge Bible Commentary: Genesis 1-11* (Cambridge: At The University Press, 1973), p.22

6. Bruce Vawter, *On Genesis: A New Reading* (Garden City, New York: Doubleday & Company, 1977), p.43

CHAPTER 25: ACCORDING TO THEIR KINDS

1. "Older, not Better," *Discover,* April 1997, p.20

CHAPTER 26: MORE BIBLICAL EVIDENCE FOR LONG CREATION DAYS

1. Gleason L. Archer, *Encyclopedia of Bible Difficulties* (Grand Rapids, Michigan: Zondervan Publishing House, 1982), p.63
2. *Torah Portions*, World Ort Union, "Navigating the Bible", 1996, April 16, 1997 <HTTP://BIBLE.ORT.ORG>
3. Herbert Lockyer, Sr., ed., *Nelson's Illustrated Bible Dictionary*, (New York: Thomas Nelson Publishers, 1986), p.411
4. I will include the text of these verses in the following chapter. The Biblical verses are Habakkuk 3:6, Psalm 90:1-6, Micah 6:2, Proverbs 8:22-31, Isaiah 46:10, and Ecclesiastes 1:3-11.

CHAPTER 28: NATURAL PROCESSES AND ACTS OF GOD

1. Jon Erickson, *"Plate Tectonics: Unraveling the Mysteries of the Earth"*, The Changing Earth Series (New York, Oxford: Facts on File, Inc., 1992), p.19
2. Tobias C. Owen, "Pluto", *McGraw-Hill Encyclopedia of Science and Technology*, 8th Ed., 1997, Vol.14, p.82
3. There is a very small group of Creationists that acquiesce to the scientific concept that all life on Earth has descended from a common ancestor over the span of billions of years. However, they disagree with the scientific belief that attributes the rise of life to strictly natural processes. These Creationists believe that God—and not nature—is the guiding force behind "descent (of life) with modification," and He has guided the progression of life through time to produce all current life, including man.
4. Creationists that embrace a strict 24-hour Creation Day believe that all plant and animal life appeared within a span of four Earth days (from the Third through the Sixth Creation Days). They would not agree with any of the dates given for the appearance of the different species of life on Earth, and would maintain that the Earth is no less

than 6,000 years old and no more than perhaps a few tens-of-thousands of years old.

5. Stephen Jay Gould, "Of it, not above it," *Nature*, Oct 26, 1995, p.681

CHAPTER 29: OTHER CREATIONIST CHALLENGES

1. Gleason L. Archer, *Encyclopedia of Bible Difficulties* (Grand Rapids, Michigan: Zondervan Publishing House, 1982), p.61
2. Richard Monastersky, "Space dust may rain destruction on Earth," *Science News*, May 9, 1998, p.294
3. Richard B. Alley and Michael L. Bender, "Greenland Ice Cores: Frozen in Time," *Scientific American*, Feb 1998, p.82

CHAPTER 30: THE PREDICTIONS OF CREATION

1. B. Bower, "Neandertals make big splash in gene pool," *Science News*, July 19, 1997, p.37

CHAPTER 31: THE THEORY OF CREATION

1. Jon Erickson, *"Plate Tectonics: Unraveling the Mysteries of the Earth"*, The Changing Earth Series (New York, Oxford: Facts on File, Inc., 1992), p.125
2. Ibid.
3. "Older, not Better," *Discover*, April 1997, p.20
4. Adam Clarke, *Commentary on the Holy Bible*, One-Volume Edition, Abridged from original six-volume work by Ralph Earl (Grand Rapids, Michigan: Baker Book House, 1967), p.16
5. Charles M. Laymon, ed., The Interpreter's One-Volume Commentary on the Bible, (New York and Nashville: Abingdon Press, and Nashville: Parthenon Press, printed and bound, 1971), p.3
6. Hugh Ross, *Genesis One: A Scientific Perspective,* Rev. Ed. (Pasadena, CA: Reasons To Believe, 1983), p.17
7. Harry M. Orlinsky, ed., *Notes on the New Translation of The Torah* (Philadelphia: The Jewish Publication Society of America, 1969), p.56

8. *Torah Portions*, World Ort Union, "Navigating the Bible", 1996, April 16, 1997 <HTTP://BIBLE.ORT.ORG>

9. John D. Davies, *Beginning Now* (Philadelphia: Fortress Press, 1971), p.45

10. Ibid.

11. Ibid., p.46

12. Ibid., p.45

13. Herbert Lockyer, Sr., ed., *Nelson's Illustrated Bible Dictionary*, (New York: Thomas Nelson Publishers, 1986), p.262

14. Gleason L. Archer, *Encyclopedia of Bible Difficulties*, (Grand Rapids, Michigan: Zondervan Publishing House, 1982), p.63

15. *Torah Portions*, World Ort Union, "Navigating the Bible", 1996, April 16, 1997 <HTTP://BIBLE.ORT.ORG>

16. Herbert Lockyer, Sr., ed., *Nelson's Illustrated Bible Dictionary*, (New York: Thomas Nelson Publishers, 1986), p.411

17. The Biblical verses which may indicate an ancient Earth are: Habakkuk 3:6, Psalm 90:1-6, Micah 6:2, Proverbs 8:22-31, Isaiah 46:10, and Ecclesiastes 1:3-11.

18. Adam Clarke, *Commentary on the Holy Bible*, One-Volume Edition, Abridged from original six-volume work by Ralph Earl (Grand Rapids, Michigan: Baker Book House, 1967), p.17

19. *The Broadman Bible Commentary*, Vol.1 (Nashville: Broadman Press, 1973), p.125

20. Nathaniel Kravitz, *Genesis: A New Interpretation of the First Three Chapters*, (New York: Philosophical Library, 1967), p.27

21. Michael Balter, "Looking for Clues to the Mystery of Life on Earth," *Science*, Aug 16, 1996, p.870

22. Jon Erickson, *"Plate Tectonics: Unraveling the Mysteries of the Earth"*, The Changing Earth Series (New York, Oxford: Facts on File, Inc., 1992), p.19

23. Ibid., p.23

24. S. Ross Taylor and Scott M. McLennan, "The Evolution of Continental Crust," *Scientific American*, Jan 1996, p.79

25. Jon Erickson, "*Plate Tectonics: Unraveling the Mysteries of the Earth*", The Changing Earth Series (New York, Oxford: Facts on File, Inc., 1992), p.19

26. Frederick Carl Eiselen, Edwin Lewis, and David G. Downey, eds., *The Abingdon Bible Commentary* (New York and Nashville: Abingdon-Cokesbury Press, 1929), p.220

27. J.H. Hertz, ed., 2nd Ed. *The Pentateuch and Haftorahs* (London: Soncino Press, 1960), p.3

28. Torah Portions, World Ort Union, "Navigating the Bible", 1996, April 16, 1997 <HTTP://BIBLE.ORT.ORG>

29. Geerat J. Vermeij, "Animal Origins," *Science*, Oct 25, 1996, p.525

30. Paul Kenrick and Peter R. Crane, "The Origin and early evolution of plants on land," *Nature*, Sept 4, 1997, pp.33-38

31. J.G.Johnson and P.H. Heckel, "Devonian", *McGraw-Hill Encyclopedia of Science and Technology*, 8th Ed., 1997, Vol.5, p.192

32. Ibid., p.197

33. Hugh Ross, *Genesis One: A Scientific Perspective,* Rev. Ed. (Pasadena, CA: Reasons To Believe, 1983), p.9

34. The Bible does not address the creation of the moon; consequently, it is unclear if we would place the moon's creation with the Earth, the universe, or our solar system.

35. Robert Jamieson, A.R. Fausset, and David Brown, *A Commentary Critical and Explanatory on the Whole Bible* (New York: Richard R. Smith, Inc., 1930), p.17

36. Gleason L. Archer, *Encyclopedia of Bible Difficulties*, (Grand Rapids, Michigan: Zondervan Publishing House, 1982), p.61

37. J.H. Hertz, ed., 2nd Ed. *The Pentateuch and Haftorahs* (London: Soncino Press, 1960), p.4

38. P.R. Ackroyd, A.R.C.Leaney, and J.W.Packer, eds., *The Cambridge Bible Commentary: Genesis 1-11* (Cambridge: At The University Press, 1973), p.21

39. Bernard Orchard, Edmund F. Sutcliffe, Reginald C. Fuller, and Ralph Russel, eds., *A Catholic Commentary on Holy Scripture* (London: Thomas Nelson and Sons Ltd, 1953), p.182

40. P.R. Ackroyd, A.R.C.Leaney, and J.W.Packer, eds., *The Cambridge Bible Commentary: Genesis 1-11* (Cambridge: At The University Press, 1973), p.21

41. Robert Jamieson, A.R. Fausset, and David Brown, *A Commentary Critical and Explanatory on the Whole Bible* (New York: Richard R. Smith, Inc., 1930), p.17

42. J.H. Hertz, ed., 2nd Ed. *The Pentateuch and Haftorahs* (London: Soncino Press, 1960), p.4

43. Stephen Jay Gould, "Of it, not above it," *Nature*, Oct 26, 1995, p.681

44. Allison R. Palmer, "Cambrian", *McGraw-Hill Encyclopedia of Science and Technology*, 8th Ed., 1997, Vol.3, p.186

45. Carl Zimmer, "Breathe Before You Bite," *Discover*, March 1996, p.34

46. Tom Waters, "First Fish," *Discover*, January 1997, p.59

47. Carl Zimmer, "Breathe Before You Bite," *Discover*, March 1996, p.34

48. Victor G. Springer and Joy P.Gold, *Sharks in Question* (Washington D.C. and London: Smithsonian Institution Press, 1989), p.30

49. Alfred S. Romer and Everett C. Olson, "Amphibians", *McGraw-Hill Encyclopedia of Science and Technology*, 8th Ed., 1997, Vol.1, p.582

50. J.G. Johnson and P.H. Heckel, "Devonian", *McGraw-Hill Encyclopedia of Science and Technology*, 8th Ed., 1997, Vol.5, p.192

51. Alan J. Charig, "Reptilia", *McGraw-Hill Encyclopedia of Science and Technology*, 8th Ed., 1997, Vol.15, p.422

52. Frank M. Carpenter, "Insecta", *McGraw-Hill Encyclopedia of Science and Technology*, 8th Ed., 1997, Vol.9, p.236

53. J.H. Hertz, ed., 2nd Ed. *The Pentateuch and Haftorahs* (London: Soncino Press, 1960), p.4

54. Adam Clarke, *Commentary on the Holy Bible*, One-Volume Edition, Abridged from original six-volume work by Ralph Earl (Grand Rapids, Michigan: Baker Book House, 1967), p.18

55. Hugh Ross, *Genesis One: A Scientific Perspective,* Rev. Ed. (Pasadena, CA: Reasons To Believe, 1983), p.12
56. Herbert Lockyer, Sr., ed., *Nelson's Illustrated Bible Dictionary,* (New York: Thomas Nelson Publishers, 1986), p.49
57. Ibid.
58. Ibid., p.48
59. Matthew Henry, *Matthew Henry's Commentary on the Whole Bible,* Vol.I., (New York, London, and Edinburgh: Fleming H. Revell Company, n.d.), p.9
60. Henry M. Morris, *The Genesis Record* (Grand Rapids, Michigan: Baker Book House, 1976), p.74
61. Hugh Ross, *Genesis One: A Scientific Perspective,* Rev. Ed. (Pasadena, CA: Reasons To Believe, 1983), p.13
62. Bernard Orchard, Edmund F. Sutcliffe, Reginald C. Fuller, and Ralph Russel, eds., *A Catholic Commentary on Holy Scripture* (London: Thomas Nelson and Sons Ltd, 1953), p.16
63. P.R. Ackroyd, A.R.C.Leaney, and J.W.Packer, eds., *The Cambridge Bible Commentary: Genesis 1-11* (Cambridge: At The University Press, 1973), p.27
64. Harry M. Orlinsky, ed., *Notes on the New Translation of The Torah* (Philadelphia: The Jewish Publication Society of America, 1969), p.59

CHAPTER 32: THE MEANING OF CREATION

1. Carl Sagan, *Cosmos* (New York; Toronto: Random House, 1980), p.1
2. Hugh Ross, *The Fingerprint of God,* 2nd Ed. (Orange, California: Promise Publishing Company, 1991), p.119
3. Ibid., pp.130-131
4. Ibid., pp.129-130
5. Patrick Glynn, *God The Evidence: The Reconciliation of Faith and Reason in a Postsecular World* (Rocklin, California: Forum, 1997), p.29

Bibliography

Bibles

International Bible Society. *The Holy Bible, New International Version.* Grand Rapids, Michigan: Zondervan Publishing House, 1984

The Holy Bible, Old and New Testaments in the King James Version. Nashville Tennessee: Thomas Nelson, Inc., 1976

The Jewish Publications Society of America. *The Torah: The Five Books of Moses.* 2nd Ed. Philadelphia: The Jewish Publication Society of America, 1967

Bible Commentaries

Ackroyd, P.R., Leaney, A.R.C., and Packer, J.W. Eds. *The Cambridge Bible Commentary: Genesis 1-11.* Cambridge: At The University Press, 1973

The Broadman Bible Commentary. Vol. 1. Nashville: Broadman Press, 1973

Clarke, Adam. *Commentary on the Holy Bible.* One-Volume Edition, Abridged from original six-volume work by Ralph Earl. Grand Rapids, Michigan: Baker Book House, 1967

Davies, John D. *Beginning Now.* Philadelphia: Fortress Press, 1971

Eiselen, Frederick Carl, Lewis, Edwin, and Downey, David G., Eds. *The Abingdon Bible Commentary.* New York and Nashville: Abingdon-Cokesbury Press, 1929

Falwell, Jerry. Exec Ed. *Liberty Bible Commentary.* Nashville: Thomas Nelson, Inc., 1983

Henry, Matthew. *Matthew Henry's Commentary on the Whole Bible.* Vol.I. New York, London, and Edinburgh: Fleming H. Revell Company, n.d.

Hertz, J.H. Ed. 2nd Ed. *The Pentateuch and Haftorahs.* London: Soncino Press, 1960

Jamieson, Robert, Fausset, A.R., and Brown, David. *A Commentary Critical and Explanatory on the Whole Bible.* New York: Richard R. Smith, Inc., 1930

Kravitz, Nathaniel. *Genesis: A New Interpretation of the First Three Chapters.* New York: Philosophical Library, 1967

Laymon, Charles M. Ed. *The Interpreter's One-Volume Commentary on the Bible.* New York and Nashville: Abingdon Press, and Nashville: Parthenon Press, printed and bound, 1971

Morris, Henry M. *The Genesis Record.* Grand Rapids, Michigan: Baker Book House, 1976

Neil, William. *Harper's Bible Commentary.* New York and Evanston: Harper & Row, 1962

Orchard, Bernard, Sutcliffe, Edmund F., Fuller, Reginald C., and Russel, Ralph. Eds. *A Catholic Commentary on Holy Scripture.* London: Thomas Nelson and Sons Ltd, 1953

Orlinsky, Harry M. Ed. *Notes on the New Translation of The Torah.* Philadelphia: The Jewish Publication Society of America, 1969

Speiser, E.A. Ed. *The Anchor Bible: Genesis.* 1st Ed. Garden City, NY: Doubleday & Company, Inc., 1964

Vawter, Bruce. *On Genesis: A New Reading.* Garden City, New York: Doubleday & Company, 1977

Encyclopedia Articles

Berry, William B.N. "Silurian." *McGraw-Hill Encyclopedia of Science and Technology*, 8th Ed., 1997, Vol. 16

Carpenter, Frank M. "Insecta." *McGraw-Hill Encyclopedia of Science and Technology*, 8th Ed., 1997, Vol. 9

Charig, Alan J. "Reptilia." *McGraw-Hill Encyclopedia of Science and Technology*, 8th Ed., 1997, Vol. 15

Coleman-Norton. P.R. "Helios." *The Encyclopedia Americana,* International Edition, 1997, Vol. 14

Haq, Bilal U. "Paleocene." *McGraw-Hill Encyclopedia of Science and Technology*, 8th Ed., 1997, Vol. 13

Johnson, J.G. and Heckel, P.H. "Devonian." *McGraw-Hill Encyclopedia of Science and Technology*, 8th Ed., 1997, Vol. 5

Koopman, Karl F. "Chiroptera." *McGraw-Hill Encyclopedia of Science and Technology*, 8th Ed., 1997, Vol. 3

"Luna." *The Encyclopedia Americana, International Edition*, 1997, Vol. 17

Mills Dawley, Powel. "Ussher, James." *The Encyclopedia Americana, International Edition*, 1997, Vol. 27

Owen, Tobias C. "Pluto." *McGraw-Hill Encyclopedia of Science and Technology*, 8th Ed., 1997, Vol. 14

Palmer, Allison R. "Cambrian." *McGraw-Hill Encyclopedia of Science and Technology*, 8th Ed., 1997, Vol.3

Pollack, James B. "Venus." *McGraw-Hill Encyclopedia of Science and Technology*, 8th Ed., 1997, Vol.19

Prothero, Donald R. "Perissodactyla." *McGraw-Hill Encyclopedia of Science and Technology*, 8th Ed., 1997, Vol.13

Romer, Alfred S. and Olson, Everett C. "Amphibia." *McGraw-Hill Encyclopedia of Science and Technology*, 8th Ed., 1997, Vol.1

Seele, Keith C. "Ancient Egypt." *The Encyclopedia Americana, International Edition*, 1997, Vol.10

"Sol." *The Encyclopedia Americana, International Edition*, 1997, Vol.25

Szalay, Frederick S. "Artiodactyla." *McGraw-Hill Encyclopedia of Science and Technology*, 8th Ed., 1997, Vol.2

Szalay, Frederick S. "Proboscidea." *McGraw-Hill Encyclopedia of Science and Technology*, 8th Ed., 1997, Vol.14

Tedford, Richard H. "Carnivora." *McGraw-Hill Encyclopedia of Science and Technology*, 8th Ed., 1997, Vol.3

Wood, Albert E. "Rodentia." *McGraw-Hill Encyclopedia of Science and Technology,* 8th Ed., 1997, Vol.15

Magazine Articles

Alley, Richard B. and Bender, Michael L. "Greenland Ice Cores: Frozen in Time." *Scientific American*, Feb 1998

Balter, Michael. "Looking for Clues to the Mystery of Life on Earth." *Science*, Aug 16, 1996

Bower, B. "Neandertals make big splash in gene pool." *Science News*, July 19, 1997

Discover. "Older, not Better." April 1997

Gould, Stephen Jay. "Of it, not above it." *Nature*, Oct 26, 1995

Kappelman, John. "They might be giants." *Nature*, May 8, 1997

Kenrick, Paul and Crane, Peter R. "The Origin and early evolution of plants on land." *Nature*, Sept 4, 1997

Kerr, Richard A. "Biggest Extinction Looks Catastrophic." *Science*, May 15, 1998

Monastersky, Richard. "Space dust may rain destruction on Earth." *Science News*, May 9, 1998

Monastersky, Richard. "Water Flowed Early in the Solar System." *Science News*, Feb 24, 1996

Monastersky, Richard. "Speedy spin kept early Earth from freezing." *Science News*, June 12, 1993

Roush, Wade. "Probing Flowers' Genetic Past." *Science*, Sept 6, 1996

Taylor, S. Ross and McLennan, Scott M. "The Evolution of Continental Crust." *Scientific American*, Jan 1996

Vermeij, Geerat J. "Animal Origins." *Science*, Oct 25, 1996

Waters, Tom. "First Fish." *Discover*, January 1997

Zimmer, Carl. "Breathe Before You Bite." *Discover*, March 1996

Zimmer, Carl. "In Times of Ur." *Discover*, January 1997

Zimmer, Carl. "An Explosion Defused." *Discover*, December 1996

General Books

Archer, Gleason L. *Encyclopedia of Bible Difficulties*. Grand Rapids, Michigan: Zondervan Publishing House, 1982

Erickson, Jon. "*Plate Tectonics: Unraveling the Mysteries of the Earth.*" The Changing Earth Series. New York, Oxford: Facts on File, Inc., 1992

Glynn, Patrick. *God The Evidence: The Reconciliation of Faith and Reason in a Postsecular World*. Rocklin, California: Forum, 1997

Harrison, Richard and Bryden, M. M.. Eds. *Whales Dolphins and Porpoises*. New York and Oxford, England: Facts on File Publications, 1990

Hawking, Stephen W. *A Brief History of Time*. New York: Bantam Books, 1988

Lockyer, Herbert. Sr., Ed. *Nelson's Illustrated Bible Dictionary*. New York: Thomas Nelson Publishers, 1986

Ross, Hugh. *Genesis One: A Scientific Perspective*. Rev. Ed. Pasadena, CA: Reasons To Believe, 1983

Ross, Hugh. *The Fingerprint of God.* 2nd Ed. Orange, California: Promise Publishing Company, 1991

Sagan, Carl. *Cosmos.* New York; Toronto: Random House, 1980

Springer, Victor G. and Gold, Joy P. *Sharks in Question: The Smithsonian Answer Book.* Washington D.C., London: Smithsonian Institution Press, 1989

Web Sites

World Ort Union. *Torah Portions.* Navigating the Bible, 1996, April 16, 1997 <HTTP://BIBLE.ORT.ORG>

Printed in the United States
5738